I would also like to recognize some of the many lenders, private collectors, contemporary artists, and institutions that have joined together to graciously participate in this exhibition. The list is extensive, given the size of the exhibition, so I am identifying only those who also provided personal assistance, commentary, and valuable feedback. Included in my acknowledgments to lenders are Patrick and Jeannie Wilshire; Greg Obaugh; Paul and LizAnn Lizotte; Jordan Berman of The Illustrated Gallery; Barry Klugerman, James Gurney; Fred, Sherry, and Kara Ross; Howard and Jane Frank; The Kelly Collection of American Illustration; Stephen Korshak; Bob Eggleton and Marianne Plumridge; Mark Corrinet; John Schoonover; and a special thanks to Muhlenburg College Library and Special Collections for their loan of the rare and unique William Blake–illustrated book *Night Thoughts* (1797) by author Edward Young.

At the Allentown Art Museum, everyone should be recognized for their contributions, hard work, and determination in bringing *At the Edge: Art of the Fantastic* to reality. The Curatorial staff and Operations orchestrated the challenge of shipping, transportation, and the design and installation of over one hundred and sixty works of art. I wish to thank Dr. Diane P. Fischer, our Chief Curator, for her leadership; Nathan Marzen, our Collections Manager; Steve Gamler, our Preparator; Sofia Bakis, our Coordinator of Collections and Exhibitions; Tom Edge, our Assistant Preparator; and Kayla O'Connor, our Adjunct Curator of Textiles. A special note of thanks is reserved for Amanda McCarthy, curatorial intern and doctoral student at Case Western Reserve University, for her work on the catalogue.

The Development and Marketing Department, led by Elsbeth Haymon, secured funding and sponsors to help underwrite the exhibition and to promote this project throughout the Lehigh Valley and beyond. We thank Rhonda Mauk, Sue Pease, Sue Small-Kreider and Carla Lindenmuth. Chris Potash, our Manager of Marketing and Public Relations, and Megan Haddad, our Marketing Coordinator, have brought exciting design elements and wonderful promotion and advertising to this project. Sharon Yurkanin, our Museum Store Manager, and her team work quietly and effectively.

Jane Kintzer and her Education Department team, including Kathy Odorizzi, Jessica Gauthier, John Pepper, and Carly Martin, created programs and activities based on *At the Edge* that will bring even more enjoyment to our members and visitors.

Let me also express my thanks to our Director of Administration, Don Gunn, and our Accountant, Janet Egbert, for their administrative and financial oversight of the exhibition; Colleen Fitzpatrick, my Executive Secretary, for her tireless and expert multi-tasking; Doug Bowerman, our Building Operations Manager, and his staff; and our Supervisor of Security Services, Joe Kimock, and his excellent security team. To everyone on staff at the Allentown Art Museum I express my appreciation for your support of *At the Edge: Art of the Fantastic.*

Lastly, I wish to recognize our sponsors and patrons through whose generosity this exhibition was made possible. Our sponsors include The Century Fund, William and Phyllis Grube, Rodale, KNBT, Julius and Kathryn Hommer Foundation, Adams Outdoor Advertising, Viamedia, The Morning Call, Amaranth Foundation, The Leon C. and June W. Holt Endowment, The Audrey and Bernard Berman Endowment Fund, The Express-Times and Lehigh ValleyLive.com, WDIY 88.1FM--Lehigh Valley Community Public Radio, The Frank Foundation, Sands Casino Resort, Holliday Inn City Center of Allentown, ICON, Laini's Little Pocket Guide, Lehigh Valley Woman, Greg Obaugh, J. David Spurlock, Paul and LizAnn Lizotte, The Illustrated Gallery, and Barry Klugerman. To all of our sponsors and patrons I express our tremendous appreciation.

J. Brooks Joyner
Priscilla Payne Hurd President and CEO
The Allentown Art Museum of the Lehigh Valley

AT THE EDGE: ART OF THE FANTASTIC
INTRODUCTION

Imagination is the voice of daring. If there is anything Godlike about God it is that. He dared to imagine everything.

—Henry Miller

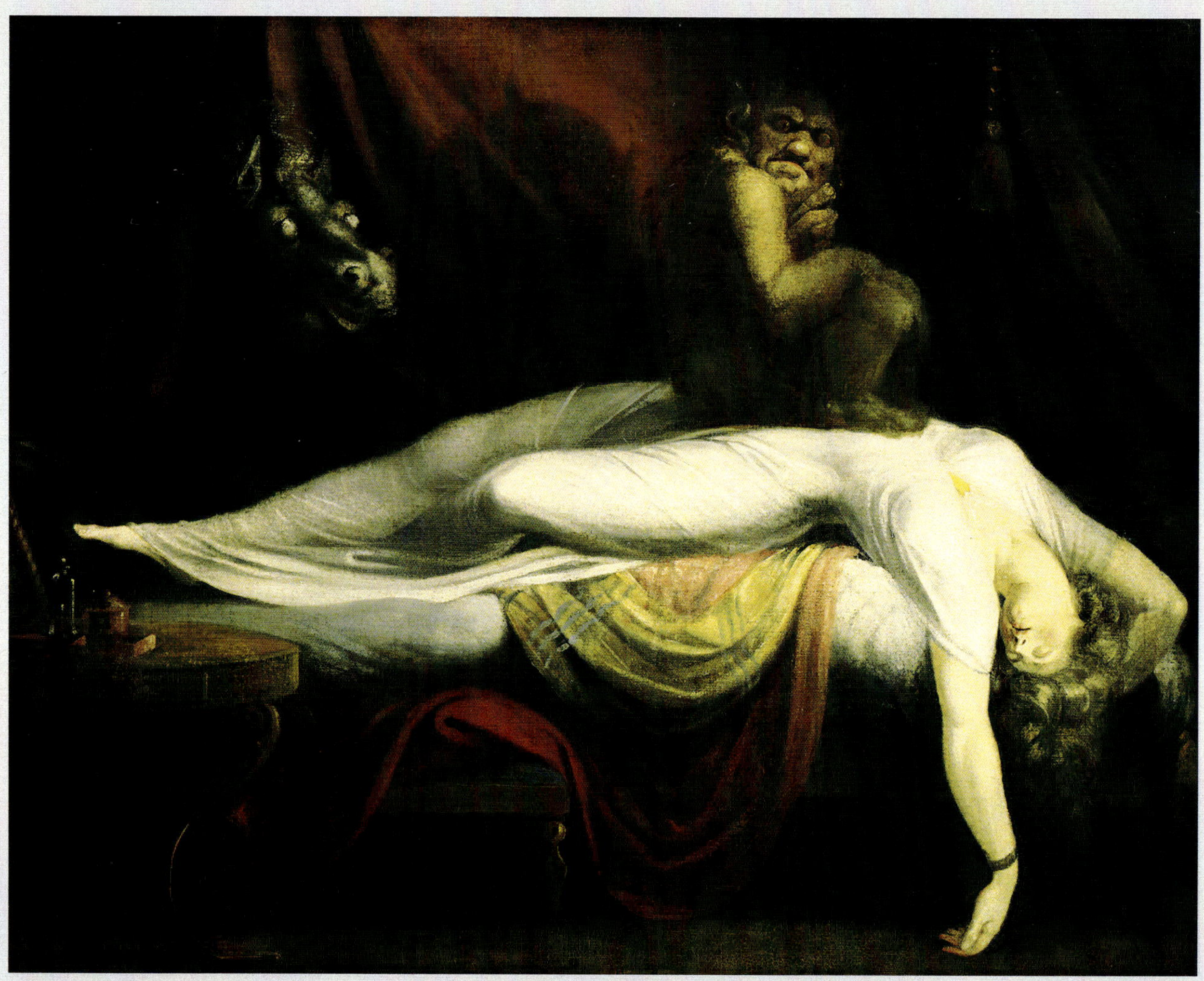

Henri Fuseli (1741–1845), *The Nightmare*, 1781, oil on canvas. Detroit Institute of Arts. Founders Society Purchase with funds from Mr. and Mrs. Bert L. Smokler and Mr. and Mrs. Lawrence A. Fleischman.

Imaginative realism brings to life worlds that have never existed but could have—or yet might. Here in this catalog are the artists of the fantastic, as presented in the exhibit *At the Edge*, populating the realms of science fiction and fantasy with their visions. They are the imagists behind the films that thrill us, the television shows we are loyal to, the games we play, and the books that take us to incredible places. Their paintings hang in museums, galleries, corporate showcases, and private collections throughout the world. Their ranks include some of the finest living realist painters whose technical virtuosity continues a long tradition of visual narrative, speaking quietly but insistently to the hidden places in all of us.

The roots of contemporary imaginative realism date back to the latter half of the eighteenth century and romanticism. Although imaginative themes were certainly common prior to this time, the romantic focus on emotion and drama differed from previous generations of artists who tended to focus on the imaginative as a tool for explaining history or faith, or as proxies for religious archetypes. From the romantics sprang the Pre-Raphaelites and their successors, the academics and the symbolists. These artists—including John Martin, Sir Edward Coley Burne-Jones, Gustave Doré, John William Waterhouse, Sir Lawrence Alma-Tadema, and Arnold Böcklin—in turn provided the main influences for the great golden age illustrators of the early twentieth century.

Between 1890 and 1920, illustrators such as N. C. Wyeth, Howard Pyle, Maxfield Parrish, Arthur Rackham and Edmund Dulac continued the imaginative tradition and bound it even more tightly to narrative and characterization as the rapidly expanding publishing market created an increased demand for imaginative imagery. This was the golden age of imaginative illustration, but it would prove to be short lived. The horrors of World War I had a sobering effect on society in both the United States and Europe, and the popular taste for the fantastic diminished. At the same time, the rise of modernism—also a reaction to the war—took fine art in a dramatically new direction, leaving many of the nineteenth century imaginative artists largely forgotten as their tradition fell into disuse.

Predominantly relegated to the low-quality pulp magazines and early science-fiction periodicals, fantastic art continued, though it became increasingly separated from its roots. Mid-century artists developed a new visual lexicon for the fantastic based on the concepts of science fiction and modern fantasy, but they did so with increasing reference to contemporary artistic trends. By the late 1950s several of the most successful imaginative artists managed dual careers, painting modernist works of fantastic art for publishers at the same time they pursued gallery careers working in contemporary styles.

It was not until the mid-1960s that an imaginative artist melded the modern conceptual imagery of science fiction and fantasy with the classical tradition of the golden age illustrators and their predecessors—Frank Frazetta. Frazetta's work electrified the field, and nearly all subsequent imaginative realists would follow his lead back to the pre-World War I tradition and beyond.

Today, themes of the fantastic are more widespread than ever in film, literature, gaming, and throughout popular culture. It may seem odd that the artists who give shape and form to the leading edge of popular culture do so from an artistic tradition dating back more than two centuries. Then again, in many ways it's not such an odd concept at all.

In previous centuries, sailors believed that the edge of the world was populated by dragons, the creatures of myth and legend, and that to cross that horizon meant coming face to face with the deepest reaches of human imagination in a place where the impossible becomes real.

Our society now actively seeks that horizon, hoping to catch a glimpse of the edge of the world.

Welcome to the edge.

Patrick Wilshire
Director
Association of Fantastic Art

William BLAKE

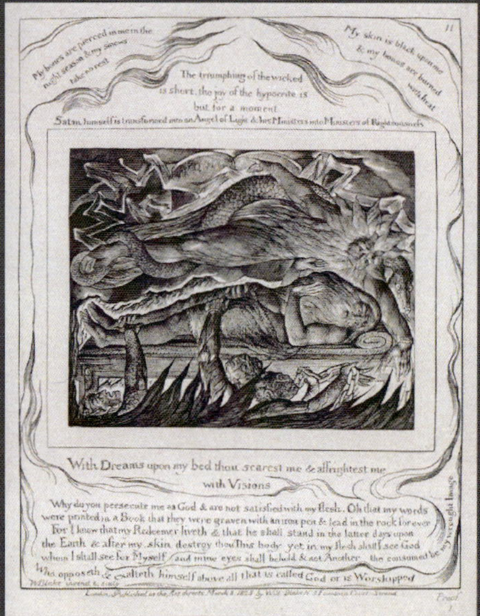

The Book of Job, 1826
Engraving on paper. Collection of the Allentown Art Museum.

British, 1757–1827

Blake is considered one of the seminal figures of the romantic movement, both for his visual and literary artistry. His paintings and engravings embody extreme creativity and expressiveness, embracing the imagination as "the body of God." Although his works are much more stylized than the later romantic artists, and much of his work is informed by his own religious fervor, he is one of the founding fathers of what would eventually become imaginative realism.

The Book of Job demonstrates Blake's power when using the normal intaglio etching, a reverse method from the unusual relief etching process that he pioneered.

Night Thoughts is an extreme rarity. Only twenty-five copies of the book were produced with full, hand-watercolored plates. Of those, only a handful have been ascribed to Blake himself, including this copy.

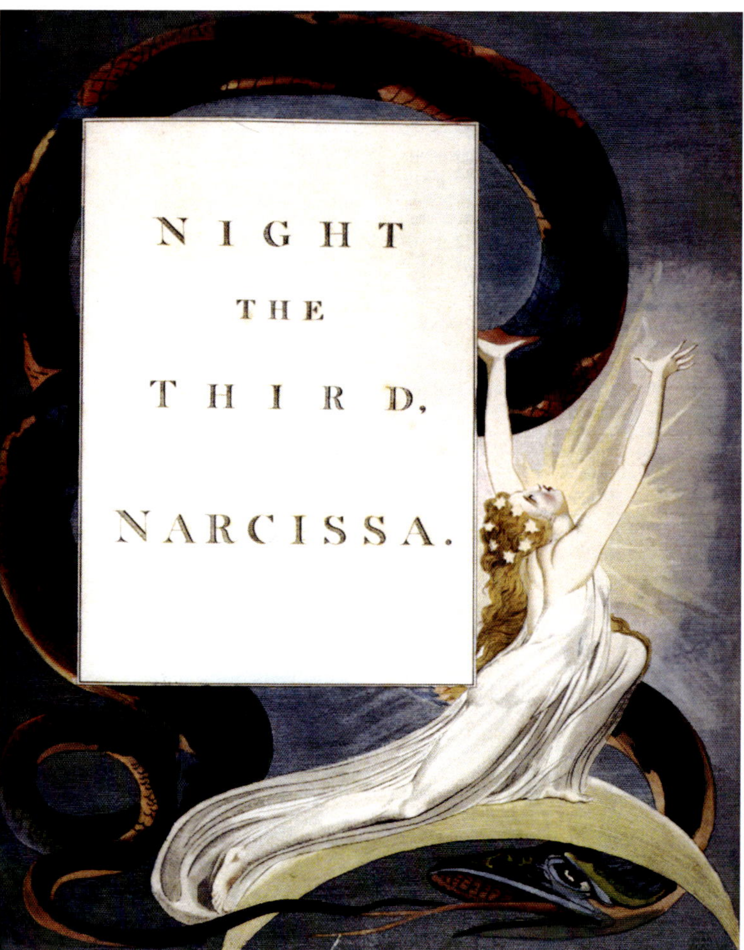

Night Thoughts, 1797
Watercolor on paper. Florence F. Tonner Collection, Muhlenberg College.

Eleanor Fortescue BRICKDALE

19th CENTURY

British, 1871–1945

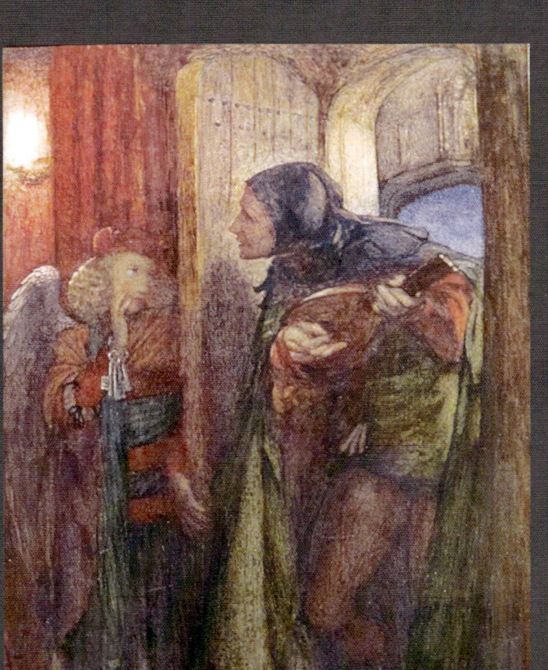

The Power of the Poet, 1903
Watercolor on paper. Private collection.

In her time, Brickdale was a well-respected illustrator and painter. In 1896 she created a lunette entitled *Spring* for the Royal Academy Dining Room, and in 1902 she had the honor of becoming the first female member of the Institute of Painters in Oils. Her works are styled in the manner of the Pre-Raphaelites such as Dante Gabriel Rossetti or William Holman Hunt, using vibrant jewel-like colors and representative nineteenth century subject matter. Tragically, Brickdale's career was cut short when she suffered a stroke in 1938 and could not paint for the remaining seven years of her life.

Many of her works also have symbolic elements as can be seen with *The Power of the Poet*. This playful and imaginative painting illustrates the power of poetry and music over not only the mortal, but immortal world as well. The poet with his mandolin has enchanted the angel, convincing her to open the door and let him in. The angel, with a coy look of adoration, dangles the keys from her wrist and bids him enter.

Likewise, *The Moth* is also a symbolic work, lamenting the coming of technology that leads to the end of the world of enchantment—a timely image considering it was created during the dark days of the First World War.

—Didactics written by Kara Lysandra Ross for 2012 exhibit at Allentown Art Museum, At the Edge: Art of the Fantastic.

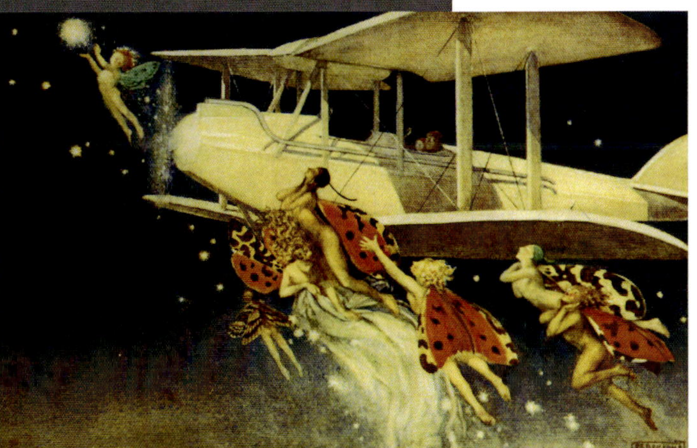

The Moth, 1917
Watercolor on paper.
Private collection.

Gustave DORÉ

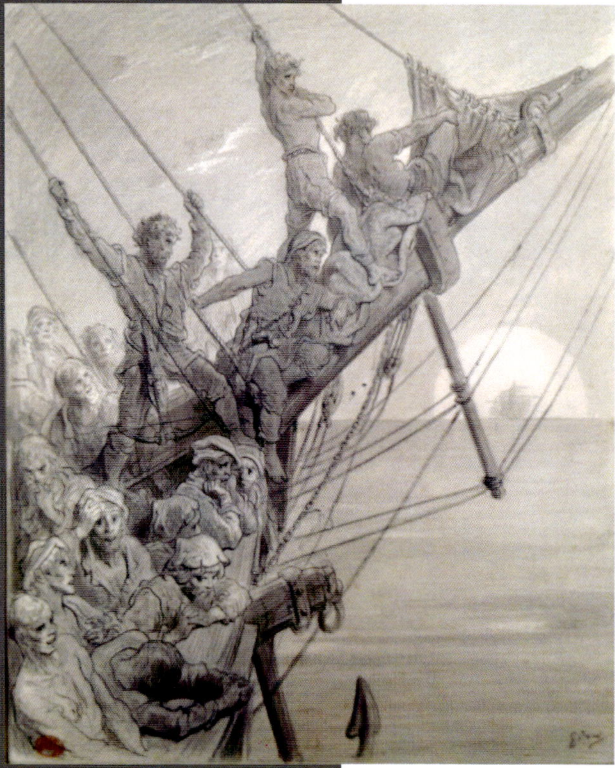

Rime of the Ancient Mariner—The Death Ship, 1870
Watercolor and ink on paper. Collection of Zaddick Longenbach.

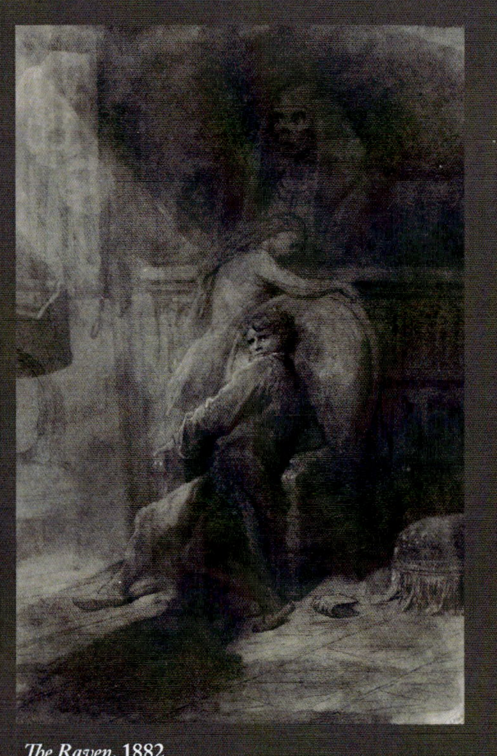

The Raven, 1882
Watercolor and ink on paper. Collection of Fred and Sherry Ross.

French, 1832–1883

Doré is one of the single most important figures in the history of imaginative realism. His stunning romantic depictions of Dante, Coleridge, Poe, and Byron influenced the work of nearly every imaginative painter who would follow in one way or another. Not only was Doré one of the most important figures of the nineteenth century, he was also one of the most successful, earning more than $2 million during the course of his career, enabling him to live a life of luxury.

During Doré's career, printing had not advanced sufficiently to allow an ink drawing to be directly transferred to a printing plate, so the artist would create a looser drawing that would then be engraved on to a printing plate. Thus, most extant Dore "originals" are the drawings that preceded the engraving process.

The Death Ship is one of Doré's illustrations for Samuel Taylor Coleridge's *Rime of the Ancient Mariner*, depicting the sailors on the cursed ship. Even in the drawing phase, the anguish of the sailors is clearly visible in their postures and gestures.

The Raven was one of the last projects Doré completed. By this time in his career printing had advanced sufficiently that he was creating more detailed original drawings for his work that could be transferred almost directly to print.

Gabriel FERRIER

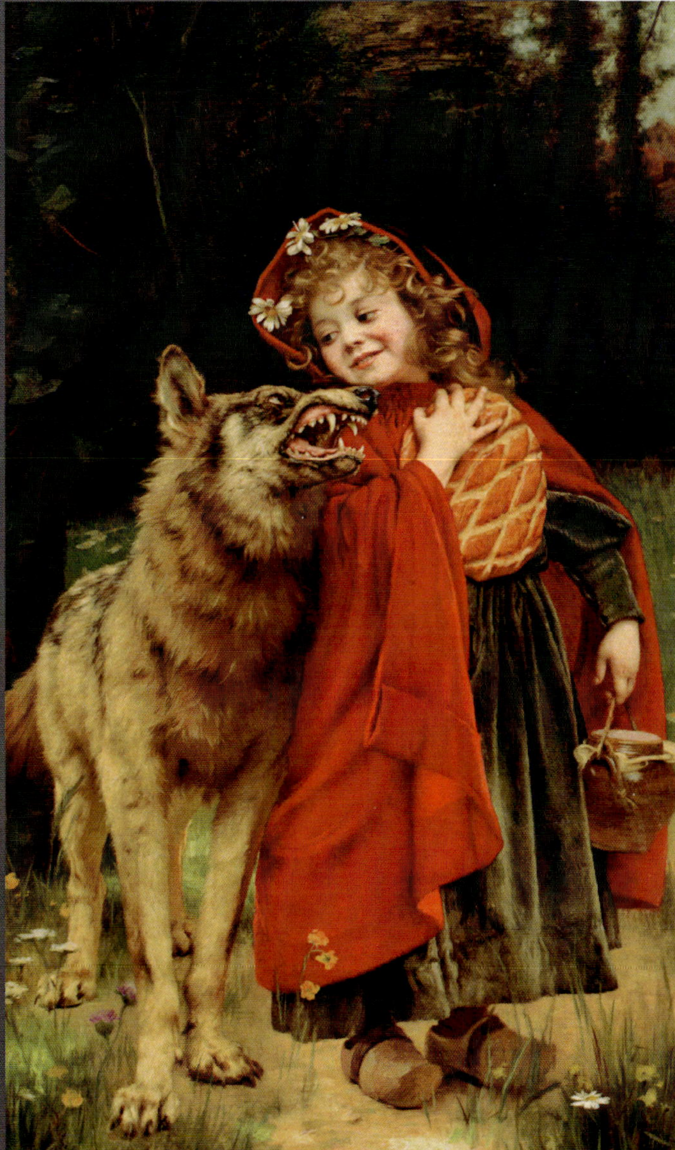

Red Riding Hood, n.d.
Oil on canvas. Collection of Fred and Sherry Ross.

French, 1847–1914

Ferrier was one of the leading figures in French academic painting. He was a professor at the École des Beaux-Arts in Paris and won the coveted Prix de Rome. His work was often filled with fantastical imagery and imaginative nudes.

Red Riding Hood is a perfect example of an important academic painting of fantasy art. Although this painting was not intended as an illustration for a book, it is interesting to note that this subject matter was considered highly desirable during the nineteenth century. This painting provides a remarkable example of the technical virtuosity that exemplified French academic painting and has proven so influential on contemporary imaginative realist painters.

—Didactics written by Kara Lysandra Ross for 2012 exhibit at Allentown Art Museum, At the Edge: Art of the Fantastic.

Edmund Blair LEIGHTON

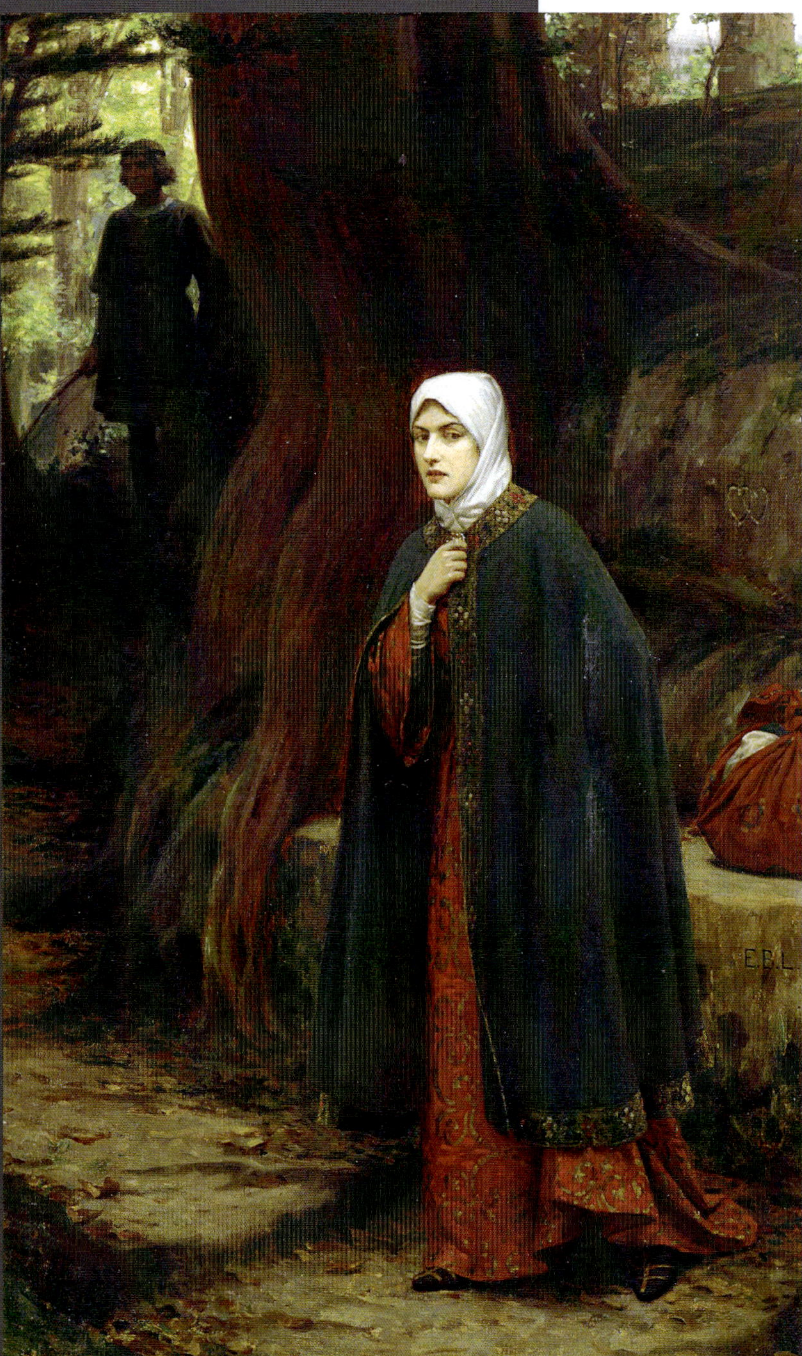

Footsteps, 1915
Oil on canvas. Private collection.

British, 1852–1922

Leighton studied at the South Kensington School of Art and the Heatherley's School of Art before gaining entry to the five-year program at the Royal Academy of Arts in 1874. He became a member of the Langham Sketch Club, and in 1880 served as its president. He was also elected to the Royal Institute of Oil Painters in 1887. He reached his professional peak around 1900. He is known for his paintings depicting romance, and although he painted many eighteenth century costume pieces with this subject, his depictions of the Middle Ages are most coveted.

Footsteps is a perfect example of Blair Leighton's subject matter. A lovely woman in medieval garb is seen sneaking into the woods, perhaps for a secret tryst. The hearts on the tree in the background suggest that she has reached her intended waiting spot and from the bundle we can infer she does not intend to return. Since a woodsman can be seen approaching in the background, it is also possible this is a rendition of the Snow White story.

—Didactics written by Kara Lysandra Ross for 2012 exhibit at Allentown Art Museum, At the Edge: Art of the Fantastic.

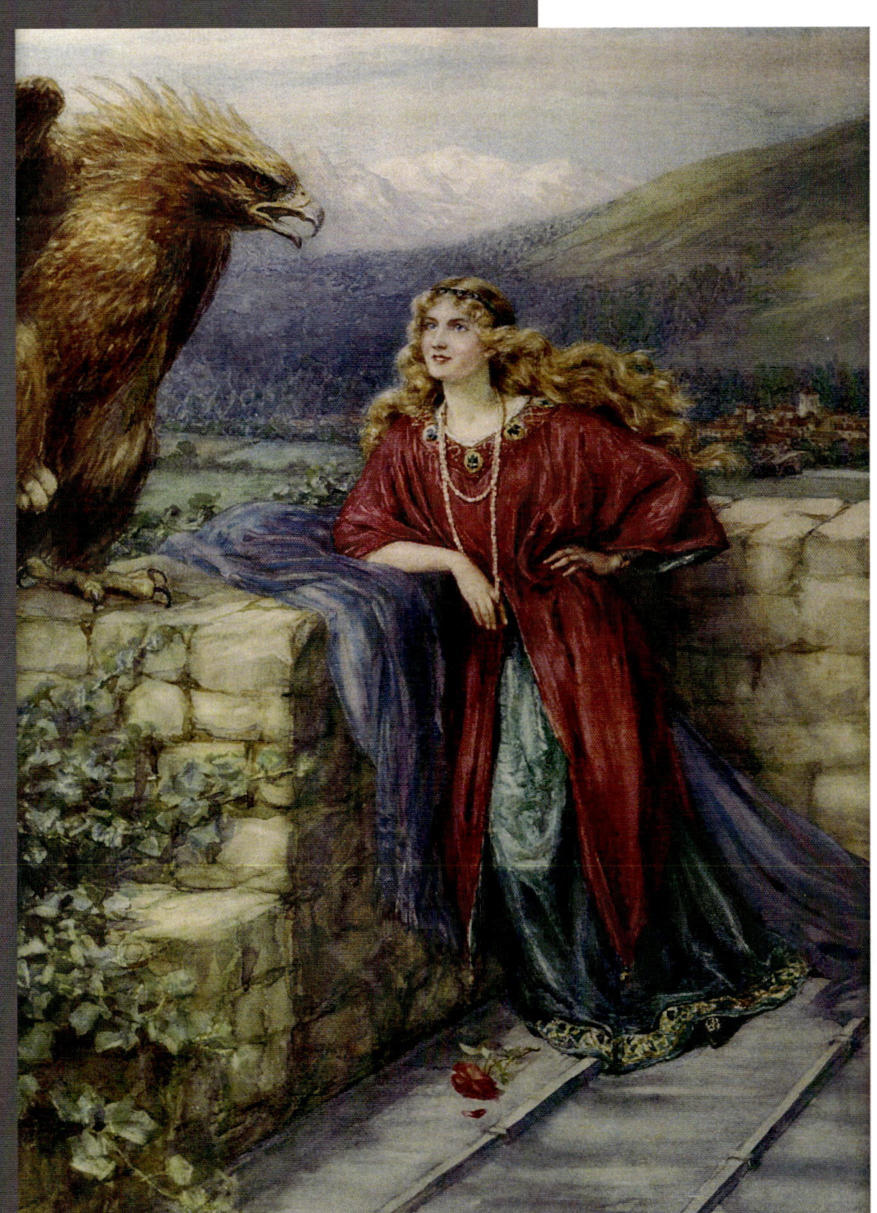

The Princess and the Eagle, c. 1895
Watercolor on paper. Private collection.

Beatrice PARSONS

British, 1860–1955

Parsons spent the majority of her career as the most renowned painter of English gardens in the world. However, at the beginning of her career in the late 1800s, she created many narrative works, her style and approach highly influenced by the Pre-Raphaelites.

The Princess and the Eagle is an example of Parsons' early narrative work, demonstrating the beautiful sense of color that would serve her well as a garden painter in the future. Although she later abandoned imaginative subjects, her early works like this one clearly demonstrate a Pre-Raphaelite influence.

Howard PYLE

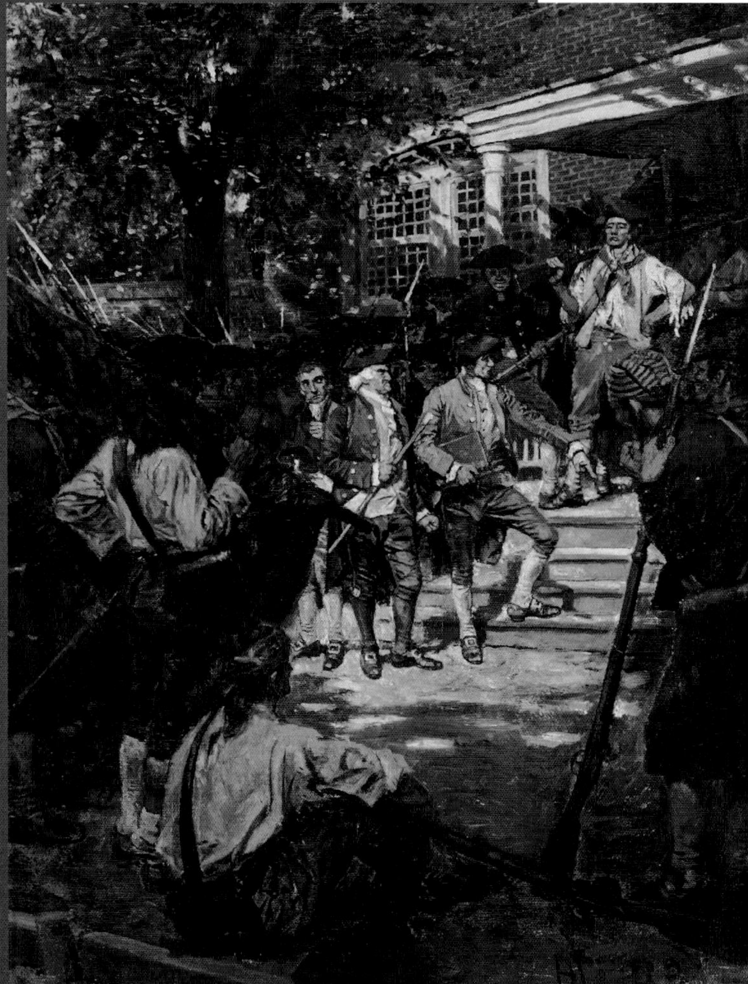

The Mob in Shay's Rebellion, 1883
Oil on canvas. Courtesy of the Illustrated Gallery.

American, 1853–1911

Pyle is the first major figure in American illustration as well as one of the most important. Not only did he produce a wide range of imaginative work, with themes from pirates to King Arthur and Robin Hood, he also founded the Howard Pyle School of Illustration Art, from which sprang the Brandywine artistic tradition, including luminaries such as N. C. Wyeth, Frank Schoonover, Harvey Dunn, and Jessie Wilcox Smith.

Pyle was also one of the first artists to specialize conceptually in illustration, thinking about painting in terms of narrative and character as opposed to mainly "meaning," technical approach, or emotional impact, although his work does not lack for any of these. His approach to narrative art impacted nearly every imaginative realist painter throughout the course of the twentieth century.

The Mob in Shay's Rebellion is one of Pyle's non-imaginative themes but demonstrates his strong feel for creating dramatic character-driven pieces.

Briton RIVIÈRE

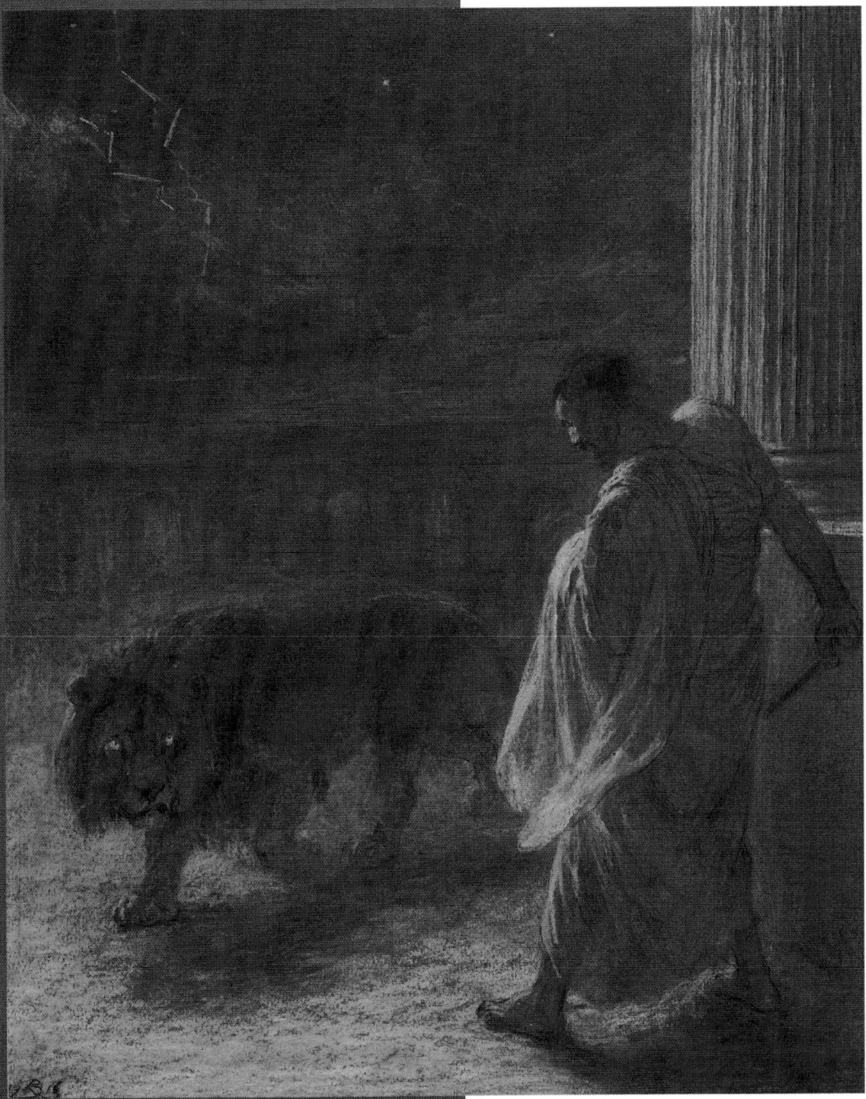

A Premonition of Imperial Rome, c. 1870
Charcoal on paper. Private collection.

British, 1840–1920

Rivière is among the finest of the Victorian animal painters, creating both glorified, romanticised paintings of wild animals and rather humanized paintings of dogs, which found a considerable market. He also created a number of works in which animals feature in a strongly imaginative narrative.

A Premonition of Imperial Rome is one of these works, in which the lion serves an allegorical purpose, thus melding animal painting and fantastic imagery.

James Edward ALLEN

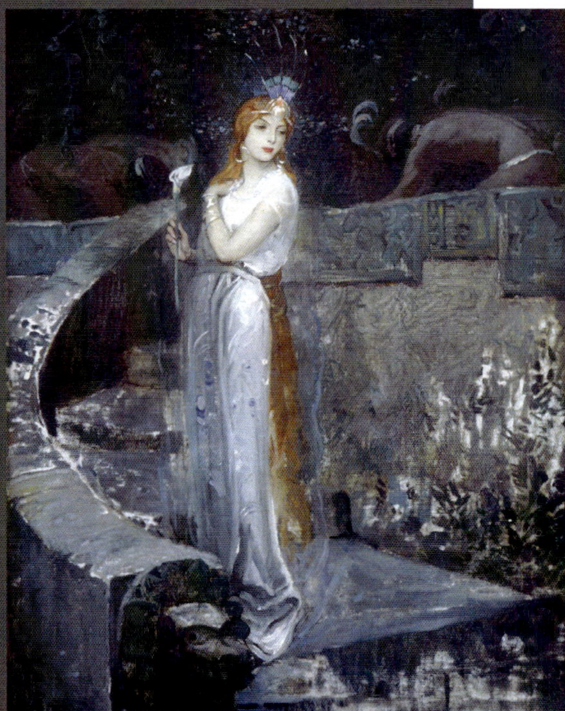

The Bride of the Sacred Well, 1928
Oil on canvas. The Kelly Collection of American Illustration.

American, 1894–1964

Allen, an illustrator and figurative printmaker, was known for his fidelity to the three-dimensional form, and actually spent years working with a sculptor to improve his sense of the human form. He also continued to insist on working directly from models rather than from reference photographs.

The Bride of the Sacred Well demonstrates Allen's familiarity with the human form as well as his acknowledged debt to both Chinese and Byzantine art.

Jaschik ÁLMOS

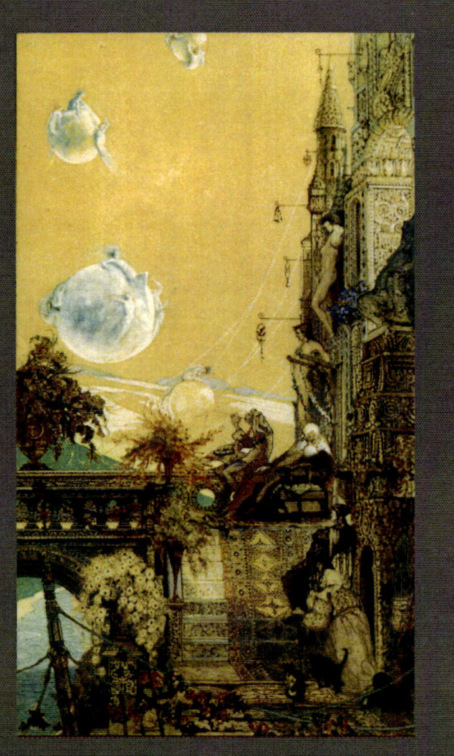

Hungarian, 1885–1950

Álmos was a superb Hungarian illustrator with a unique imagination. He illustrated collections of weird stories (including ones by Poe and H. G. Wells) in the 1920s for a variety of Hungarian publishers. He worked in a highly detailed and decorative watercolor style showing both orientalist and academic influences. His work is relatively little-known today. Unlike his more famous countryman, Willy Pogany, Álmos never left Hungary and so hardly any of his work appeared in either Western Europe or the United States.

Slaves of the Spheres is a wonderfully imaginative work. Its place of publication is unknown, although it likely served as an illustration for a Hungarian book.

Slaves of the Spheres, c. 1925
Watercolor on paper. Private collection.

James AYLWARD

THE GOLDEN AGE

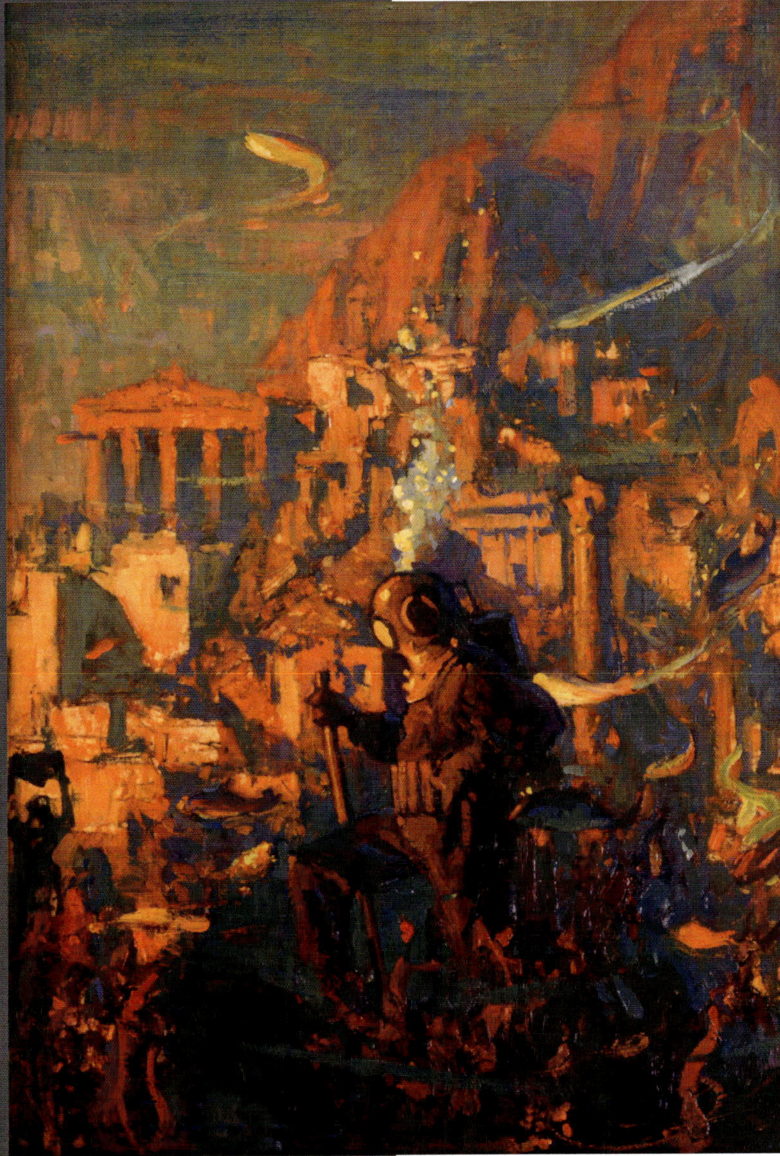

Twenty Thousand Leagues Under the Sea, 1925
Oil on board. The Kelly Collection of American Illustration.

American, 1875–1956

Aylward was an illustrator who specialized in maritime art, turning his love of the sea into memorable paintings for classics such as Jack London's *Sea Wolf* and Jules Verne's *Twenty Thousand Leagues Under the Sea*. Aylward was selected as one of only eight artists officially designated by the United States Army to chronicle World War I.

Twenty Thousand Leagues Under the Sea shows Aylward at his best, portraying the legendary Captain Nemo at the ruins of Atlantis.

Wladyslaw T. BENDA

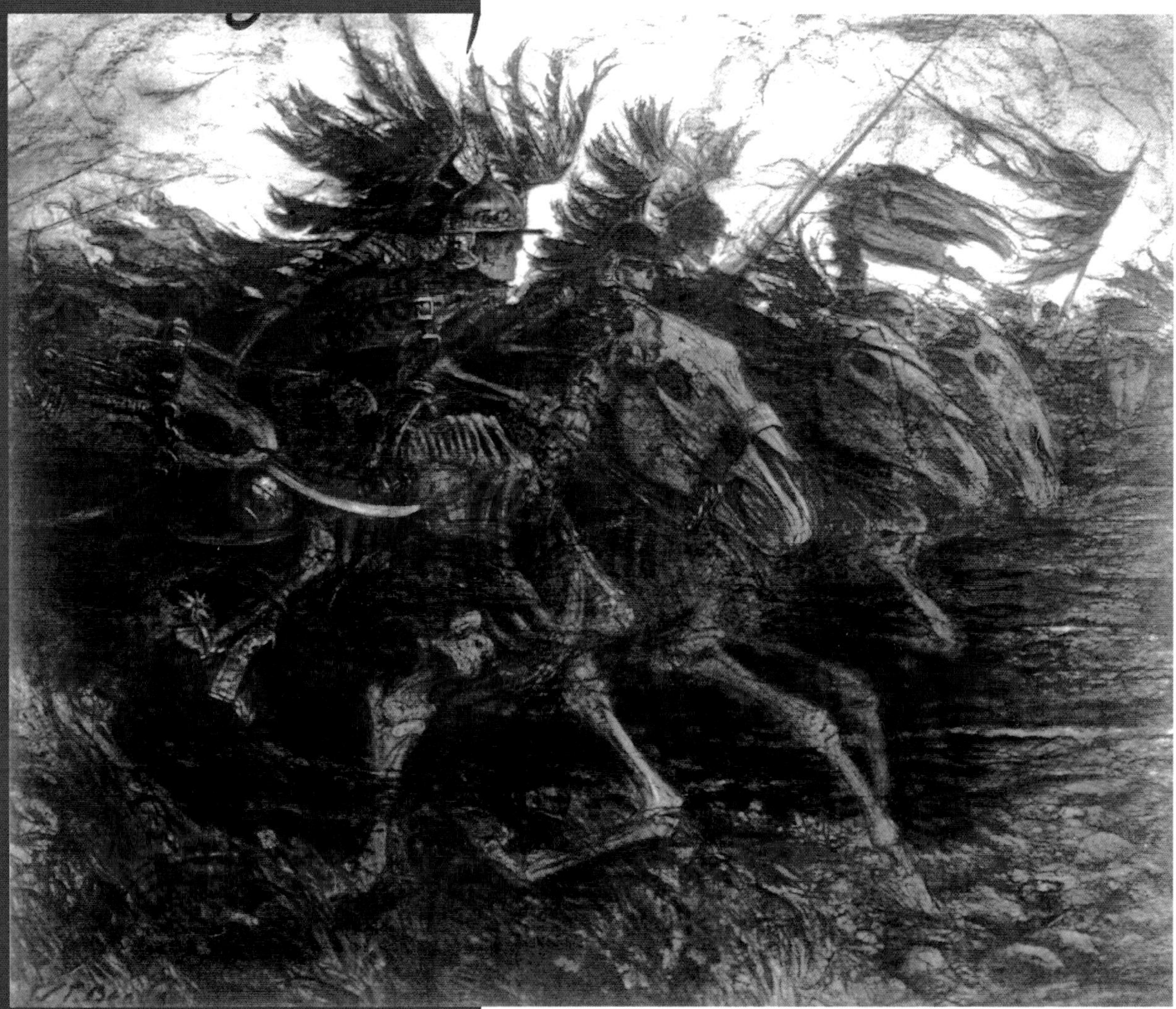

The Army of the Dead, c. 1917
Charcoal on paper. Private collection.

Polish/American, 1873–1948

Benda was born and studied in Poland, then emigrated to the United States in 1902, where he attended the Art Students League of New York and the William Merritt Chase School. He eventually became one of the most famous illustrators of his day, equally as well known as Norman Rockwell, N. C. Wyeth or Maxfield Parrish. He was renowned for his depictions of mysterious women, very different from the all-American girl look created by other artists, and also for his strange, theatrical masks and costume designs.

The Army of the Dead is an unusual work for Benda, who rarely worked with outright fantastic themes. It was produced at the outbreak of World War I as a recruiting poster for the Polish army, and depicts a legendary Polish cavalry brigade. It appears, however, that it was deemed too extreme and grotesque by the commission, as no record exists of the poster having been produced.

Franklin BOOTH

American, 1874–1948

Booth is widely acknowledged as one of the finest pen-and-ink artists in history. His highly distinctive technique of using closely spaced line to control light and density came from a misunderstanding. As a young artist, Booth carefully copied magazine illustrations, believing they were pen-and-ink works instead of engravings. As a result, his ink style replicates the feel of steel engraving. He had a tremendous influence on later artists, particularly Roy Krenkel and Bernie Wrightson.

Flying Islands of the Night—Mid-Air Spirit shows that Booth also had the ability to handle color, although he did so fairly infrequently.

In the Golden Land of Dreams is one of Booth's masterpieces, in which both his exquisite technique and imaginative grandeur are on full display.

Flying Islands of the Night—Mid-Air Spirit, 1913
Watercolor and ink on paper. Collection of Zaddick Longenbach.

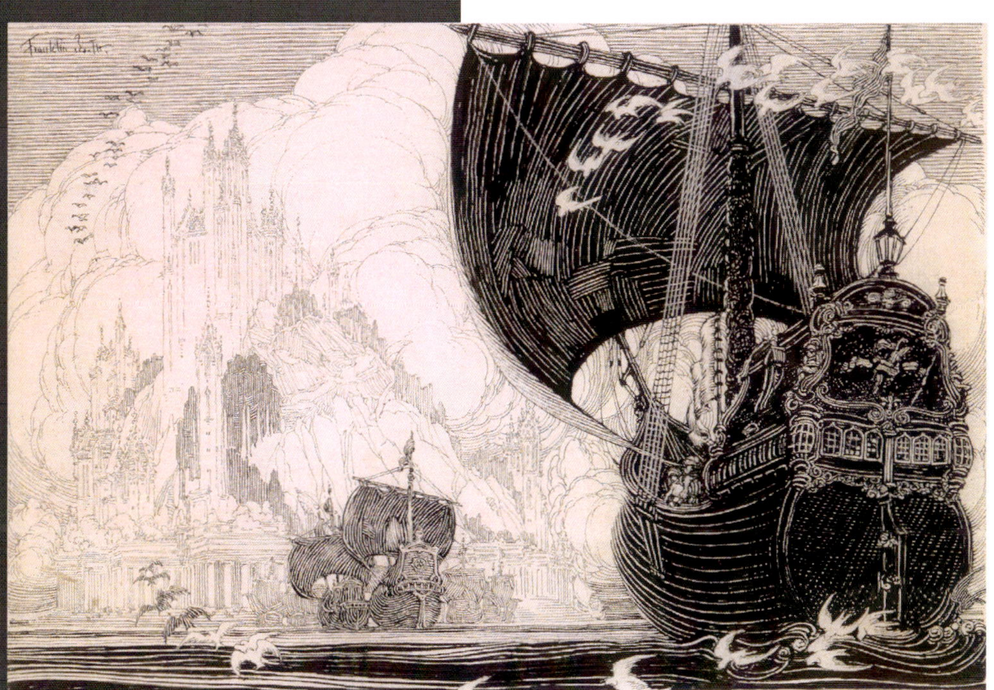

In the Golden Land of Dreams, 1913
Ink on paper. Kelly Collection of American Illustration.

Howard Chandler CHRISTY

American, 1873–1952

Christy was an extremely popular illustrator during the golden age, being best known for his creation of the Christy Girl, a more approachable version of the Gibson Girl that was also popular. Although Christy did very little work with fantastic themes, his approach to the female form lent itself well to the work he did do, including *The Lady of the Lake*.

Lady of the Lake (Rob Roy and Lady McGregor) provides a beautiful example of a Christy Girl transported into a romantic, medievalist setting.

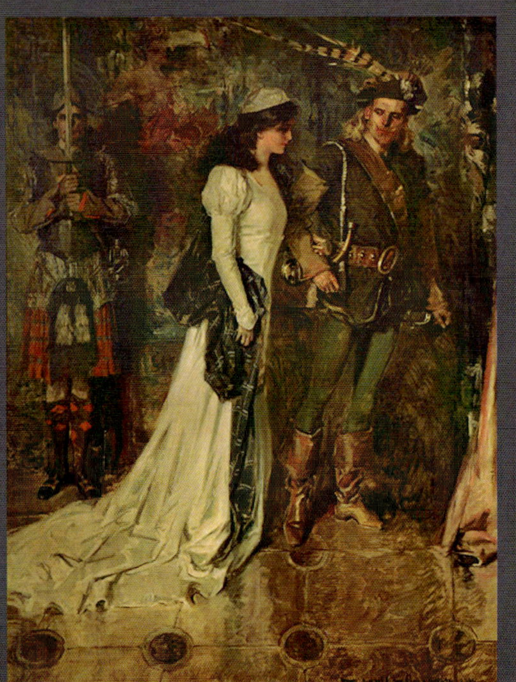

Lady of the Lake (Rob Roy and Lady McGregor), 1910
Oil on canvas. Courtesy of the Illustrated Gallery.

Harry CLARKE

Irish, 1889–1931

Clarke, a leading figure in the Irish arts and crafts movement, is renowned for both his illustration and his work in stained glass that show the influence of Art Nouveau and decadent art. His imagery often draws comparisons to those of Aubrey Beardsley, but Clarke's work is more disturbing than that of his peer. Part of the uniqueness of Clarke's style is his transposition of stained glass techniques to pen and ink, picking lines out of a background in an incredibly detailed manner.

The Pit and the Pendulum is a classic work from Poe's *Tales of Mystery and Imagination*, the publication that made Clarke's reputation as a book illustrator.

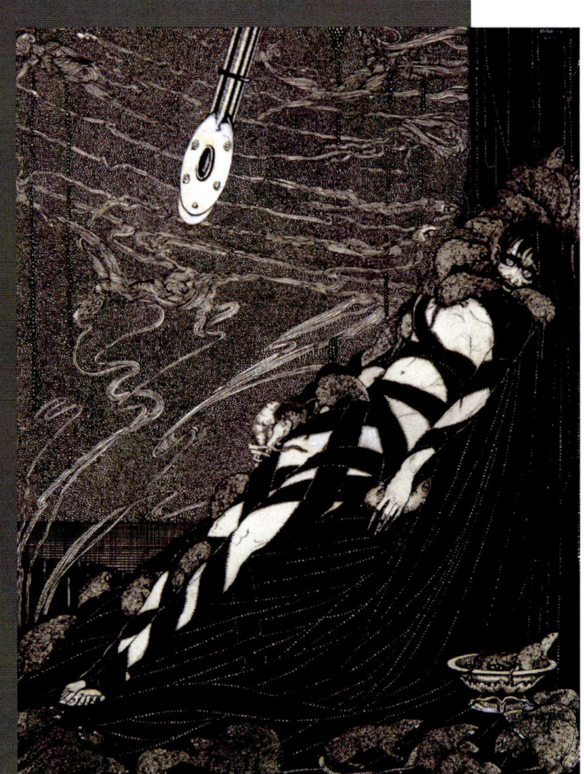

Tales of Mystery and Imagination—The Pit and the Pendulum, 1919
Ink on paper. On loan from the Korshak Collection, Orlando, FL.

Joseph Clement COLL

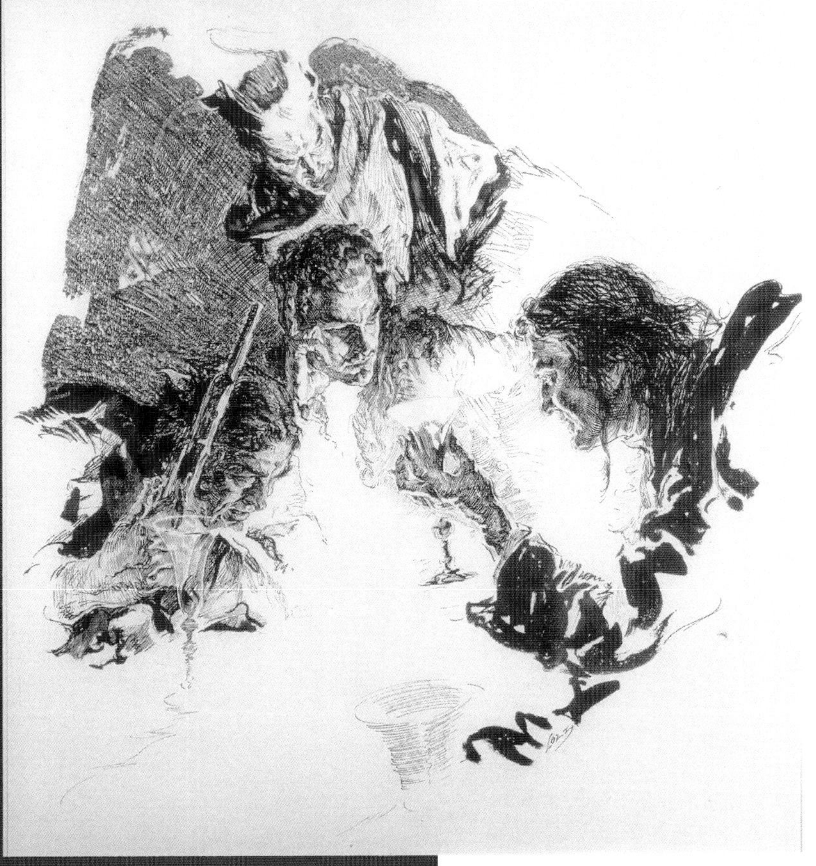

The Conspirators, c. 1915
Ink on paper. The Kelly Collection of American Illustration.

American, 1881–1921

Coll, along with Daniel Vierge, is credited with having created the "heroic" narrative style in pen and ink. His powerful, instinctive linework—seemingly effortlessly executed—created depth, deep shadows and psychological impact that would prove to be tremendously influential, particularly on the work of Frank Frazetta.

The Conspirators demonstrates Coll's remarkable ability to achieve a high sense of drama and lighting within the constraints of pen and ink, mixing areas of tightly rendered detail with pure blacks and whites to produce a depth rarely seen in black-and-white work.

Lee F. CONREY

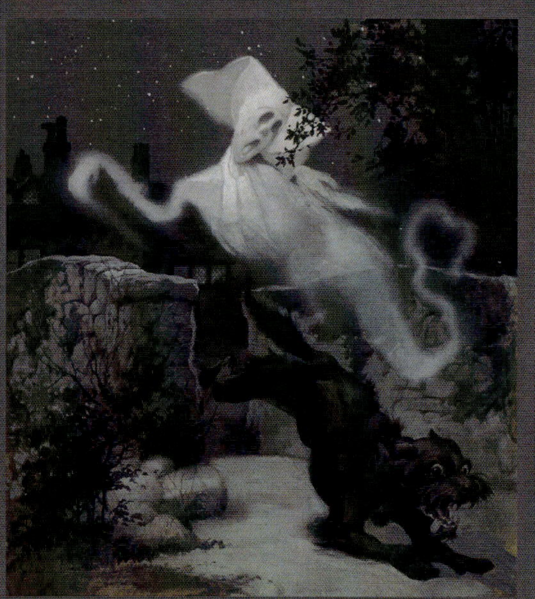

The Spirit of the Canoness, c. 1940
Watercolor on paper. Private collection.

American, 1883–1976

Conrey is one of the unsung heroes of the famed *American Weekly Magazine* and a master of drybrushing, a technique that produces a characteristic scratchy look by painting with very little pigment on the brush's bristles. He had a long and prolific career beginning around 1915. His work remains little known today because it typically appeared in a newspaper supplement in black and white at a time when color was much more popular.

The Spirit of the Canoness appeared in *American Weekly Magazine* in the late 1930s or early 1940s, illustrating a passage from *Lord Halifax's Ghost Stories*.

Dean CORNWELL

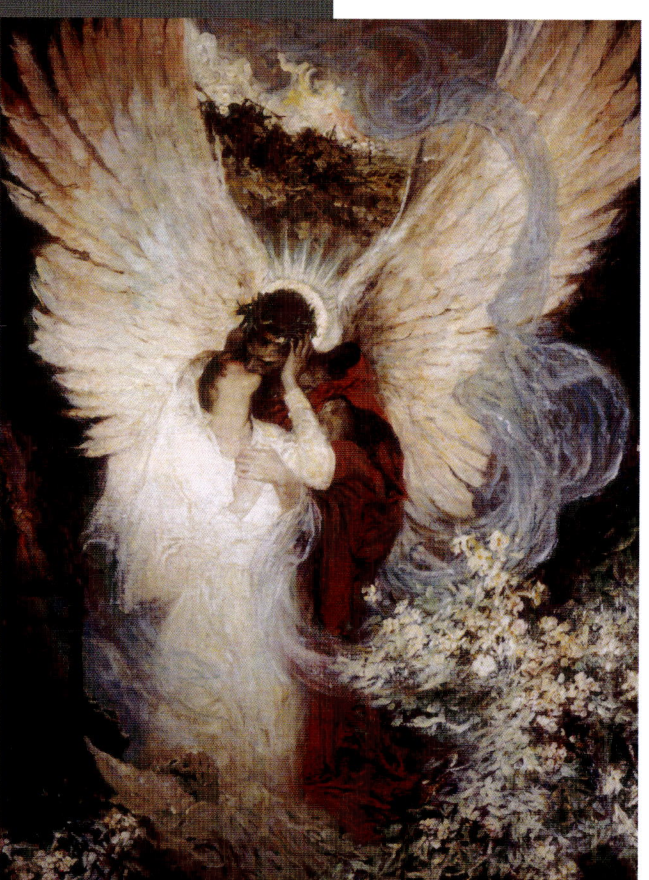

American, 1892–1960

Cornwell is one of the major figures of the later golden age of illustration. At his peak, he was one of the most famous illustrators in America as well as a highly sought-after muralist, known among his peers as the Dean of Illustration. While he is perhaps best known for his advertisements and war posters, he was completely at home with the fantastic, creating rich narratives and lushly handled paint reminiscent of his artist mentors, Harvey Dunn and Frank Brangwyn.

The Other Side demonstrates Cornwell's flair for the dramatic, his rich, loosely painted style, and his strong sense of narrative.

The Other Side, 1918
Oil on canvas. The Kelly Collection of American Illustration.

Edmund DULAC

The Tempest—Full Fathoms Five, 1908
Watercolor, gouache and ink on paper.
On loan from the Korshak Collection, Orlando, FL.

French, 1882–1953

Along with Arthur Rackham and Kay Nielsen, Dulac was one of the dominant figures in high-end illustrated book publication in Britain during the golden age. Unlike Rackham, who worked predominantly with line filled with color, Dulac, who had studied as a painter, used pure color. His work is sharply divided into two periods, centering around the year 1913. Before this time his work is cool and rich, showing the influence of Western art. After 1913 his work becomes brighter and more stylized.

Full Fathoms Five is one of Dulac's most famous images from his 1908 edition of Shakespeare's *The Tempest*, showing the rich, mellow blues and cool hues that were typical of his pre-1913 work.

William Russell FLINT

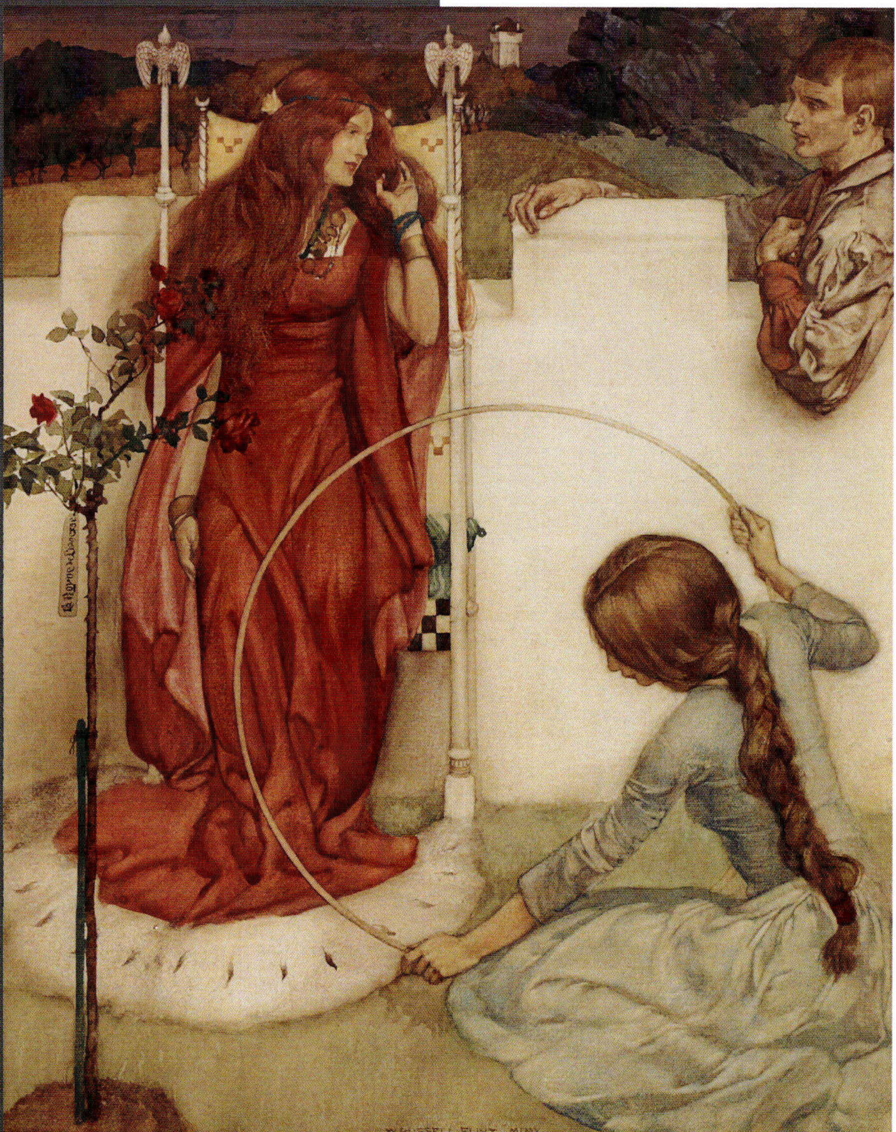

Sir Gareth and the Lady Lyonesse, 1910
Watercolor on paper. Private collection.

Scottish, 1880–1969

Early in his career, Flint's work showed almost a prototypical post Pre-Raphaelite influence in terms of his mostly highly romanticized depictions of beautiful, sometimes sensualized women. Painting in watercolor, he was highly respected during his career and was knighted by the British government in 1947. Although the peak of his artistic career came after World War II, it is his early illustrations for Sir Thomas Malory and Geoffrey Chaucer that served as the high points for his work in the field of imaginative art.

Sir Gareth and the Lady Lyonesse is an image from Sir Thomas Malory's *Le Morte d'Arthur*, and shows the strong influence of John William Waterhouse and Herbert Draper on Flint's early work.

Frederick R. GRUGER

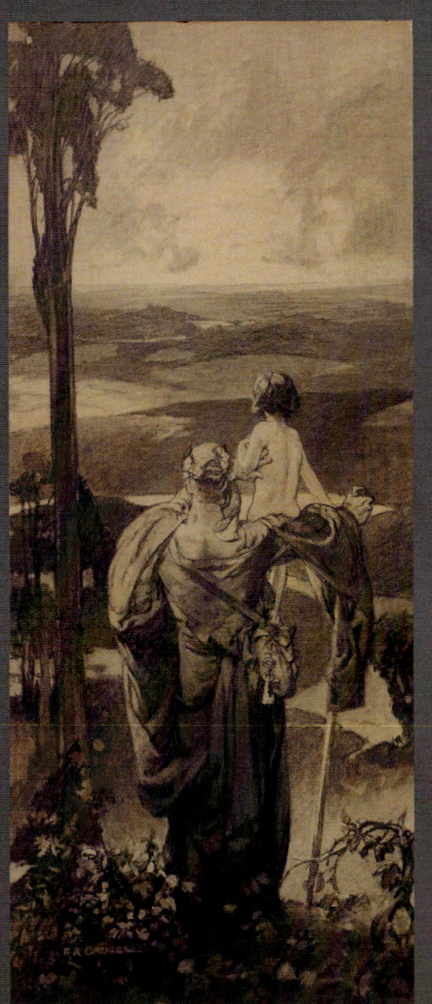

The Passing of Summer, c. 1920
Graphite on board. Private collection.

American, 1871–1953

Gruger was an extremely popular illustrator between 1900 and 1940, creating nearly three thousand works for the *Saturday Evening Post* alone. He worked predominantly with Wolff pencil (a combination of graphite and charcoal) on a thin cardboard that was eventually produced and sold as "Gruger Board"—a mainstay for illustrators for decades. Although Gruger rarely worked with outrightly fantastic themes, his method of working purely from imagination allowed him to produce masterful results when he did turn his hand to the imaginative.

The Passing of Summer is one of Gruger's most famous works. It is an allegorical work that references the great artists of the nineteenth century (including Gruger's greatest inspiration, Edwin Austin Abbey) in its highly romantic mood and feel.

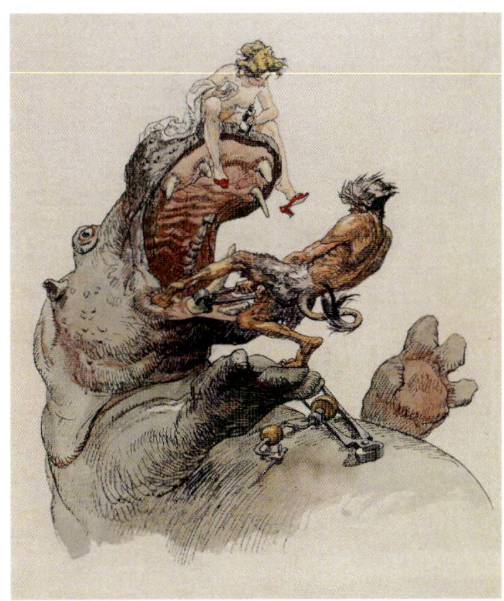

The Dental Technician, c. 1925
Watercolor and ink on paper.
Private collection.

Heinrich KLEY

German, 1863–1945

Although Kley spent much of his career painting industrial scenes and machinery, his darkly humorous and often erotic pen and ink drawings have led to his greatest recognition. Walt Disney was an ardent admirer of Kley and built a large private collection of his work. Kley's influence can be seen in Disney productions such as *Fantasia*.

The Dental Technician is a perfect example of Kley's work, including the satyr, nymph, and hippopotamus themes that are so clearly referenced in Disney's *Fantasia*.

Frank Xavier LEYENDECKER

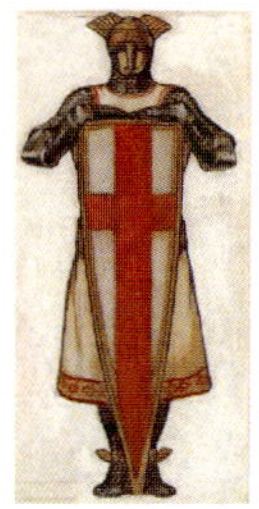

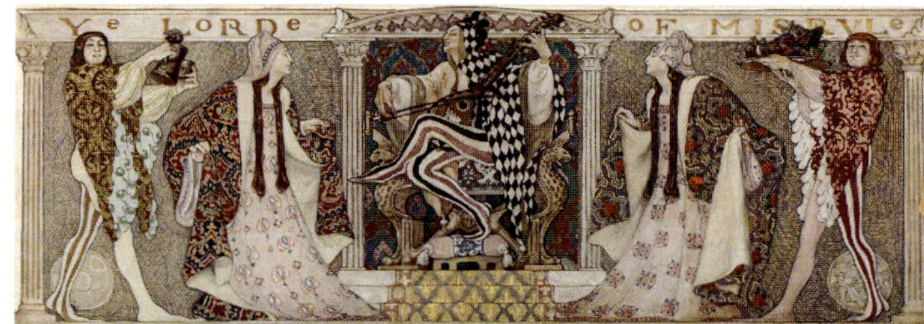

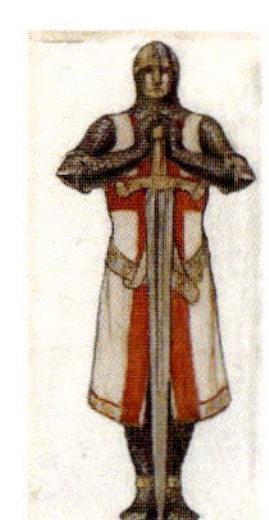

Ye Lorde of Misrule, c. 1915
Oil on canvas. Courtesy of the Illustrated Gallery.

American, 1877–1924

Frank Leyendecker failed to achieve the fame of his older brother Joseph but produced a wide range of successful illustrative work. He painted in similar manner to Joseph, but with a more delicate touch that lacked the power of his brother's imagery.

Ye Lorde of Misrule is an excellent example of the younger Leyendecker's work, showing his more decorative approach to an imaginative theme.

Joseph Christian LEYENDECKER

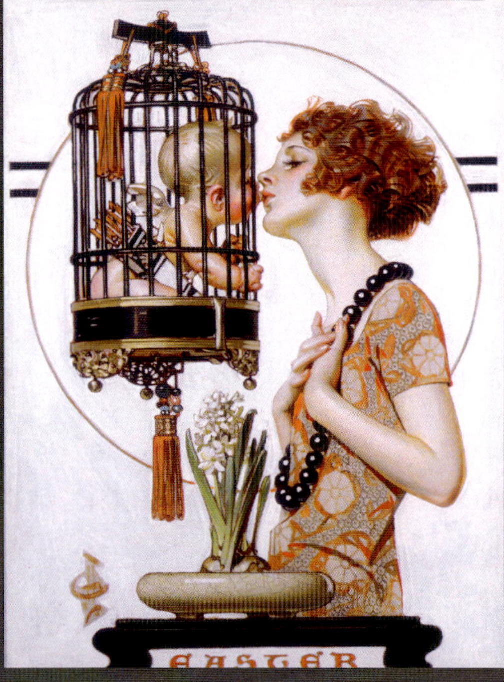

Woman Kissing Cupid, 1923
Oil on canvas. The Kelly Collection of American Illustration.

American, 1874–1951

Joseph Leyendecker, like his brother, studied at the Académie Julian in Paris, then returned to the United States. He immediately became one of the most demanded artists in the field. He produced more than three hundred covers for the *Saturday Evening Post* and served as a tremendous influence on his friend Norman Rockwell, who was a pallbearer at his funeral. Leyendecker is equally famous for his New Year Baby series of *Post* covers, his striking war posters, and his iconic advertising work, including the debonair Arrow Collar Man.

Woman Kissing Cupid is a superb exemplar of Leyendecker's work for the *Saturday Evening Post*, using his iconic cupid to inject a touch of the fantastic and whimsical into that very mainstream publication.

Fortunino MATANIA

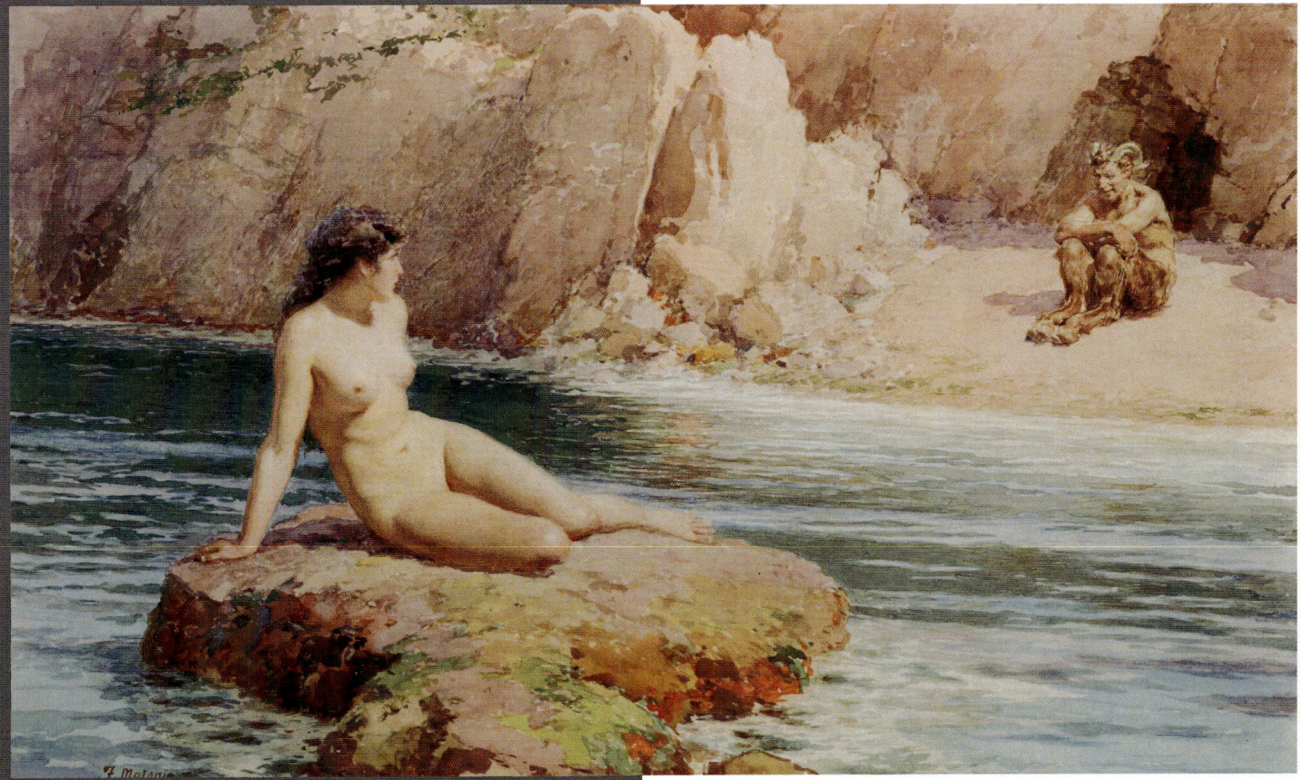

Checkmate, c. 1930
Watercolor on paper. On loan from the Korshak Collection, Orlando, FL.

Italian, 1881–1963

Matania began his career producing highly detailed illustrations of World War I and later produced historical and mythological themes. The latter work, including voluptuous nudes, cemented his position as one of the most popular illustrators of the time. He is best known for his highly detailed ink drawings, but he also produced many works in color that are equally noteworthy.

Checkmate demonstrates Matania's draughtmanship and his gift for color, as well as his wry sense of humor.

Alphonse MUCHA

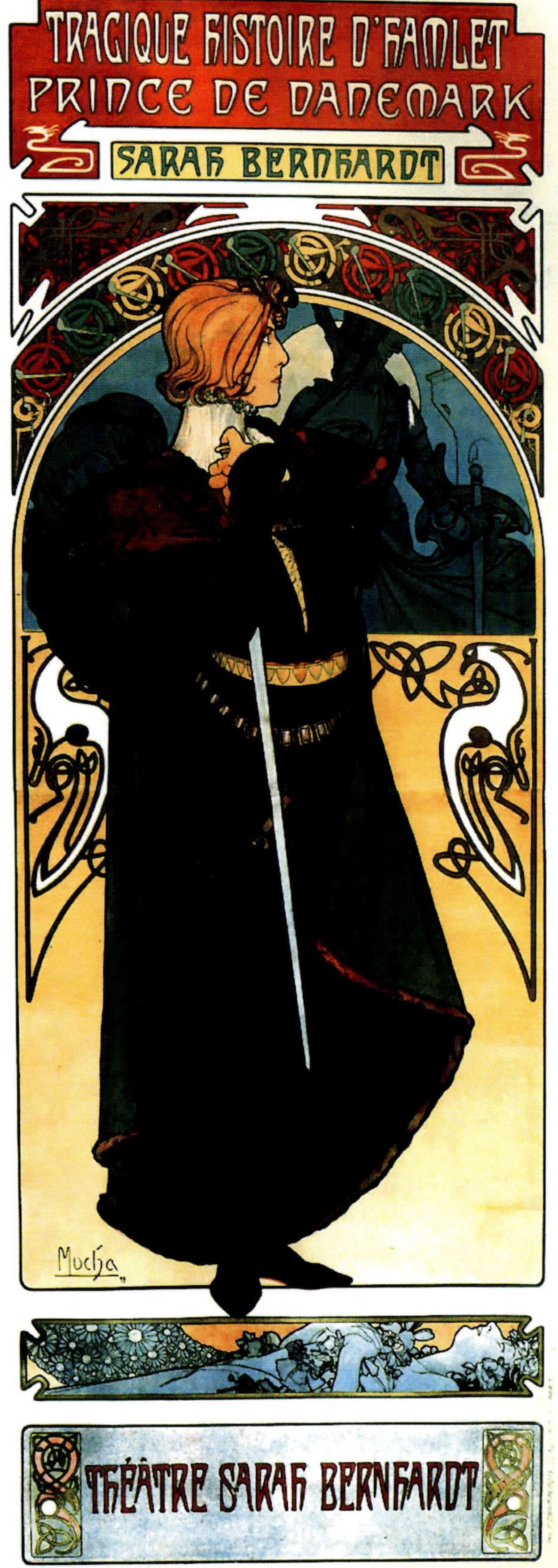

Czechoslovakian, 1860–1939

Mucha is generally recognized as the preeminent voice of the French Art Nouveau style just before the turn of the twentieth century, mixing classical looking women with an ornate design scheme. He achieved fame creating lithographic posters, although his output included lithographs as well as paintings, drawings, theater sets and costume designs. The vast majority of his work resides today in the Mucha Museum in Prague, and his work—other than lithographs—is rarely seen in the United States. His influence on the imaginative artists of the late twentieth century is hard to overstate.

Hamlet is an example of one of Mucha's early lithographic posters done for Sarah Bernhardt, the most famous actress of her time. In lithography, the image is laid directly on to stone and printed one color at a time. When the process is complete the stones are ground down. Thus, these lithographs are the only originals that exists, even though they exist in a multiple edition.

Hamlet, 1899
Lithograph on paper. Courtesy of the Illustrated Gallery.

William Andrew ("Willy") POGANY

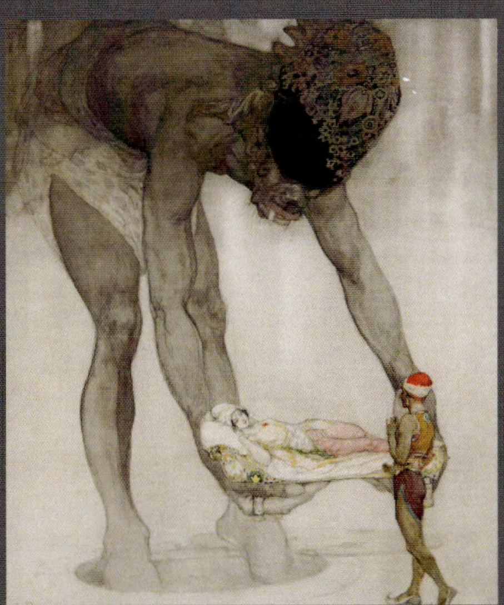

Tales of the Persian Genii—The Sultan Nisnar, 1917
Watercolor on paper. On loan from the Korshak Collection, Orlando, FL.

Hungarian, 1882–1955

Pogany was a prolific illustrator of children's books and limited edition "gift" books featuring classic myths and legends, which were the artist's favorite subject. Pogany left Hungary for Great Britain and then the United States early in his career. He worked in a wide range of styles, varying his approach to suit each individual project.

The Sultan Nisnar is an illustration from *Tales of the Persian Genii* and shows Pogany using a more orientalist style—as suits the subject matter—rather than the more ornate Art Nouveau influences seen in some of his earlier works, like Richard Wagner's operas or Samuel Taylor Coleridge's *Rime of the Ancient Mariner*.

Arthur RACKHAM

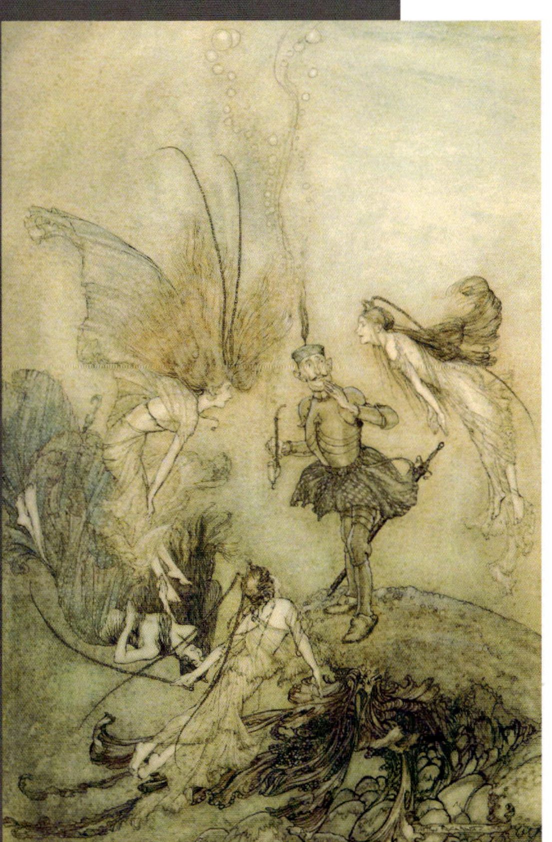

Sir Rupert the Fearless, 1907
Watercolor and ink on paper. On loan from the Korshak Collection, Orlando, FL.

British, 1867–1939

Rackham's name is synonymous with golden age British fantastic illustration. He is the most famous British watercolorist, both during his lifetime and today. Rackham worked in a distinctive style that used ink lines to bound color, where the inking is the primary means of image-making with the color layered in with beautiful transparent washes. His work has influenced contemporary watercolorists from Brian Froud to Tony DiTerlizzi and Omar Rayyan.

Sir Rupert the Fearless is a beautiful example of Rackham's work, containing many of the thematic elements that define his art, including fairylike women, twisted trees, a soft, gentle sense of humor and a muted, earth-tone palette.

Harry ROUNTREE

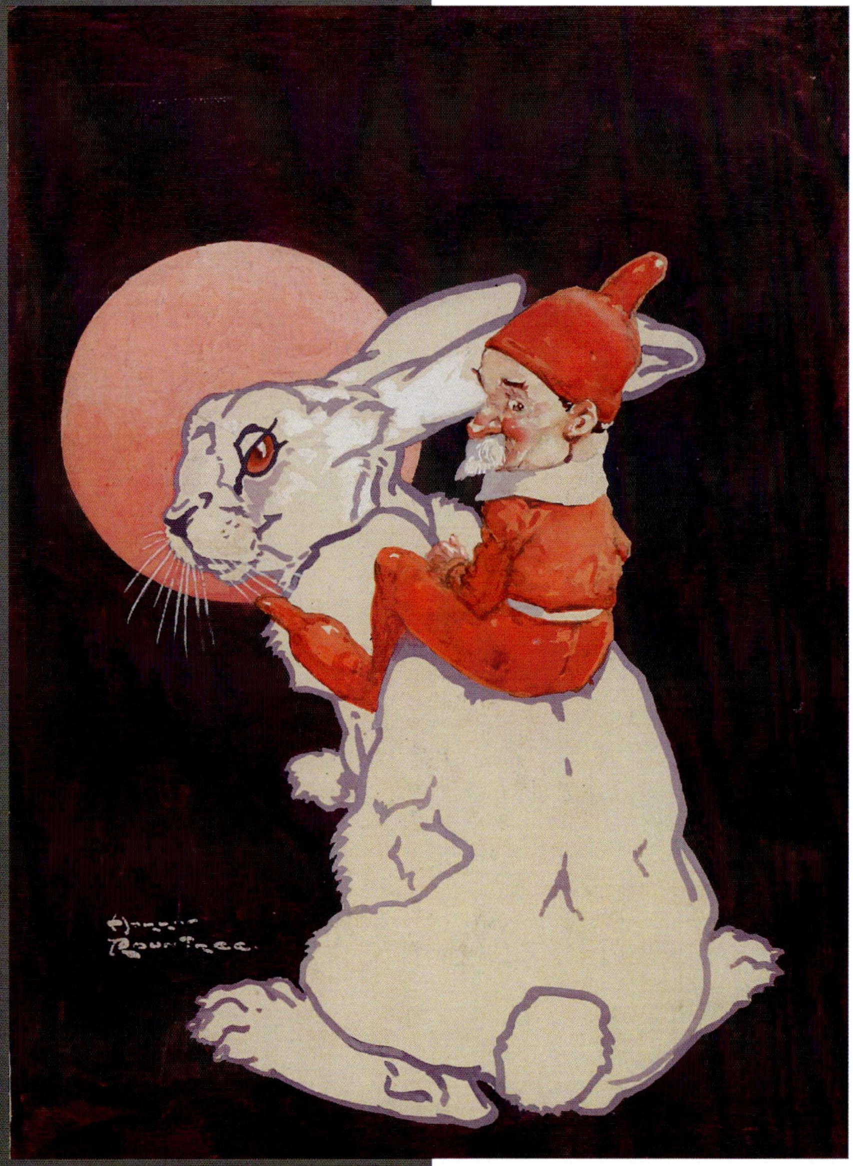

Rabbit Moon, 1922
Watercolor on paper. Private collection.

British, 1878–1950

Born in New Zealand, Rountree relocated to London in 1901. He was one of the most successful illustrators of children's animal stories in the golden age. He worked with other themes, but his depictions of fairy-tale animals, including Brer Rabbit and others in *Alice in Wonderland* and *Aesop's Fables,* made him famous. Working in ink and watercolor, Rountree's illustrations capture a feeling of joy and energy that is perfectly suited to the subject matter.

Rabbit Moon shows Rountree's ability to blend humans and animals in an image with great effect, even when the animals are not overtly "fairy tale-ish."

Frank E. SCHOONOVER

In Fierce Rushes the Spanish Advanced, 1917
Oil on canvas. The Kelly Collection of American Illustration.

American, 1877–1972

Schoonover was one of the original group of students studying under Howard Pyle at the Drexel Institute in Philadelphia. He helped form the Brandywine School of painting along with classmates like N. C. Wyeth, William Aylward, and Harvey Dunn. Like these artists, Schoonover worked with a wide range of themes, including the fantastic, in his illustrations for authors Edgar Rice Burroughs, Jonathan Swift, and Johann Wyss. Along with Pyle and Wyeth, he is one of the greatest Brandywine influences on modern artists.

In Fierce Rushes the Spanish Advanced demonstrates Schoonover's ability to capture intense drama and action in a highly complex scene that reads quickly and powerfully.

Swiss Family Robinson shows the other end of Schoonver's range of talents with a simple composition and vibrant colors combined with a single exotic element producing an image that immediately immerses the viewer in the narrative of the painting.

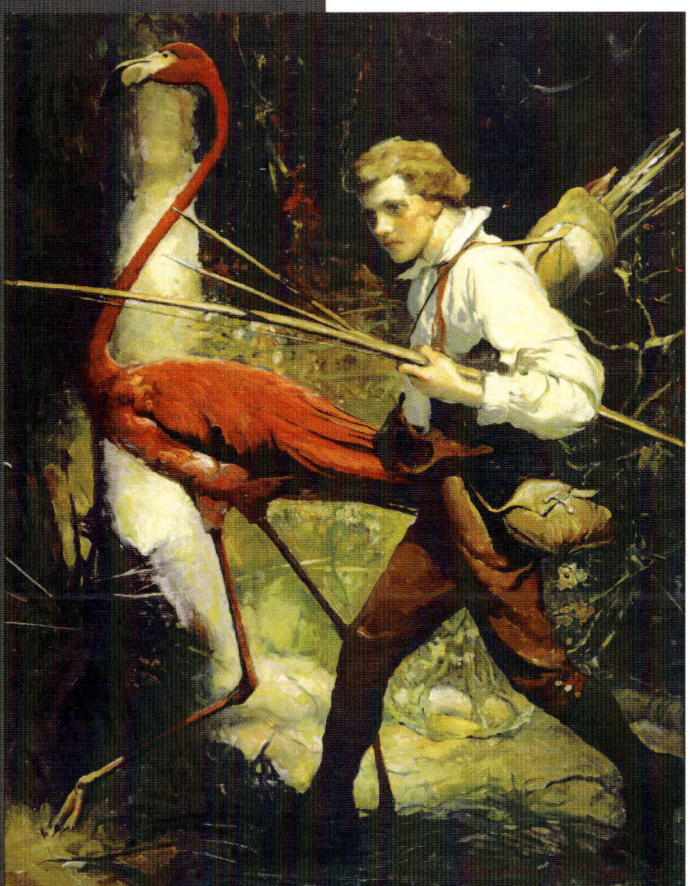

Swiss Family Robinson, 1921
Oil on canvas. Collection of Dr. Edward R. Burka.

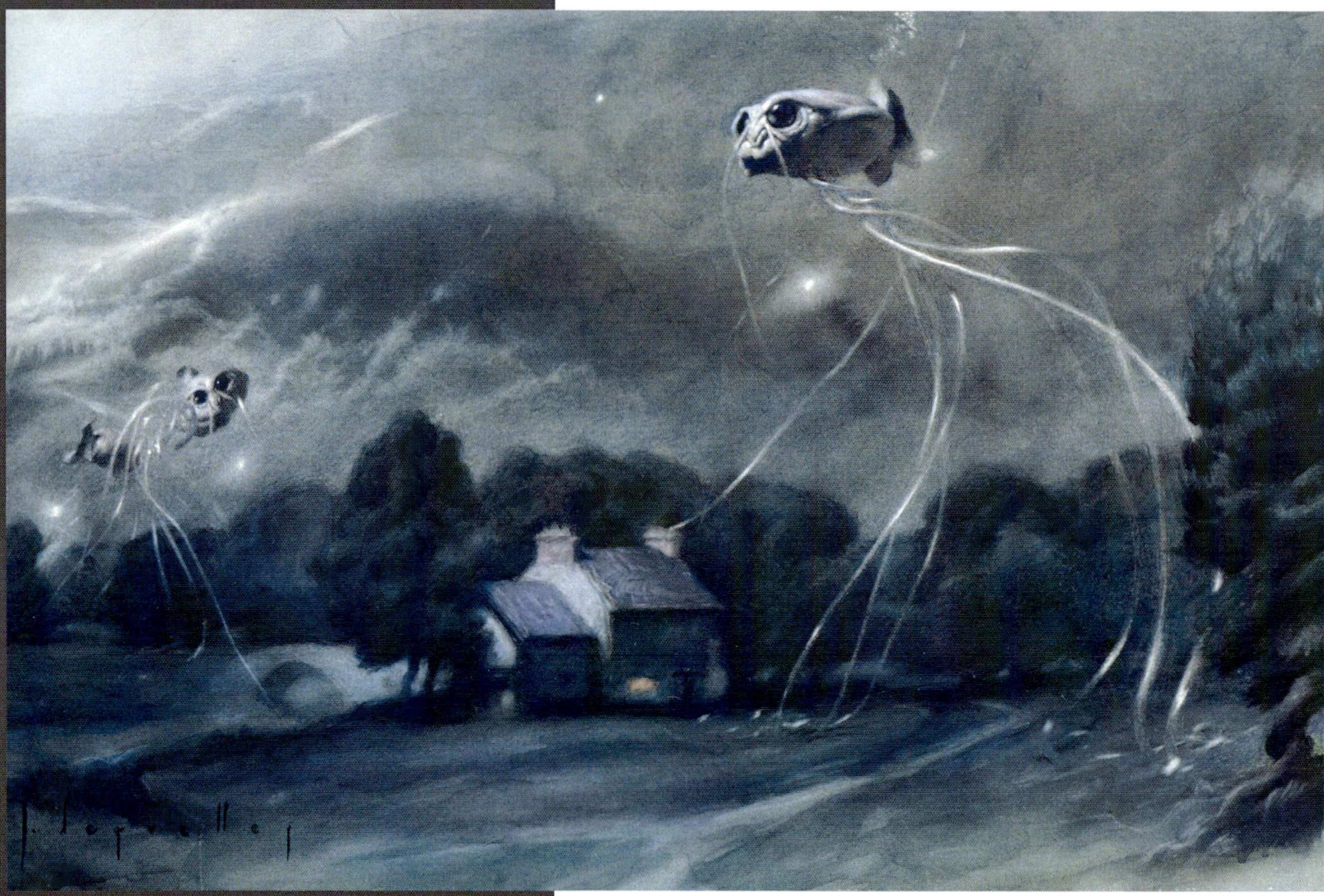

War of the Worlds, c. 1910
Watercolor on paper. On loan from the Korshak Collection, Orlando, FL.

José SEGRELLES

Spanish, 1885–1969

Until fairly recently, Segrelles has been the best-kept secret in golden age illustration. Although he did have an exhibition in New York during his lifetime, the vast majority of his work was done for Spanish publications. His work is characterized by a remarkable sense of composition and conceptual richness, and his watercolor technique allowed him to utilize this talent to its fullest. Although he was barely known in the United States in the 1960s, he was appreciated by Roy Krenkel, who shared this work with Frank Frazetta, leading to the obvious influence of Segrelles's work on Frazetta's own paintings.

War of the Worlds is an illustration for the H. G. Wells novel of the same name. It provides an excellent example of Segrelles's flair for the otherworldly, as his depictions of the famous Martian tripods is unique and disturbing in a way that no other illustrator has managed to capture.

Sidney SIME

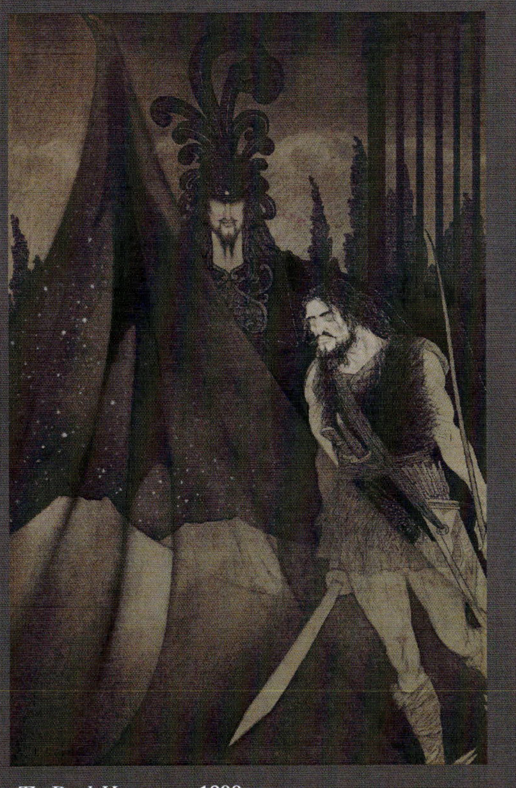

The Dark Huntsman, 1899
Watercolor and ink on paper. Private collection.

British, 1867–1941

Sime developed a reputation throughout his career for creating fantastic and often disturbing imagery, especially for the early fantasy author Lord Dunsany. Many of these works conceal a biting sense of satire beneath the fantastical trappings. Although Sime did work in color, the vast majority of his output was rendered in black and white. Among contemporary artists, Roger Dean has specifically cited Sime as an influence.

The Dark Huntsman is one of Sime's best illustrations, done in 1899 for *Pall Mall Magazine* illustrating the short story "The Mountains of the Moon."

Jesse SMITH Wilcox

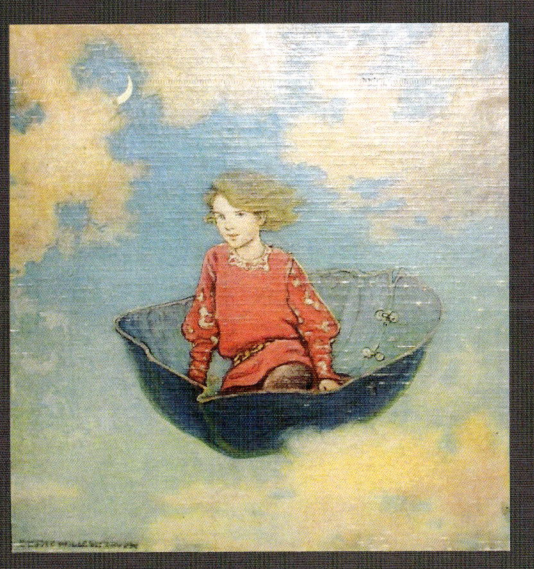

The Little Lame Prince, 1923
Watercolor on paper. Courtesy of the Illustrated Gallery.

American, 1863–1935

A native of Philadelphia, Smith was one of several well-known female artists who studied under Howard Pyle. She is most recognized for her covers for *Ladies' Home Journal* as well as children's book illustrations, including for Charles Kingsley's *The Water Babies*. She was the second woman to be inducted into the Society of Illustrators Hall of Fame, and in recent years her original paintings have reached price levels normally reserved for Pyle and Wyeth.

The Little Lame Prince is a fine example of Smith's work as her career began to focus increasingly on children as subjects, in this case depicting a character from *Boys and Girls of Bookland*.

Austin Osman SPARE

British, 1886–1956

Spare baffled critics in his own day, producing a wide range of fantastic and symbolic works often connected to his own considerable development as a magus, or sorcerer. Critics praised his draughtsmanship but found themselves at a loss when considering his overall image-making. While he has since been considered by critics to be both a proto-surrealist and pop artist, he is probably more accurately described as the last of the great British symbolists.

The Magus is a unique work, painted on the vellum cover of a specially bound edition of one of Spare's own books on "magick." The image depicts the magus preparing to enter his own mind, eliminating all external distractions in a form of psychological repression.

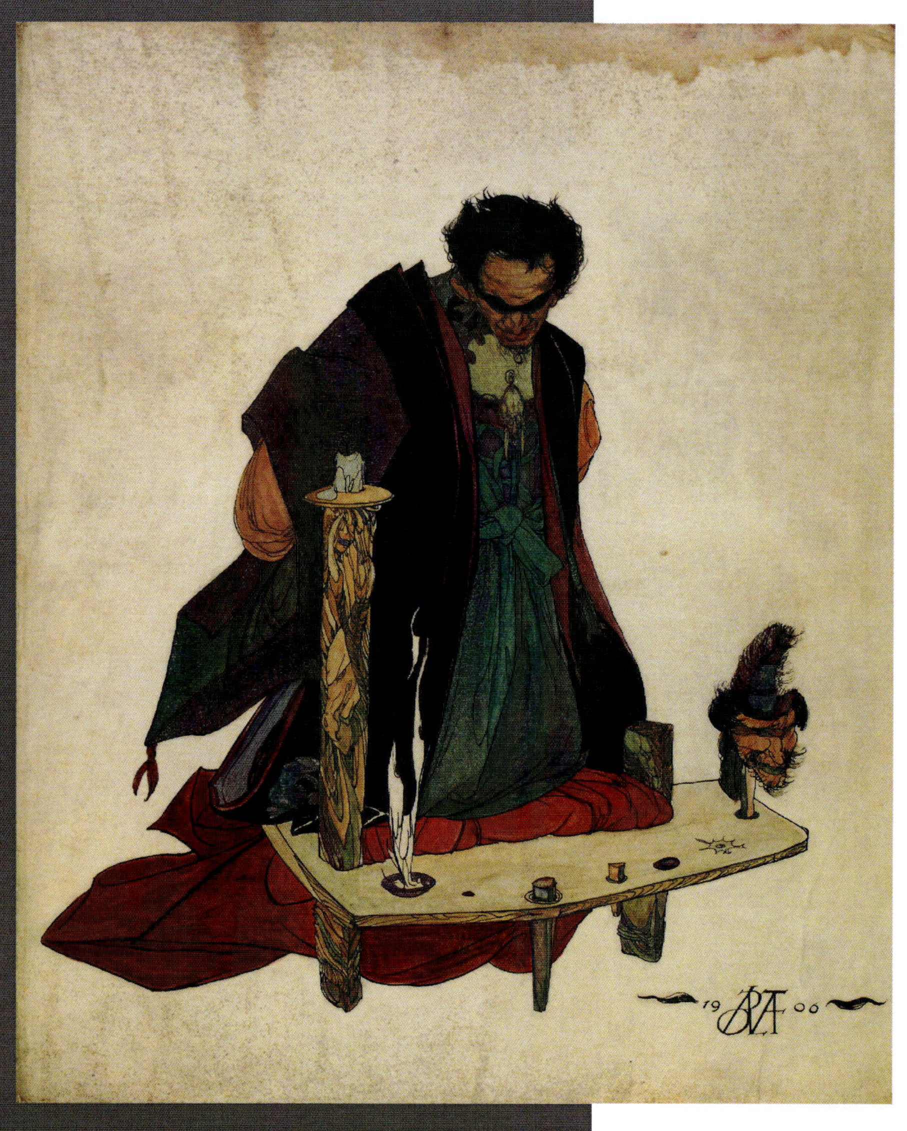

The Magus, 1906
Watercolor and ink on vellum.
Private collection.

J. Allen ST. JOHN

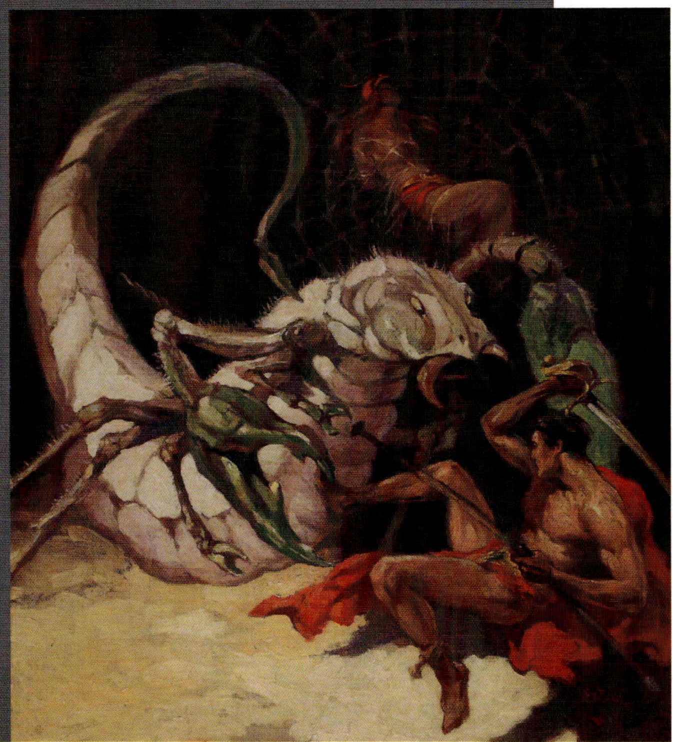

Buccaneers of Venus, 1933
Oil on canvas. Collection of Zaddick Longenbach.

American, 1872–1957

St. John may be considered the godfather of contemporary imaginative realism as his turn-of-the-century illustrations for the works of Edgar Rice Burroughs proved to be immensely influential on both Roy Krenkel and Frank Frazetta. In 1891, St. John began studying at the Art Students League of New York and later enrolled at the Académie Julian in Paris. Thus, St. John was well versed in the French academic tradition as well as that of the Brandywine painters.

Buccaneers of Venus is an illustration created for the *Weird Tales* pulp to depict a Burroughs-esque story by another writer. It shows St. John's skill at depicting action and movement, something no other artist in the field would equal until Frazetta.

Edmund Joseph SULLIVAN

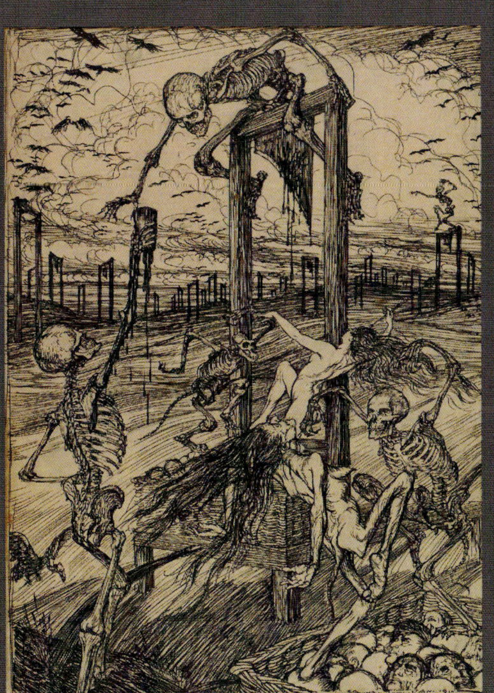

The Gods Are Athirst, 1910
Ink on paper. Private collection.

British, 1869–1933

Sullivan, working from the late nineteenth century into the early twentieth, merged the classic British illustration tradition with influences such as Art Nouveau to produce a style that was most aptly described as that of a more romantic Aubrey Beardsley. His penchant for skeletons and macabre imagery brought an almost symbolist flair to his work. His single most famous drawing, a skeleton with roses, was immortalized by Stanley Mouse and Alton Kelley for a Grateful Dead poster in 1966.

The Gods Are Athirst is typical of Sullivan's macabre imagery, his tightly spaced lines providing a remarkable sense of depth and movement to his inks.

Gustaf TENGGREN

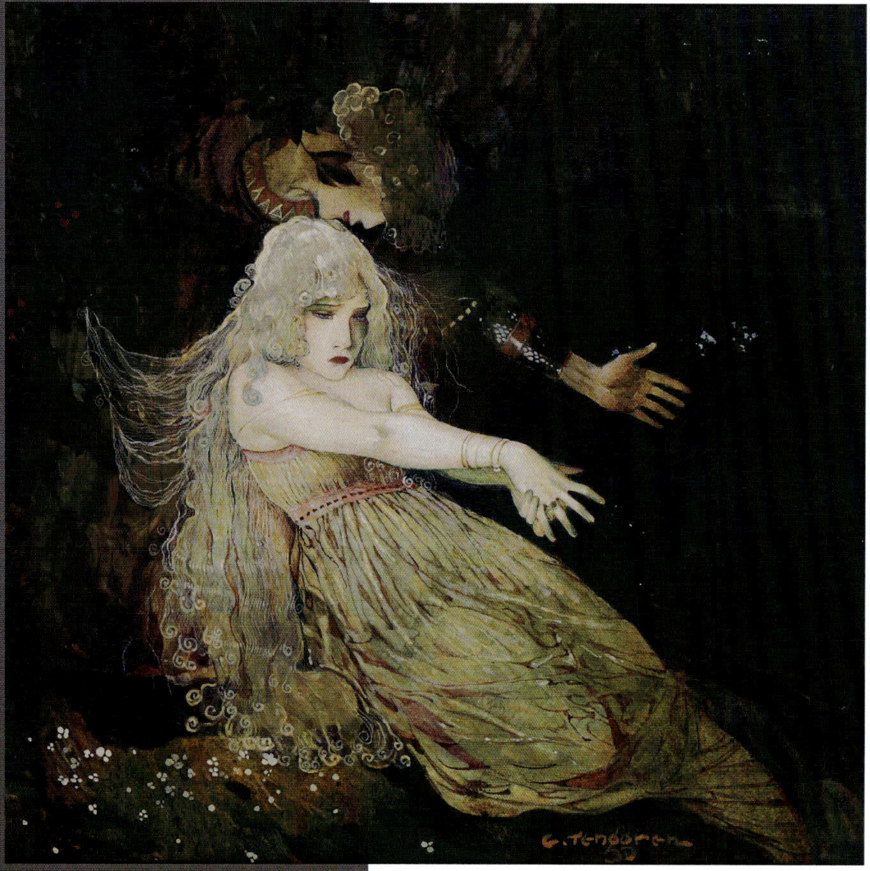

The Linden Maid, c. 1930
Watercolor on paper.
Private collection.

Swedish, 1896–1970

Tenggren began his career in Sweden, taking over the illustration duties for the popular annual *Among Elves and Trolls* from John Bauer, working in a similar eerie watercolor style. In 1920 he emigrated to the United States and in 1935, he was recruited by Walt Disney to be the art director for *Snow White*, the first full-length animated film. Tenggren's Rackham-like style fit the story perfectly, and he continued to work with Disney on several subsequent films. After he left Disney in 1939, he continued his career as a highly successful illustrator but changed his style completely, illustrating classic children's books such as *Little Black Sambo* and *The Poky Little Puppy* with no trace whatsoever of his imaginative stylistic roots.

The Linden Maid is a beautiful example of Tenggren's work during his time with Disney, featuring the most complete expression of his style, mixing the best of Arthur Rackham and John Bauer with his own, unique characterizations.

N. C. WYETH

American, 1882–1945

Newell Convers Wyeth, one of the first generation of Howard Pyle students, is considered one of America's greatest illustrators. Wyeth's emotional paintings illustrating such classics as *Treasure Island*, *The Boy's King Arthur* and *Robin Hood* defined the Brandywine ideal and have impacted every imaginative realist painter since Frazetta. His mastery of light and shadow brought a heightened tension to his work, particularly in his earlier years when his rich palette and tremendous narrative sense combined with his affinity for Pyle's subject matter—pirates and medieval scenes—to create moody masterpieces. As his career progressed Wyeth moved away from oils and to egg tempera, painting landscapes, still lifes, and portraits for exhibition in a variety of styles but never achieving the recognition that his illustrations brought.

Allan and the Holy Flower shows a different side of Wyeth, in this case illustrating an Allan Quartermain story by H. Rider Haggard for a magazine cover. This earlier work depicts a character with relatively little paint as befit the need to cover the right side of the painting with a significant amount of text.

The King's Henchman is a beautiful example of Wyeth's work, bringing his control of light, shadow, color, and value to the fore in a striking work. It has been suggested that this painting was the inspiration for comic artist Hal Foster to create the iconic Prince Valiant, who looks very much like the male figure in this painting.

Allan and the Holy Flower, 1915
Oil on canvas. Courtesy of the Illustrated Gallery.

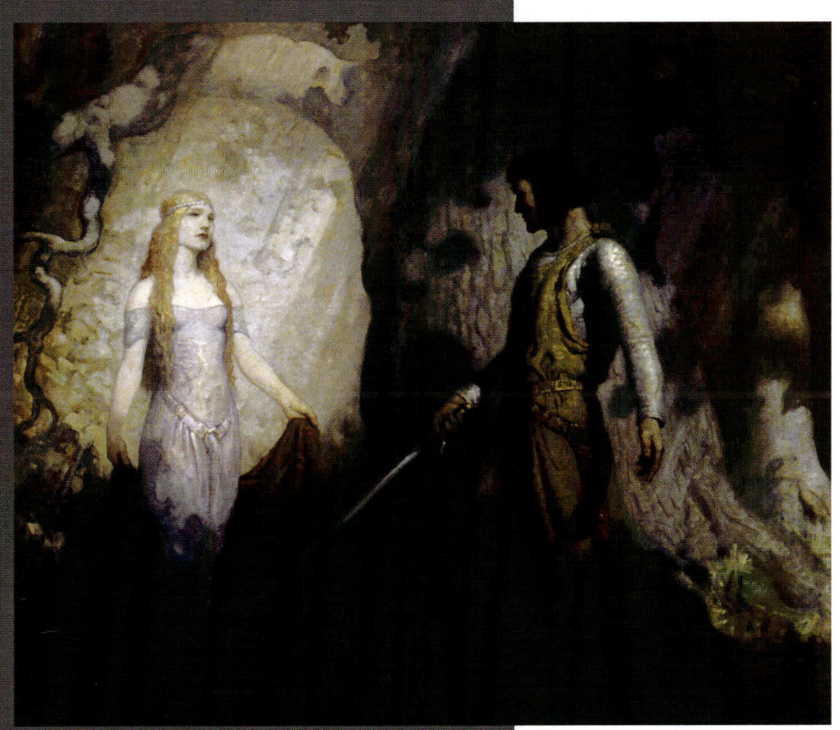

The King's Henchman, 1927
Oil on canvas. The Kelly Collection of American Illustration.

Earle BERGEY

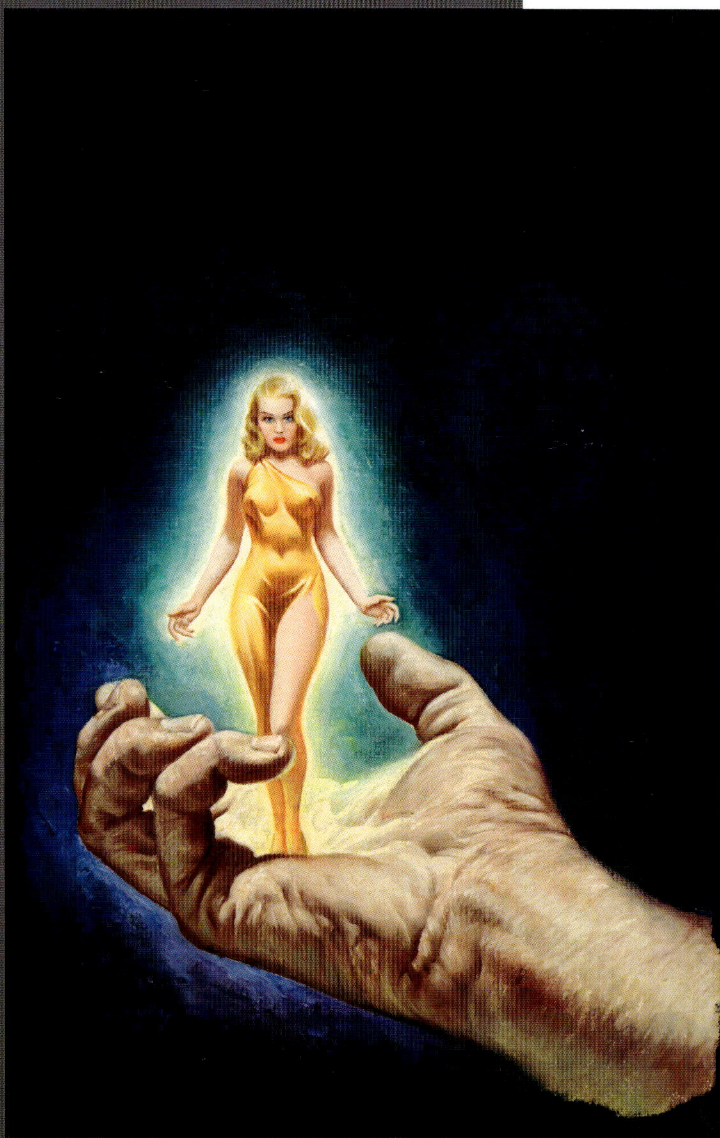

Vulcan's Dolls, 1952
Oil on board. Collection of Joshua David Bergey.

American, 1901–1952

Painting tastefully brazen portraits of women in space decades before man set foot on the moon, Bergey transformed science-fiction art from architectural to human and elevated the emerging genre to iconic heights. Educated at the Pennsylvania Academy of the Fine Arts, he fast became one of the most prolific American illustrators of the twentieth century, an unbridled force in all genres of pin-up, pulp fiction, and paperback art. His work displays a mastery of visual storytelling, uncommon ease depicting anatomy, lushly conceived female figures who appear unusually self-possessed, and a salient gift for animating scenes with exaggerated light.

A seminal painting from the zenith of Bergey's career, *Vulcan's Dolls* electrified the cover of *Startling Stories*, the quintessential American science-fiction and fantasy pulp magazine, in February 1952. The signature Bergey Girl arises out of the artist's own hand, glistening like a fleshy phoenix, a seductive vision of pulp fiction's influential past and fantasy's boundless future.

—*Didactics written by Joshua David Bergey for 2012 exhibit at Allentown Art Museum,* At the Edge: Art of the Fantastic.

Hannes BOK

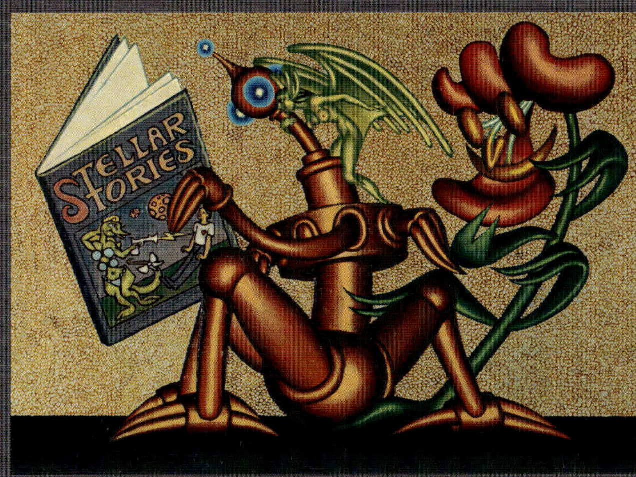

Stellar Stories, 1950
Oil on board. The Frank Collection.

American, 1914–1964

Bok is regarded as one of the most important artists of the 1940s, instantly recognizable for his highly stylized approach. Although his work shows a great deal of technical influence from Maxfield Parrish, his design sense stemmed from a much wider base, including tribal art and the cubist painters. Equally at home in black and white or color, Bok was one of the relatively few pulp artists to make a transition to paperback covers and magazines in the 1950s before leaving the field completely to pursue his interests in astrology.

Stellar Stories demonstrates Bok's unique sense of design, both in color and figural depictions. The small, pixie-ish sprite on the robot's shoulder is typical of Bok's style, although this piece does lack the Parrish-like backgrounds and landscapes that were commonly part of the artist's work.

MID-CENTURY

Chesley BONESTELL

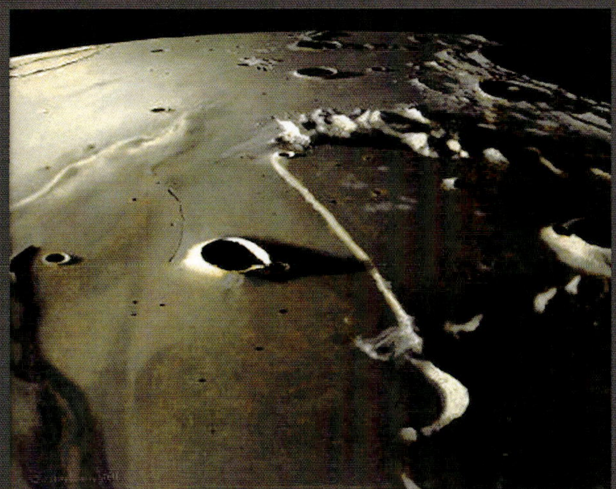

1961 Moon Landscape, 1961
Oil on board. Collection of Stuart Schiff.

American, 1888–1986

Bonestell is considered the father of astronomical art. His early career was spent in architecture, but in the early 1940s Bonestell began a series of space paintings that appeared in *Life* magazine. From that point on he specialized in astronomical paintings, producing stunningly realistic renderings of planets, moons, and other heavenly bodies. In addition, Bonestell worked in Hollywood in the 1950s creating matte paintings for many of the classic science-fiction films of the period, including *Destination Moon*, *When Worlds Collide*, and *War of the Worlds*. Upon his death in 1986, the Association of Science Fiction and Fantasy Artists renamed its annual award the Chesley Award as a tribute to his influence.

1961 Moon Landscape is a relatively simple painting by Bonestell, but even this piece demonstrates his near-photographic technique. Note that this painting was produced eight years before man would set foot on the surface of the moon.

Ed EMSHWILLER

Regan's Planet, 1964
Oil on board. The Frank Collection.

American, 1925–1990

Emshwiller was one of the most prolific and popular artists of the 1950s and 1960s, working for a wide range of magazine and book publishers. His work was characterized by "the inventive hardware of space travel, the juxtaposition of large foreground figures with smaller background figures to show depth, abstract elements used as science fiction leitmotivs and imaginative backgrounds." (Jane Frank. *Science Fiction and Fantasy Artists of the Twentieth Century: A Biographical Dictionary*. Jefferson, NC: McFarland, 2009.) Always interested in film, Emshwiller began to move away from illustration toward film in the 1960s, eventually becoming an award-winning independent filmmaker and video producer whose credits include the early classic of computer animation *Sunstone*, created in 1979. In addition to his illustration work, Emshwiller maintained an active gallery career as an abstract expressionist.

Regan's Planet demonstrates many of the key elements of Emshwiller's style: large foreground figures, scale, and abstract elements.

Virgil FINLAY

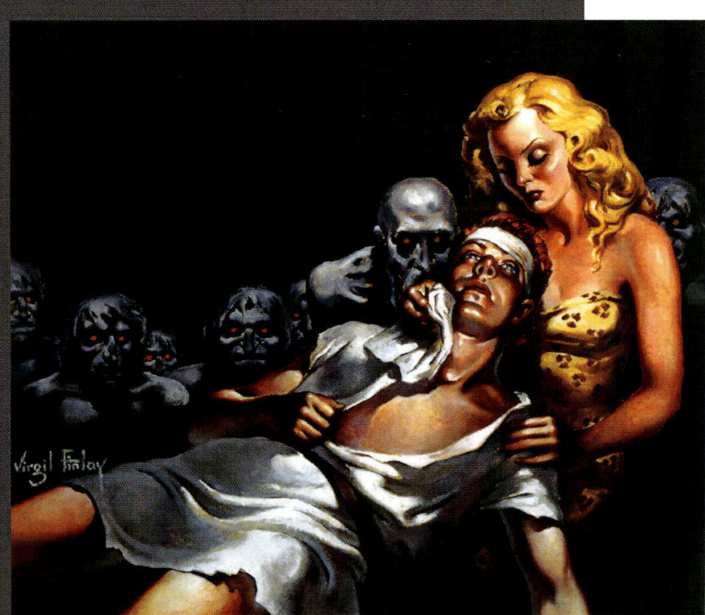

Beyond the Great Oblivion: Dawn and Darkness #2, 1940
Oil on board. The Frank Collection.

American, 1914–1971

Finlay is considered among the most important illustrators working in black and white of the twentieth century, ranking alongside golden age masters J. C. Coll and Franklin Booth. His incredibly detailed stipple technique, greatly inspired by Gustave Doré, was time-consuming but produced stunning results. Finlay was also a highly popular cover artist during the pulp period, but he never successfully made the transition to books. When the pulp market declined, he turned to creating interior art for astrology magazines from the 1960s until his death. Inarguably, Finlay served as a major source of inspiration for most of the mid-century artists, and nearly every contemporary black and white artist owes a great debt to his virtuoso work.

Beyond the Great Oblivion: Dawn and Darkness #2 is an example of Finlay's work in color, of which fine examples are relatively scarce. This early work already demonstrates Finlay's classical feel for beautiful women, something he would hone throughout his career.

Frank Kelly FREAS

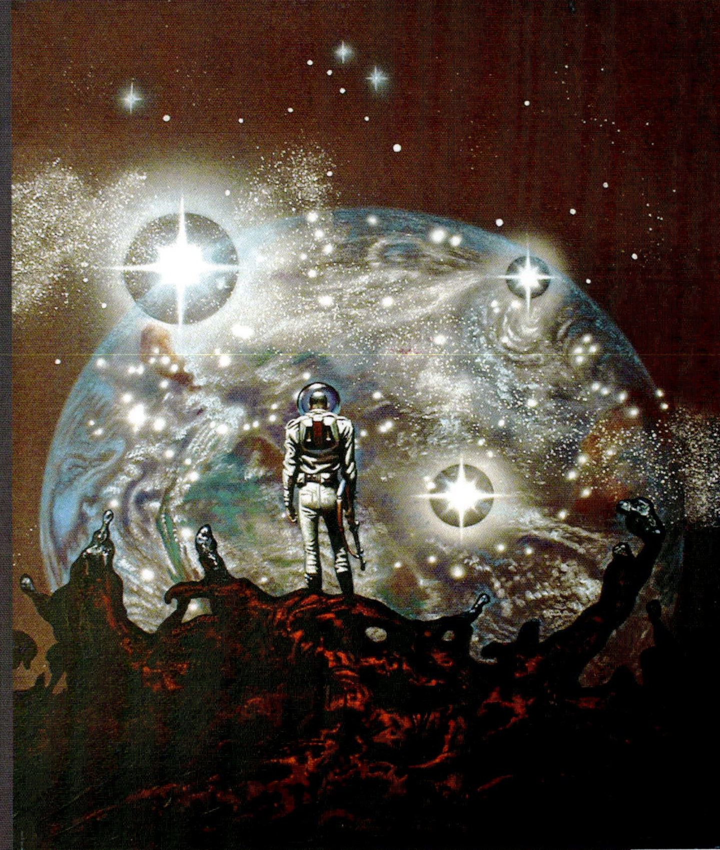

Green Hills of Earth, 1977
Acrylic on board. Collection of Mark, Barbara, and Matthew Corrinet.

American, 1922–2005

Freas is recognized as the single most popular artist in the history of the field, as well as being one of the most prolific, enjoying a fifty-year career remarkable for its consistency and breadth. Freas began his career in the early 1950s, working for the twilight of the pulps, magazines, and the book market, creating both color paintings and black-and-white interiors. (Among his more recognized works is the first illustration of Alfred E. Neuman, the mascot of *MAD* magazine.) His influence even spread from science fiction to science, as NASA selected him to design a shoulder patch for Skylab I, designated him the official NASA artist for seven space missions, and used his work in their own educational program. Perhaps his most widely known work outside the field is the cover for Queen's album *News of the World*.

Freas worked predominantly in acrylics and was widely noted for both his use of witty humor as well as his interest in realism, preferring to render characters with flaws rather than idealized figures.

Green Hills of Earth is classic Freas, although more melancholy in tone than many of his works. This painting has been identified by many ex-military men as the perfect expression of the feelings of a soldier far from home.

Roy G. KRENKEL

Bearers of the Fire, 1976
Charcoal and white on paper. Private collection.

American, 1918–1983

With the exception of Frazetta, no mid-century illustrator had a bigger influence on the sword and sorcery subgenre than Krenkel, and without Krenkel there would not have been a Frazetta. Krenkel, regarded by contemporary imaginative realists as the consummate draughtsman, would mentor Frazetta, introducing him to the great artists of the past—a familiarity which allowed Frazetta to meld their classical painting styles with his bravura approach to picture making. Krenkel always regarded himself as a draughtsman first and a painter second, and it is in his wonderfully flowing drawings that his genius is most clearly identifiable.

Bearers of the Fire is probably Krenkel's single greatest work in the fantasy genre; relatively few illustrators working in the field of the fantastic have produced a work of equal quality. The sense of wonder in the piece is breathtaking.

Paul LEHR

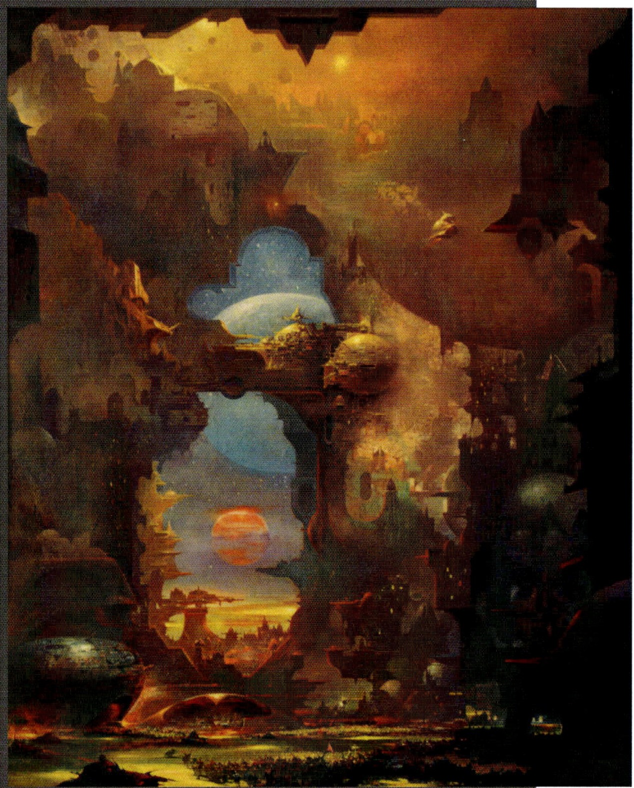

Cosmic Assembly, c. 1990
Acrylic and oil on Masonite. Collection of the Lehr family.

American, 1930–1998

Lehr is a prime example of the illustrator whose greatest works were not illustrations. His work dominated science-fiction covers from the mid-1960s through the mid-1970s, but it is the work done after he stopped illustrating that defines Lehr's legacy. As styles changed in the late-1970s, demand for Lehr's unique approach dropped off, and his cover assignments dwindled to almost nothing. As a result, the artist began creating personal works, taking the surrealist motifs and innovative color solutions that he'd developed throughout his career to a higher level, creating works that straddle the border between surrealism and imaginative realism.

Cosmic Assembly is typical of Lehr's personal work—grand in both scale and vision, it depicts a sprawling, disjointed city of immense size, populated by crowds in conflict. War and aggression, on a cosmic scale, are perhaps the single most common thematic strand in Lehr's late work.

Harold McCAULEY

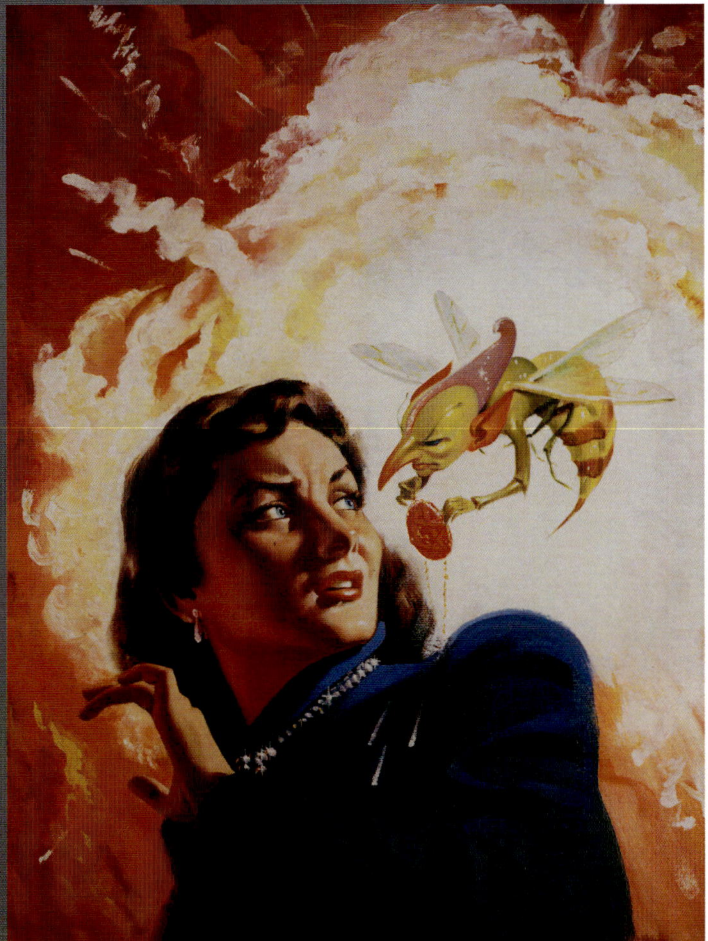

Mr. Yellowjacket, 1951
Oil on canvas board. The Frank Collection.

American, 1913–1977

McCauley's work has a more direct connection to the golden age than most of his contemporaries—he studied under J. Allen St. John, who ignited his passion for the fantastic. The creator of the Mac Girl, McCauley was one of the finest fantastic pin-up artists in the history of the field, blending classic post-war pin-up imagery, fantastic themes, and a classically influenced painting approach. Like many of his contemporaries, McCauley also worked in other fields, including advertising and calendar art.

Mr. Yellowjacket is arguably McCauley's finest single painting. Though it lacks the classic pin-up structure of much of his work, the composition, narrative, and paint quality of this piece make the clear connection to the work of the golden age in a way that much of McCauley's saucier work did not.

Stanley MELTZOFF

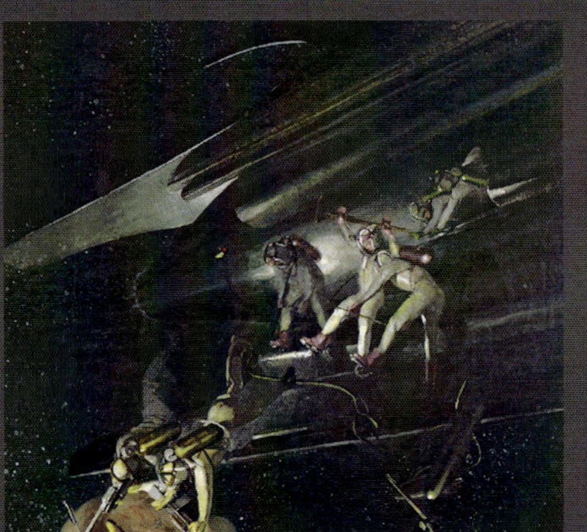

Destination Universe, 1953
Oil on board. Collection of Robert K. Wiener.

American, 1917–2006

Meltzoff is known for perhaps having the greatest effect on the field of fantastic art on a per-painting basis of any artist in history. Predominantly a mainstream illustrator, Meltzoff created a series of early paperback cover paintings in the first half of the 1950s that were, for the first time, largely free of the influence of the pulps. These works—perhaps as few as ten in number—helped to demonstrate at an early time that science fiction, both as literature and as art, could be taken seriously. His work had a profound influence on the following generation of artists, most notably Paul Lehr and John Schoenherr, both of whom mirrored some of Meltzoff's more surrealistic themes.

Destination Universe is a classic Meltzoff science-fiction image—one of as few as half a dozen that are still extant—that clearly shows both his realistic tendencies as well as the complete lack of pulp bombast that made his work so influential in later years.

Leo MOREY

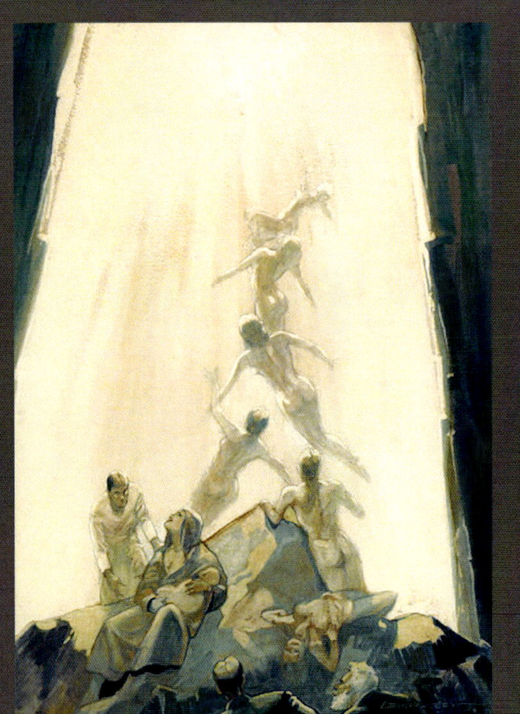

Amazing Stories, 1934
Oil on canvas. Courtesy of the Illustrated Gallery.

American, 1899–1965

Morey began working in the fantastic art field in 1930, painting covers for *Amazing Stories* after Frank R. Paul left to work for another publisher. Although he never attained the popularity of Paul, Morey's early entry to the field made him one of the first pulp artists to paint rocket ships, aliens, and robots.

Amazing Stories shows Morey's approach to the fantastic: loosely painted and crude by modern standards but dramatic and—although not in this case—often colorful.

Frank R. PAUL

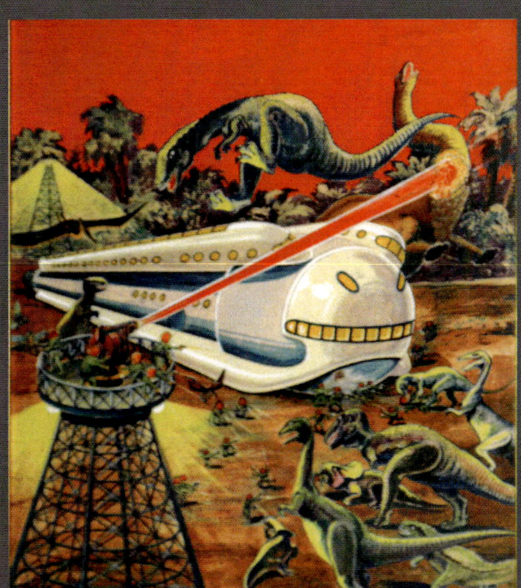

One Prehistoric Night, 1934
Oil on board. The Frank Collection.

American, 1884–1963

Paul was the first great science-fiction illustrator. Although he was technically less skilled than many of the later artists to come into the field (Paul's strength was architecture and design), he played a seminal role in the development of the visual lexicon of science fiction. "More than any other illustrator, he epitomized the 'sense of wonder' that was a prominent feature of early science fiction." (Jane Frank. *Science Fiction and Fantasy Artists of the Twentieth Century: A Biographical Dictionary*. Jefferson, NC: McFarland, 2009.) Paul had a prosperous career in both the pulp and magazine fields, often working with pioneering publisher Hugo Gernsback. But when Gernsback's last magazine ceased publication in 1954, Paul left the field, although he continued to illustrate on a very limited basis elsewhere.

One Prehistoric Night is a perfect example of Paul's exuberant approach to science fiction, with dinosaurs, rockets ships, ray guns, and spacemen all together in a glorious frenzy of activity. Although other artists would paint all of these elements more effectively, much of their mental imagery would come from Paul's work.

Richard POWERS

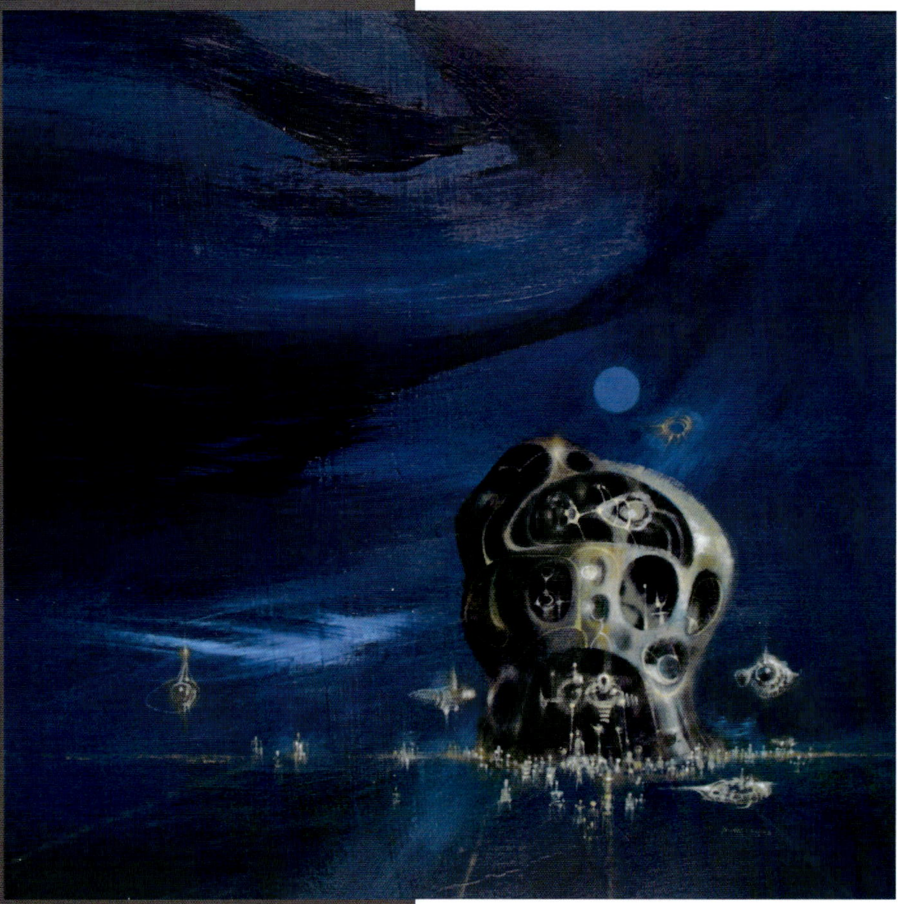

Pstalemate, 1971
Oil on board. Collection of Vincent Di Fate.

American, 1921–1996

Powers provided a unique voice to fantastic art beginning in the 1950s. Unlike most of his peers, Powers had no background in science fiction, commercial illustration or the pulps, or even in classical realism. As a result, his work drew from a completely different range of artistic influences, including Joan Miró, Roberto Matta, and Yves Tanguy, as well as contemporary abstract expressionists. His early work contained clear narrative elements, but as his career progressed his art became more experimental and more purely abstract, created with a wide range of experimental techniques including collage and the use of found materials. His work came to define "serious" science fiction in the 1950s and early 1960s, and was highly influential on many of the artists to follow including John Schoenherr, Jack Gaughan, Paul Lehr, Vincent DiFate, and many others. Like several other artists in the field at the time, Powers also maintained a successful mainstream art career, including being featured as part of a four-man show at the Museum of Modern Art in 1952.

Pstalemate is a classic example of Powers at his height, his abstracted and surreal forms just hinting at a narrative but creating a clear mood of otherworldly mystery and drama.

Norman SAUNDERS

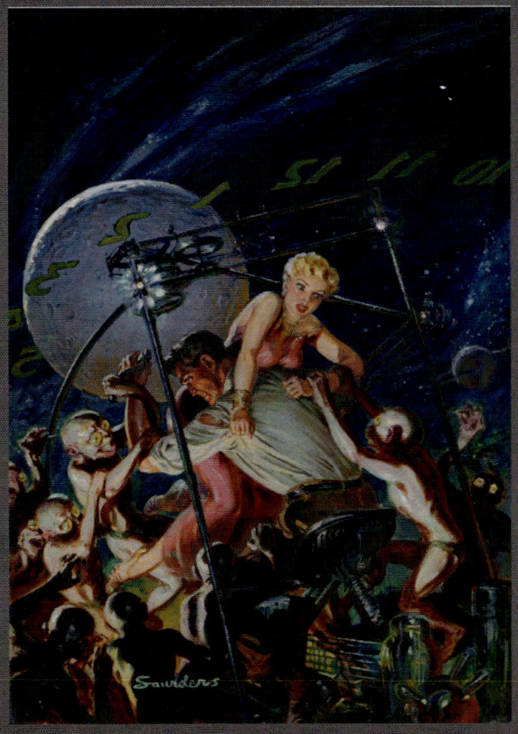

Famous Fantastic Mysteries, 1950
Oil on board. Collection of Zaddick Longenbach.

American, 1907–1989

Saunders was one of the most prolific of the pulp artists in the pre–World War II period (creating 876 cover paintings between 1935 and 1942) who then moved easily into the paperback, comic, and trading-card markets in the post-war period. He worked in all genres, with fantastic art being the one in which he worked the least. He was nonetheless influential on later artists in the field. His best-known work is actually not cover art but the classic trading card series *Mars Attacks* produced for Topps in 1962, which has been referenced by everyone from comic artists to Tim Burton.

Famous Fantastic Mysteries is a representation of the classic H. G. Wells novel *The Time Machine*, and it demonstrates the classic pulp elements—high action and beautiful damsels in distress—that characterized much of his best work.

John SCHOENHERR

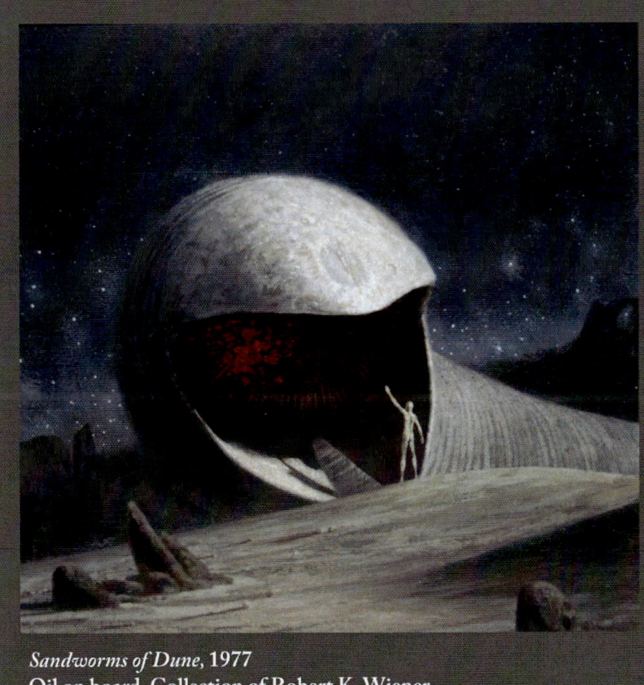

Sandworms of Dune, 1977
Oil on board. Collection of Robert K. Wiener.

American, 1935–2010

Schoenherr is best known in the imaginative field for his iconic work on Frank Herbert's *Dune* series, creating the canonical images of the sandworms that would be followed by all other painters and filmmakers. His work was popular in the 1960s and early 1970s, using elements of surrealism like Powers but to a much more limited extent, making his works far more narrative. At the same time, Schoenherr also developed a successful mainstream art career, eventually leaving the commercial field altogether to focus on his highly acclaimed wildlife paintings.

Sandworms of Dune is the archetype of the Schoenherr painting, depicting not only his most famous visual creation but also providing a beautiful example of his mix of surrealist feel with narrative representationalism.

Opposite page: Eternal Champion provides a good example of Frazetta's handling of a bright, rich palette. While many of his works are somber in tone, he was equally adept and managing deep, rich colors, much like his Brandywine predecessors. Like many of Frazetta's paintings, this one aims for the high point of action, producing adrenaline rather than tension. In this, Frazetta is more a child of the Baroque than the Brandywines.

Eternal Champion, 1970
Oil on masonite. Collection of Mona Pavesi.

Jungle Girl, 1962
Ink on paper. Collection of Scott Williams.

Jungle Girl demonstrates Frazetta's remarkable deftness with brush and ink. In 1962 he was commissioned to provide a series of ink illustrations for Canaveral Press's deluxe editions of Edgar Rice Burroughs novels. The twenty-seven published pieces Frazetta created for those books are considered the high point of his black-and-white career, and some historians consider them superior to his paintings. This piece was created for the books but not used in print.

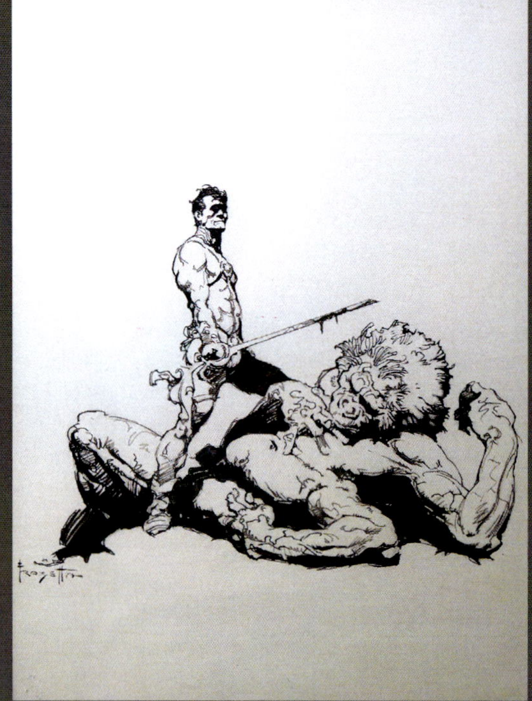

Gods of Mars, 1972
Ink on board. Private collection.

Gods of Mars is a later ink piece, created in 1973 for Doubleday Book Club editions of the *John Carter of Mars* series. At this point Frazetta is working more with line and not using much brushwork, unlike the Canaveral inks. *Gods of Mars* demonstrates his remarkable ability to hone an image and character to its essence, with no line out of place.

FRANK FRAZETTA

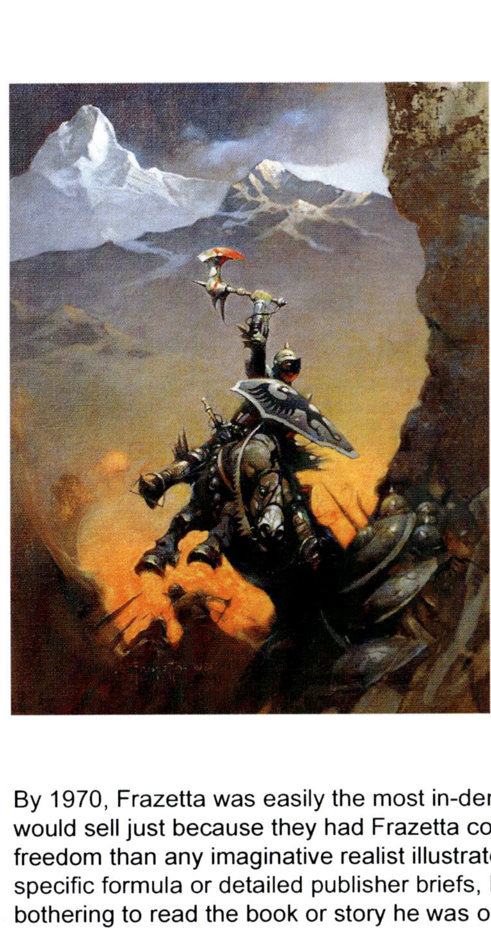

American, 1928–2010

Frazetta is unquestionably the most important imaginative realist painter of the second half of the twentieth century and may be the most significant single artist to ever work in the field. After beginning his career in the 1950s in comics, he transitioned to illustration beginning in the early 1960s. Although his very early work in the field showed the influence of his contemporaries and his own comic background, he quickly began to produce work directly connected to the earlier romantic and Brandywine traditions.

In 1966 he painted the first of his iconic *Conan* covers for Lancer Books, *Conan the Barbarian*. His work between 1966 and 1970 is, without question, the most significant of any four-year span in the history of imaginative realism. Working for both paperback and magazine publishers, he created a series of milestones—including additional *Conan* covers, *Cat Girl*, *The Sea Witch*, *Egyptian Queen*, *Vampirella #1*, and *Princess of Mars*—and completely transformed the field.

By 1970, Frazetta was easily the most in-demand artist in the field. Publishers found that books would sell just because they had Frazetta covers, and Frazetta found himself with far more artistic freedom than any imaginative realist illustrator had secured in decades. Rather than being tied to a specific formula or detailed publisher briefs, Frazetta painted whatever he wanted, often not even bothering to read the book or story he was ostensibly "illustrating," as with the *Conan* paintings:

> I didn't read any of it. It was too opposite of what I do. I told them that. So, I drew him my way. It was really rugged. And it caught on. I didn't care about what people thought. People who bought the books never complained about it. They probably didn't read them.

In a time when many artists working in the field held a rather low view of their own work, rarely even bothering to retrieve their original paintings from publishers, Frazetta never doubted his own significance. He was the first artist to demand his original paintings be returned, and also the first artist to maintain the copyrights to his commissioned works. It was a rare confluence of ego and groundbreaking talent that allowed Frazetta to dominate the field and inform the work of nearly every artist to follow, even more than forty years after those initial masterpieces. In short, Frazetta was the first imaginative realist in decades to view himself as a painter rather than an "illustrator."

But what was it that made Frazetta so special? At a time when most imaginative realists had lost their connection with their roots in the early twentieth century and earlier, Frazetta rediscovered his roots in the works of artists like Pyle and Wyeth, Doré and even Leonardo da Vinci, whose powerful pyramidal compositions inform many of Frazetta's most significant paintings. As a result, his paintings showed a power and a classicism that had long been absent from the field, and his paintings stood out as entirely different creations from the works around them.

Frazetta's influence holds in the marketplace as well. Of all of the twentieth century imaginative painters, he is one of only three to have paintings reach the one million dollar mark in price (the others being golden age legends N. C. Wyeth and Maxfield Parrish).

It is impossible to overstate the influence of Frazetta on contemporary imaginative painters. Even those who weren't directly influenced to follow Frazetta's style were inspired to look back in history for their own progenitors, ensuring that the field of imaginative realism would be profoundly changed for decades to come.

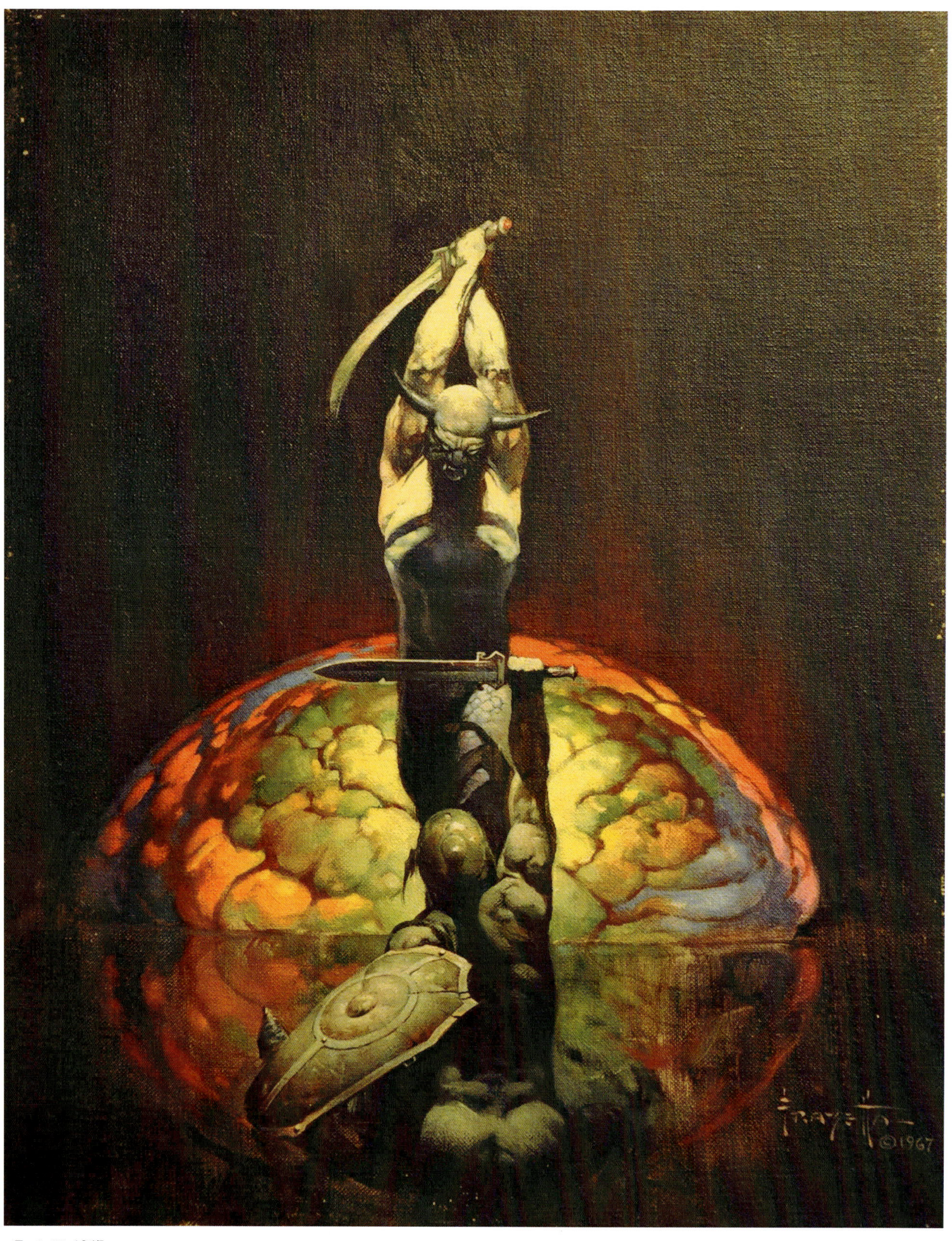

Eerie #8, 1967
Oil on canvas. Courtesy of Heritage Auctions - HA.com.

Eerie #8 is one of the classic covers Frazetta created for Warren Publishing's iconic trio of magazines (*Eerie*, *Creepy*, and *Vampirella*) beginning in the mid-1960s. This piece, subtitled *The Brain*, demonstrates the power of Frazetta's brushstrokes and composition, here highlighting the key moment in a life-or-death struggle.

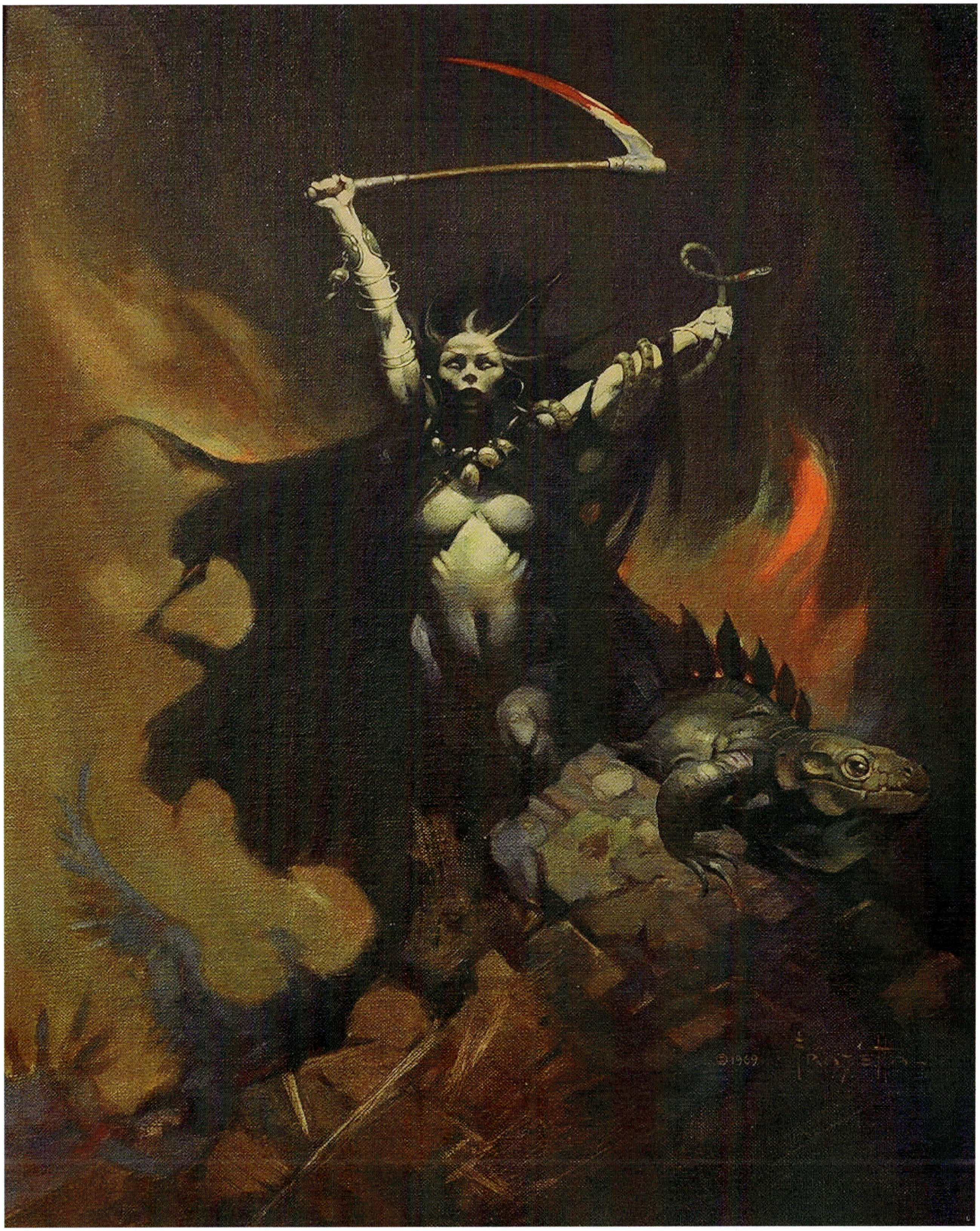

Vampirella #11, 1969
Oil on canvas. Courtesy of Heritage Auctions - HA.com

Vampirella #11 provides a great example of Frazetta's approach to painting. This piece is not, in any way, a painting of Vampirella—it's an example of Frazetta painting what he wanted to paint and publishers happily using those images regardless of whether or not they exactly matched their editorial concepts.

Doug BEEKMAN

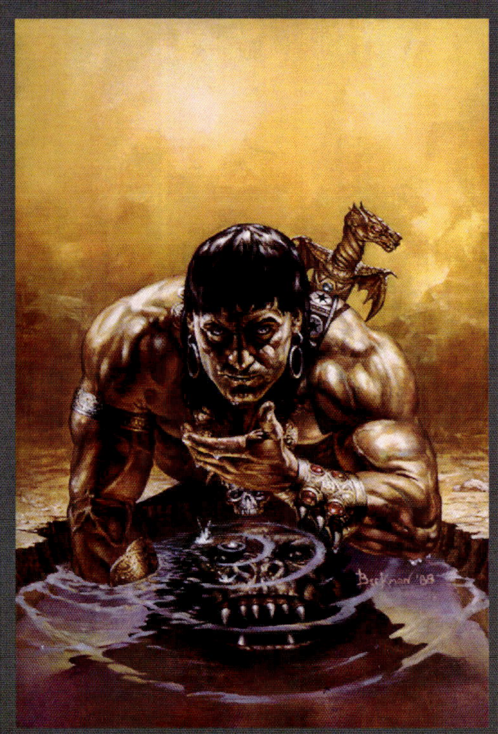

Killing Thirst, 1986
Oil on board. Collection of the artist.

American, born 1952

Beekman began his professional career in the mid-1970s working on a wide range of topics, from fantasy to science fiction. In the 1980s he began perhaps his most well-known association: painting images of the iconic character Conan for an extended series of magazine and paperback covers. Beekman works in a highly narrative, painterly style, predominantly in oils.

Killing Thirst is one of Beekman's most famous Conan paintings. While most of his Conan paintings feature Conan at the height of conflict, this piece is particularly notable for its dramatic foreshadowing of action about to occur.

Julie BELL

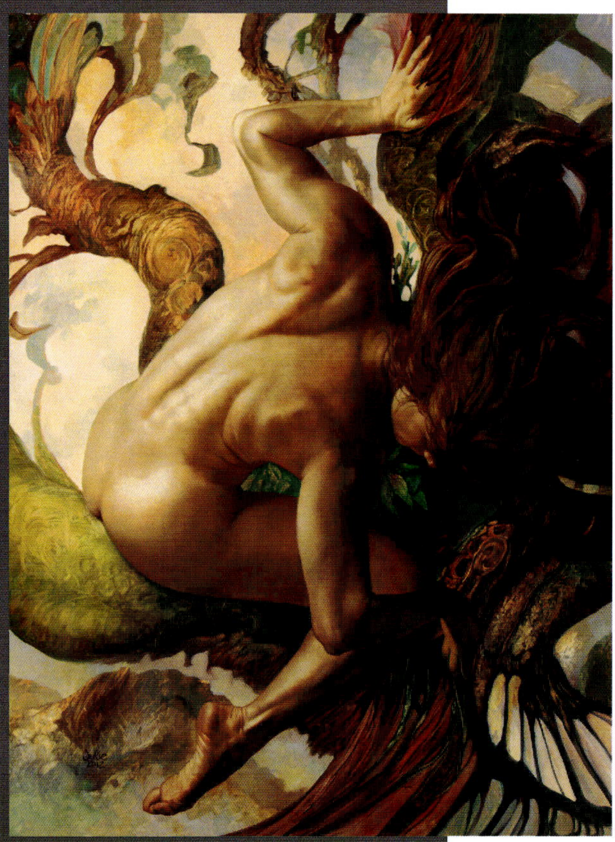

American, born 1958

One of the most famous contemporary imaginative realists, Bell is married to iconic painter Boris Vallejo, and her early paintings show the clear influence of Vallejo's training. However, Bell has taken her work in a different direction, with a flair for color and romanticism uniquely hers, and as much interest in painting animal figures as human. (Bell is also a successful wildlife painter.) She is unquestionably the best-known living female imaginative realist.

A Dream About a Dragon and a Tree is the newest and largest painting Bell has done to date, created especially for the *At the Edge* exhibition. It features her distinctive color sense and fondness for sinuous, flowing forms and designs, as well as her unparalleled skill at rendering the human form.

A Dream About a Dragon and a Tree, 2012
Oil on canvas. Collection of the artist.

John BERKEY

CONTEMPORARY

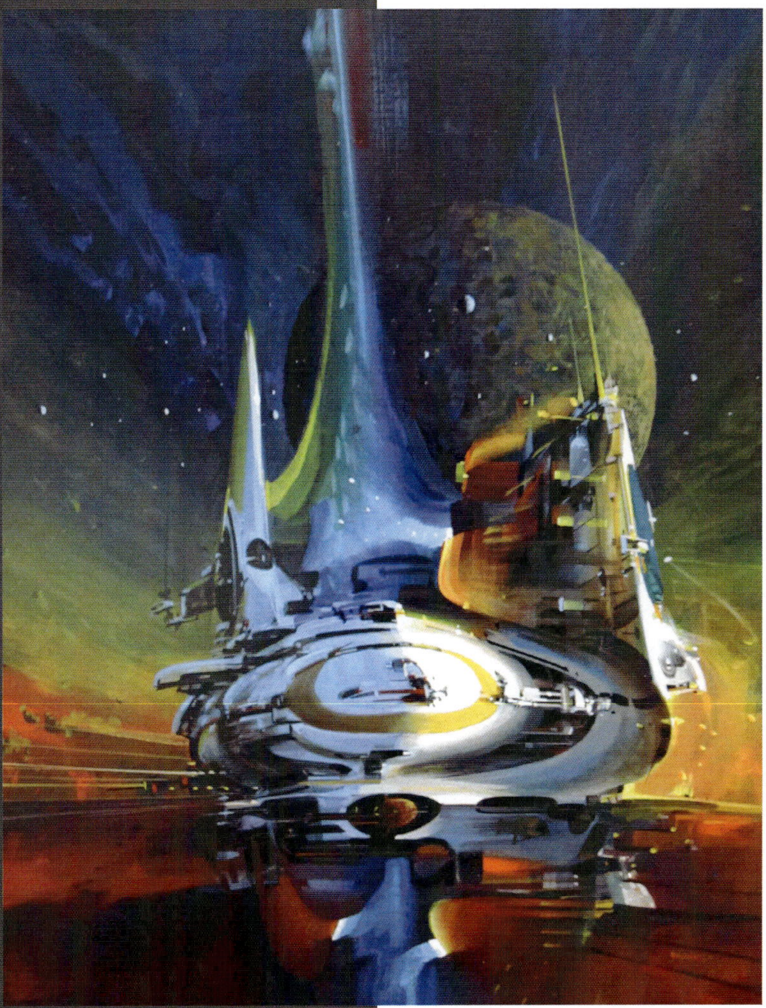

Carrier Destroyer, c. 1985
Acrylics and casein on board.
Collection of Paul and LizAnn Lizotte.

American, 1932–2008

Berkey is best known for his renderings of space hardware in a distinctive, almost impressionistic style that builds shape with color rather than line or shading. During the 1970s Berkey also created some of the most iconic imaginative movie-poster art of the decade, including for the movies *King Kong* (1976) and *Star Trek* (1979). Berkey's ability to build form, mass, and movement out of sheer color has influenced many of the artists working in the science-fiction field. Berkey is a member of the Society of Illustrator's Hall of Fame.

Carrier Destroyer is an excellent example of Berkey's space paintings, the vivid color and dynamic presence displaying mass, power, and movement all at the same time.

Rick BERRY

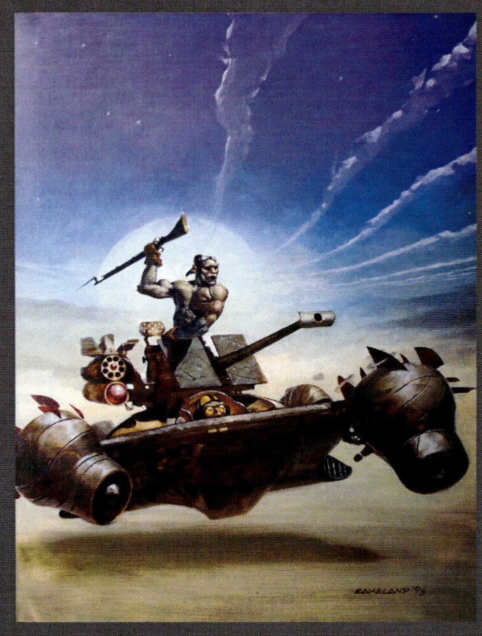

Overlords of Bonparr, 1992
Oil on board. Private collection.

American, born 1953

Berry is known for his mix of powerful figurative oils as well as being a groundbreaking early adopter of digital technologies. He is credited with the first digitally created book cover art, for William Gibson's *Neuromancer* (1984). Berry's work tends to evoke dramatic movement and kinetic impact. He is closely associated with artist Phil Hale, having served as Hale's mentor and then frequent artistic foil throughout the 1990s.

Overlords of Bonparr is an excellent example of Berry's illustrative work, created in the early 1990s and bearing his pseudonym, Sam Rakeland, which he used to distinguish his classical illustration from his more personal stylistic work.

Thomas BLACKSHEAR

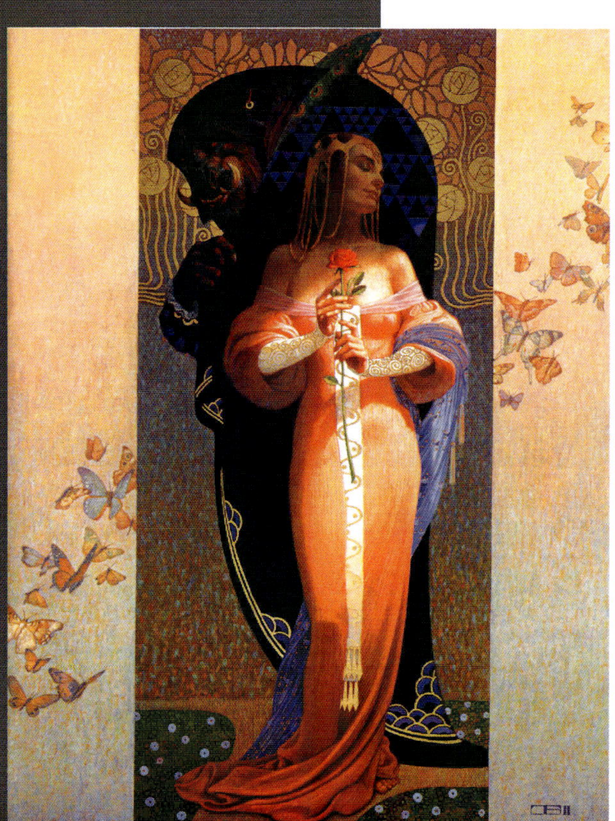

American, born 1955

Blackshear began his career as an illustrator before turning to the fine art market, producing a wide range of works including the development of the Ebony Visions series and what he terms Afro-Nouveau. As an illustrator he produced paintings in a variety of genres, winning numerous awards including the coveted Society of Illustrators' Gold Medal.

Beauty and the Beast is a stunning example of Blackshear's narrative work, bringing Nouveau influences such as Gustav Klimt and Maxfield Parrish to a timeless fairy tale.

Beauty and the Beast, 1994
Oil on canvas. Collection of the artist.

Richard BOBER

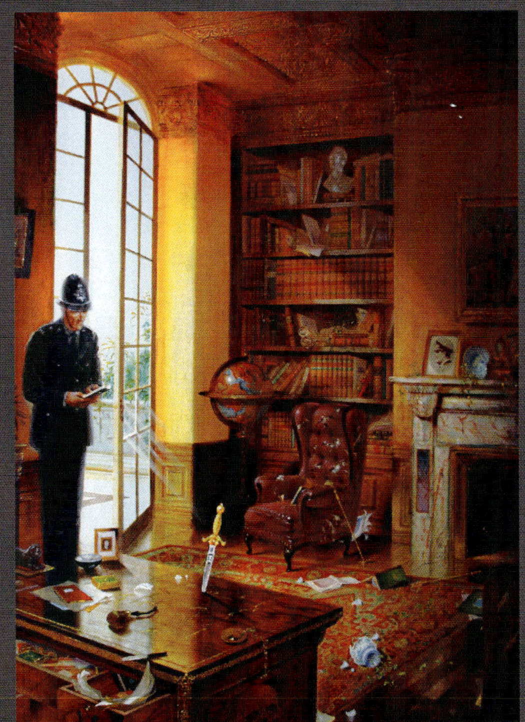

A Very Particular Murder, 1989
Oil on board. The Frank Collection.

American, born 1943

From a technical perspective, Bober is possibly the finest imaginative realist painter of the twentieth century. Heavily influenced by nineteenth century artists like J. M. W. Turner, the complex layering, glazing, and building of his works takes a tremendous amount of time; as a result, Bober has a low output compared to most of his contemporaries. The majority of his work has covered either fantastic or mysterious themes.

A Very Particular Murder is a fine example of a Bober painting, blending both mystery and the eerie edge of the fantastic with the kind of ornate design and peerless paint handling that makes him such a distinctive voice in the field.

Gerald BROM

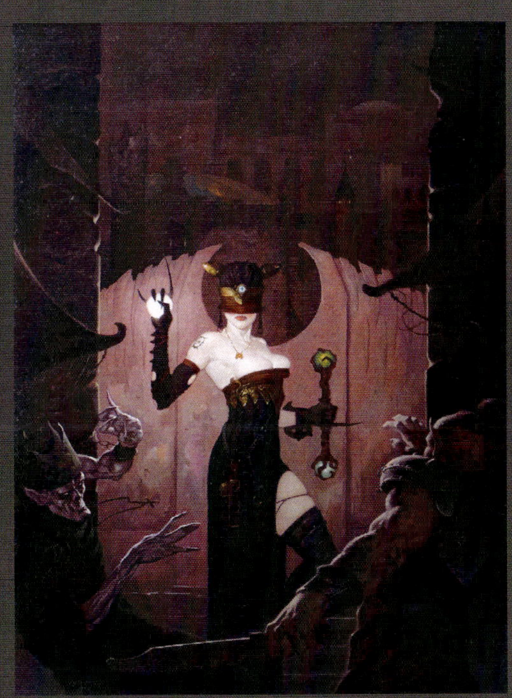

Radiance, 1997
Oil on board. Private collection.

American, born 1965

Brom is one of the best-known figures in contemporary imaginative realism, both for his painting and, in recent years, for his illustrated novels. Generally credited with having launched the Goth movement in the field in the mid 1990s, Brom's artwork mixes dark, edgy themes with a very classical Brandywine painting style. He has probably had more impact on the current look of imaginative realism than any single artist in the past twenty-five years.

Radiance is an archetypal painting by Brom, demonstrating many of the hallmarks of his style: subdued palette; pale, almost luminescent skin; and an eye for details that border on the fetishistic, creating a look that is both ultramodern and yet in some ways eerily Victorian in feel.

Jim BURNS

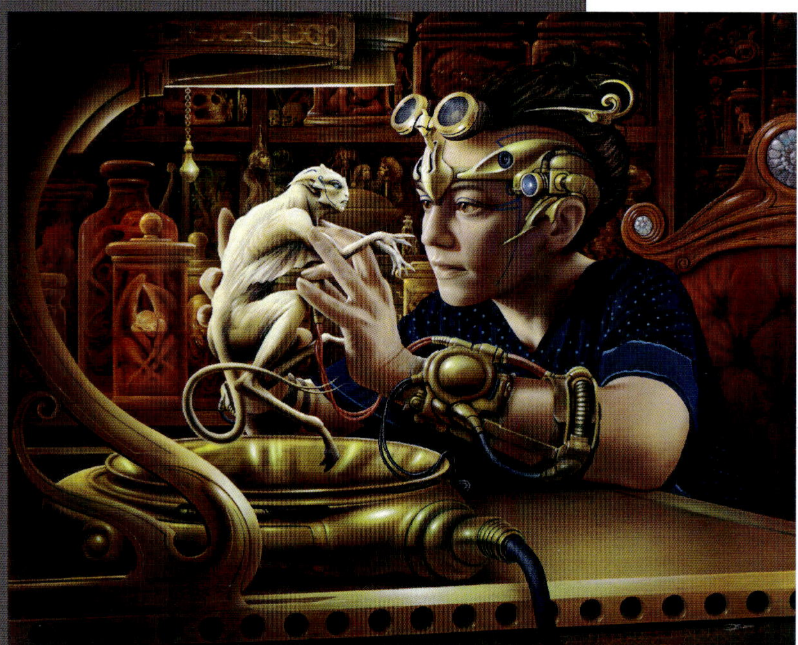

Homuncularium, 2010
Acrylic on canvas. Collection of the artist.

British, born 1948

Burns is one of the relatively few artists in the field—mostly British—who focus almost exclusively on futuristic imagery, doing very little work with fantasy themes. His work is typified by brilliant colors and an almost hyper-real, tightly rendered style. Burns has won more awards in the field than any other British artist, has been involved in numerous exhibitions both in the United States and overseas, and has been the subject of a BBC Wales documentary.

Homuncularium touches on one of Burns's favorite themes, the idea of communication between disparate characters. It demonstrates his signature artistic style, mixing beautiful human figures with flowing, organically styled hardware and bizarre aliens, beautifully rendered in rich, vivid colors.

Clyde CALDWELL

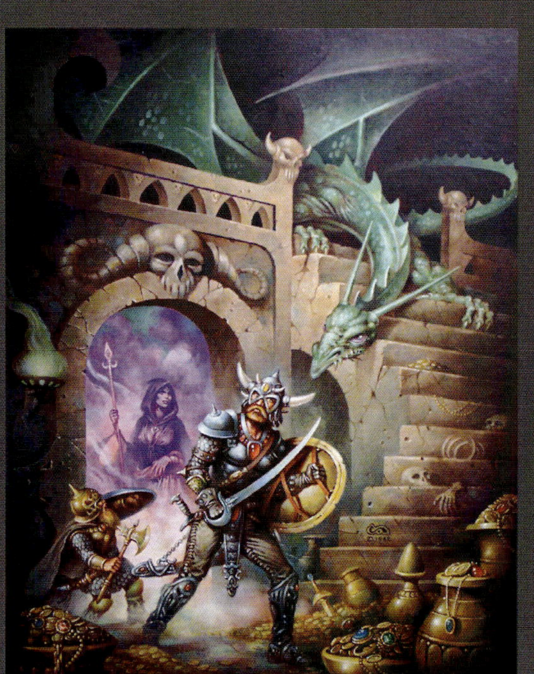

The Dragon's Lair, 1982
Oil on board. Collection of Greg Obaugh.

American, born 1948

Caldwell is best known as one of the four horseman of TSR in the 1980s, where he was responsible for helping to define the look of the *Dungeons & Dragons* world. His work is tightly rendered and highly distinctive, from clothing to the designs of common thematic elements like dragons. Caldwell left TSR in early 1992 but has maintained a successful freelance career while doing increasing numbers of personal paintings.

The Dragon's Lair is a classic Caldwell painting from early in his career with TSR. Originally created for *Dragon* magazine, it showcases Caldwell's work well, from the stylized designs of characters and the dragon to the wry narrative twist that runs through much of his work from this period.

Jeremy CANIGLIA

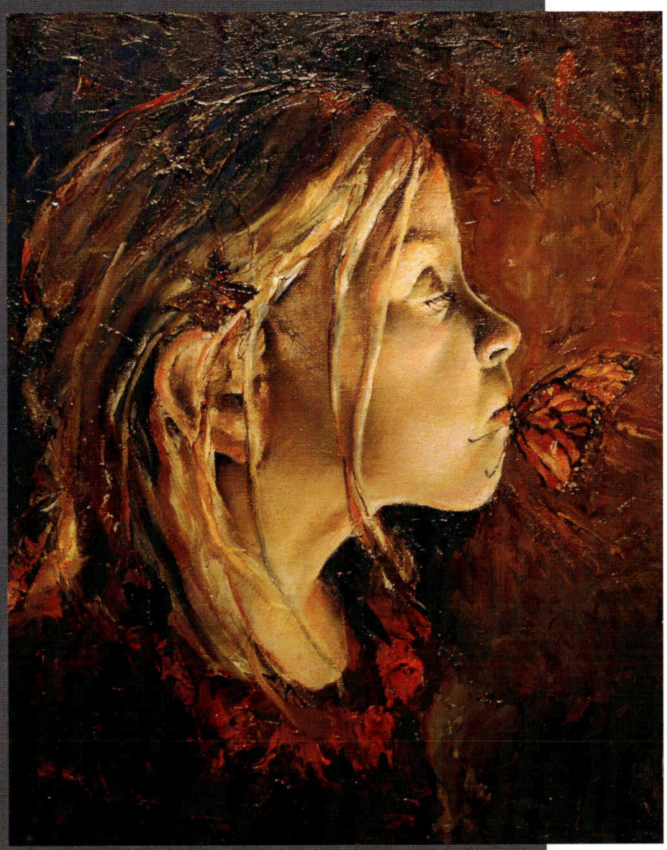

Birth of Spring, 2007
Oil on canvas. Collection of the artist.

American, born 1970

Caniglia walks the fine line between beauty and horror in many of his works, treating themes of birth and death, often in the same piece. With a style reminiscent of the old masters, his work is less narrative than many of his contemporaries but rife with symbolic meaning. Caniglia works both as an illustrator and a gallery artist, treating both commercial and private commissions with a similar approach.

Birth of Spring is one of Caniglia's best-known works. The young girl and butterfly are both beautiful, but the juxtaposition creates a slightly disturbing feeling to the painting.

Thomas CANTY

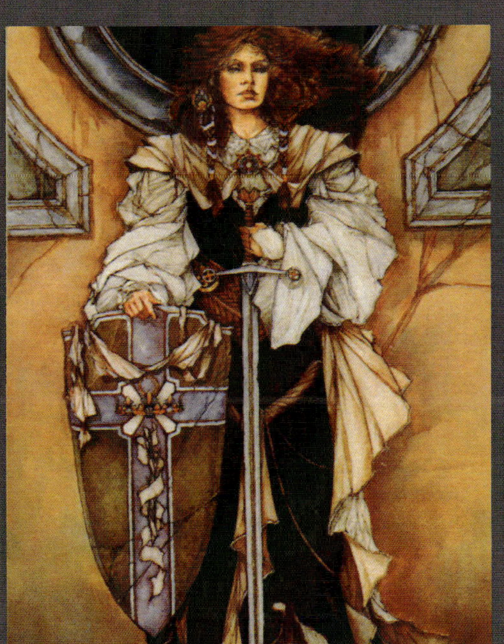

The Silver Branch, 1996
Oil on paper. Collection of Robert K. Wiener.

American, born 1952

Canty is one of the foremost practitioners of what author Terry Windling has called New Romanticism, or the updating of classical nineteenth century romantic imagery for the late twentieth century. Drawing thematic approaches from the Pre-Raphaelites and technical details from the Aesthetic movement and Art Nouveau, Canty's work harkens more directly back to the antecedents of imaginative realism than most of his contemporaries. Working with a layering of oil washes and glazes, he creates a delicate feel to his work that is much more reminiscent of watercolor than the oil paints he uses.

The Silver Branch typifies Canty's work. The highly stylized figure, clothing, and design elements are all drawn directly from the nineteenth century. Canty is one of the very few contemporary imaginative realists who has little artistic debt to Frank Frazetta, instead referring directly to Sir Edward Coley Burne-Jones, Arthur Rackham, and Gustav Klimt.

Travis CHARESTS

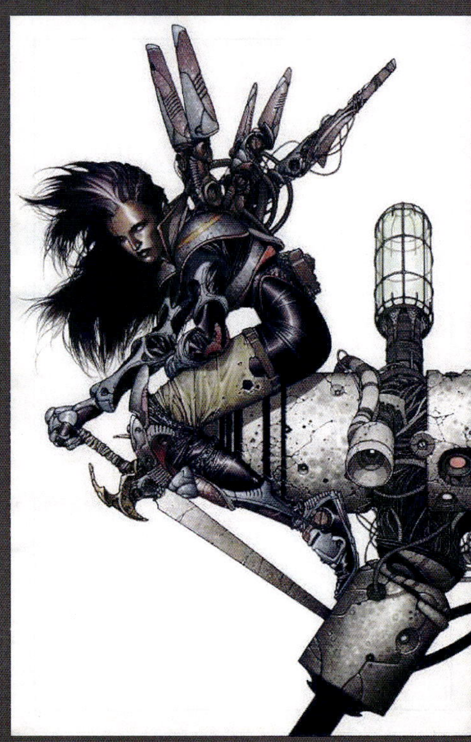

New Horizons, 1997
Watercolor and ink on paper.
Collection of Scott Williams.

Canadian, born 1969

Charest represents the finest of the contemporary artists working in the field of comics, producing exquisite drawings and watercolors that stand on their own as isolated images, particularly his covers. His highly detailed ink technique shows more influence from the work of Japanese artists such as Masamune Shirow than the golden age artists that inform most imaginative realists.

The comic field is related but distinct from imaginative realism, drawing from a different historical tradition. However, there is a great deal of crossover between the two disciplines, and influence has flowed both ways in the past several decades. Several contemporary comic artists have been particularly influential, including Charest, James Jean, and Todd McFarlane.

New Horizons typifies much of Charest's work with its focus on beautiful futuristic women, although he has shown equal facility in the past with film noir or other period treatments. Although he is, at heart, a pen-and-ink artist, this piece shows that he has a remarkable facility with color as well, the delicate washes enhancing but not obscuring his brilliant technical linework.

Richard CORBEN

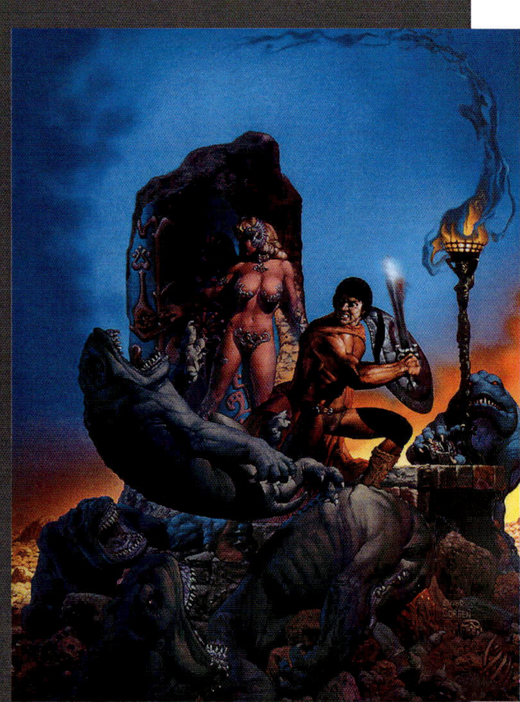

Pilgor and the Boonthas, 1980
Oil on board. Collection of Zaddick Longenbach.

American, born 1940

Corben has spent his career as something of a renaissance man, working in comics, illustration, animation, and publishing. As a result, his illustrative output is far less than most of his contemporaries, but the striking distinctiveness of his work has contributed to a profound influence. Initially coming to prominence working for the French *Metal Hurlant* with Moebius and Philippe Druillet, then *Heavy Metal* in the United States, his work in many ways echoes his early career in the underground comics movement, making him a perfect exemplar for the cross-pollination of comics and imaginative realism.

Pilgor and the Boonthas is an excellent example of Corben's color sense and unique figurative style that renders his work immediately identifiable, although it presents less of his trademark light-hearted eroticism than much of his oeuvre.

Kinuko CRAFT

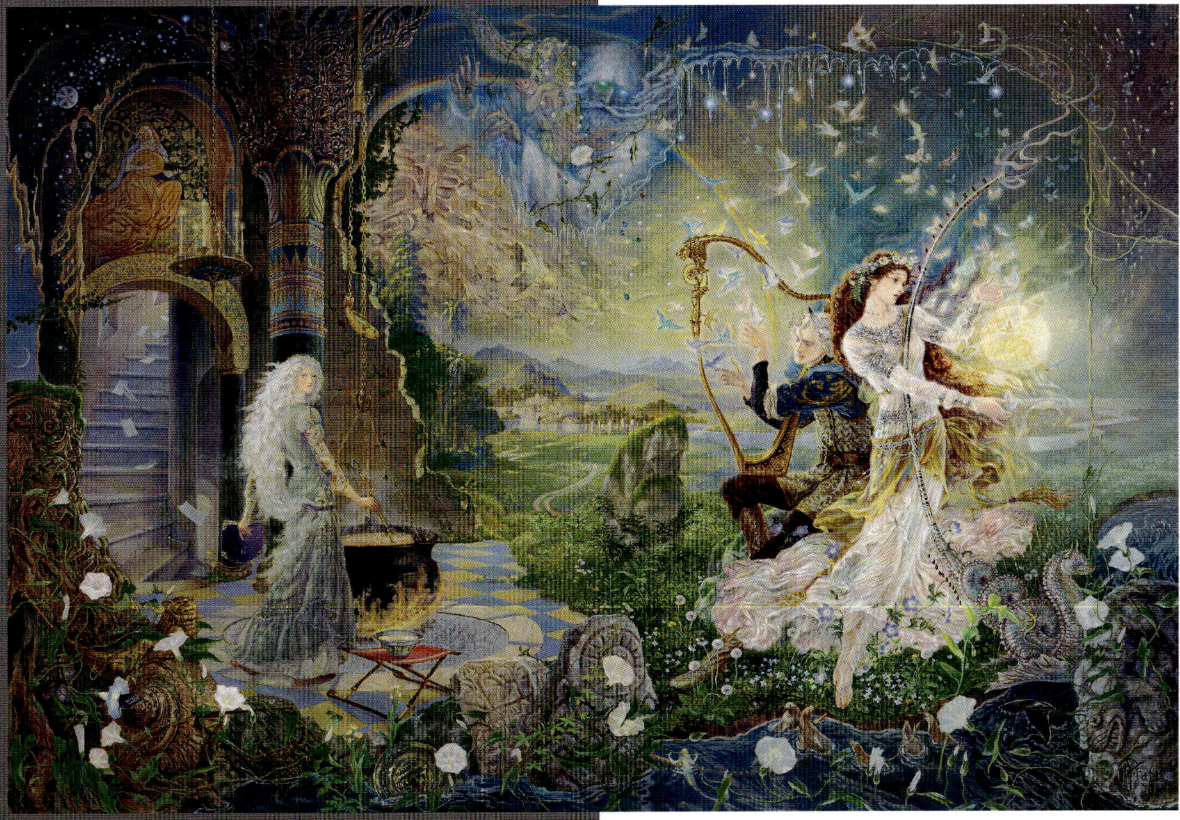

Bards of Bone Plain, 2010
Oil over watercolor on paper. Private collection, New York.

American, born 1940

Craft is renowned for her delicate, ornately constructed work that draws heavily from the works of the nineteenth century Aesthetic movement as well as Japanese influences. Her technique, working with thin oil glazes over watercolor, is unique in the field and gives her work an unparalleled depth and mystique. Over the course of her career she has won more than one hundred graphic artist awards, making her one of the most decorated artists to ever work in the genre.

Bards of Bone Plain is a privately commissioned work that demonstrates every aspect of Craft's artistry, including delicate, extremely complex details, romantically stylized figures, and the medievalist feel that typified much of the work of Pre-Raphaelite artist Dante Gabriel Rossetti, one of Craft's key influences.

Roger DEAN

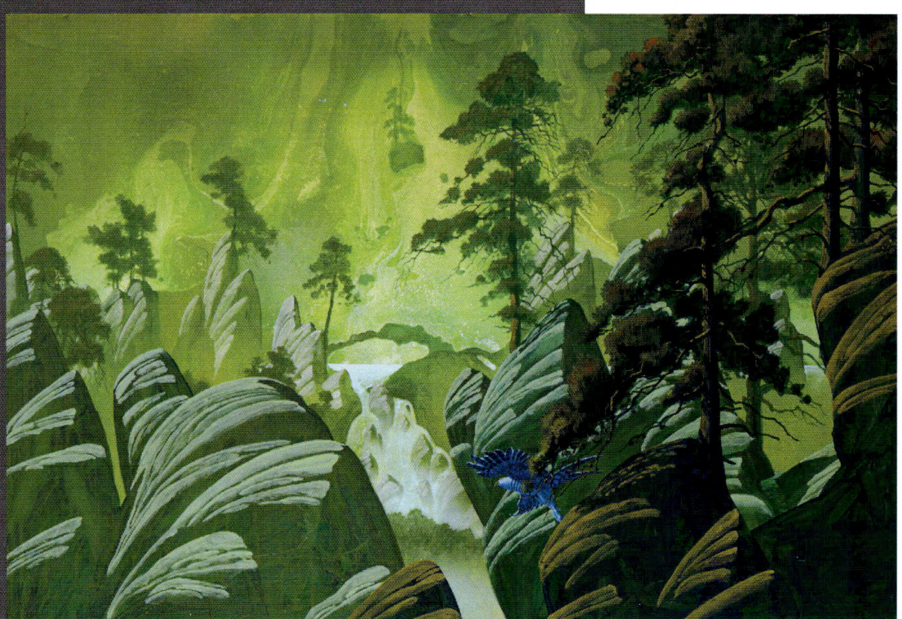

Fly from Here, 2010
Oil on board. Collection of the artist.

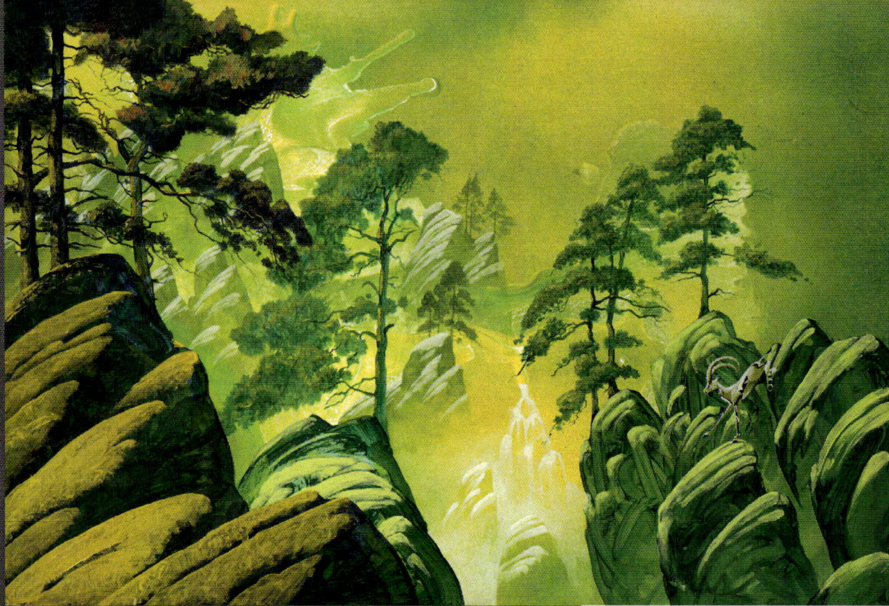

The Leap, 2010
Oil on board. Collection of the artist.

British, born 1944

Dean is one of the artists responsible for reawakening the imaginative realist tradition in Britain in the early 1970s. He has achieved worldwide fame for his album-cover art, including his iconic work for the bands Yes and Asia. He has held record-breaking solo exhibitions of his work all over the world.

Dean is the founder of Dragon's Dream publishing, the first publisher dedicated solely to producing art books on imaginative realists. Dean's own 1975 contribution to the company, *Views*, reached #1 on British bestseller lists and went on to sell more than a million copies, making it the best-selling book of all time in the field. Dragon's Dream would later become Paper Tiger, the company responsible for publishing many of the finest books in the field.

Fly from Here and *The Leap* are a set of paintings created for the 2011 Yes album *Fly from Here*. Both paintings feature Dean's iconic imaginative landscapes filled with carven rocks and distinctive trees in a stunning palette of greens and golds.

Olivia DeBERARDINIS

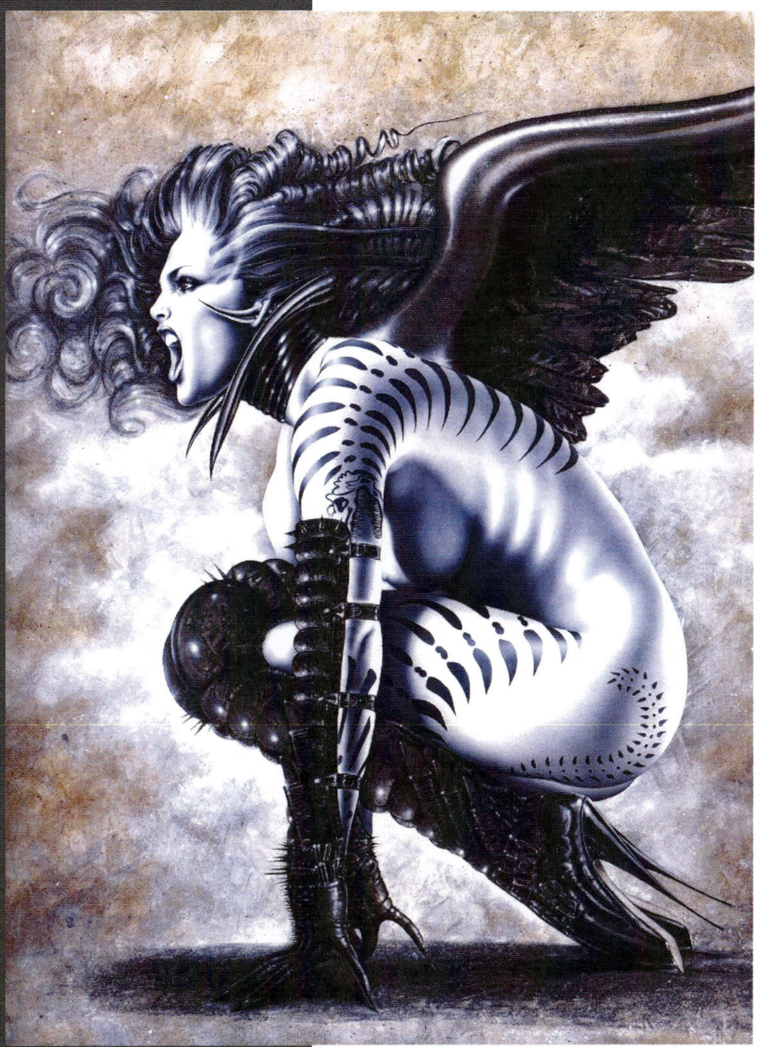

Banshee, 1987
Acrylic on paper. Collection of Julie Strain.

American, born 1948

Olivia (who paints under her first name only) is the most widely recognized contemporary pin-up artist in the world. While most pin-up painting is devoid of fantastic elements, Olivia has maintained a long-standing interest in the fantastic as well, and her melding of the fantastic with the pin-up in the early 1980s had a tremendous impact on imaginative realism. Together with other artists such as Christos Achilleos, Hajime Sorayama, and Dave Stevens, she elevated the fantasy pin-up to its own subgenre within the field. While artists in the field had often combined sensuality—or raw eroticism—with their imaginative narratives, Olivia helped to popularize the pin-up structure within the field, highlighting a single female figure with little narrative beyond background or accessory elements.

Banshee is one of Olivia's most iconic imaginative pin-ups, initially featured on the cover of *Heavy Metal* magazine. The migration of the elements of Olivia's pin-up work into the broader field of contemporary imaginative realism continues to this day.

Joe DeVITO

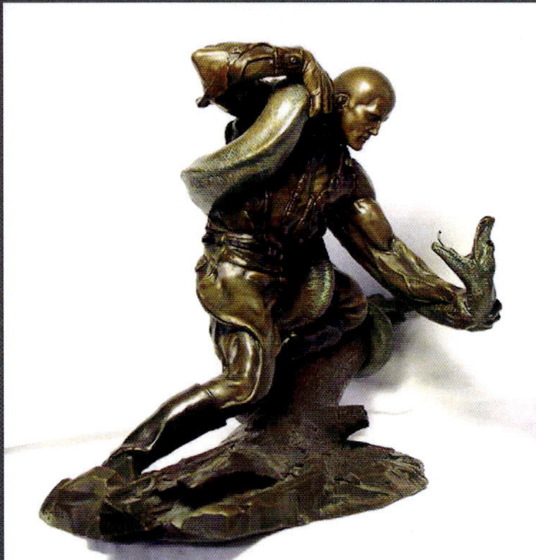

Doc Savage, 2001
Bronze. Collection of the artist.

American, born 1957

DeVito is a highly successful artist working in both two and three dimensions, and is represented in *At the Edge* in both forms. His powerful, classical style features richly painted oils in a variety of thematic approaches, including his magnum opus, the continuation of the classic Merian C. Cooper story of King Kong, *Kong: King of Skull Island.*

Doc Savage presents DeVito's representation of classic pulp hero Doc Savage, bringing his sculpting prowess to bear on an action-packed depiction of the character, drawn from Steve Holland—the original model for James Bama's iconic series of *Doc Savage* paperback covers.

Kong: King of Skull Island is the cover of DeVito's illustrated prequel and an excellent example of both his painting and his narrative vision.

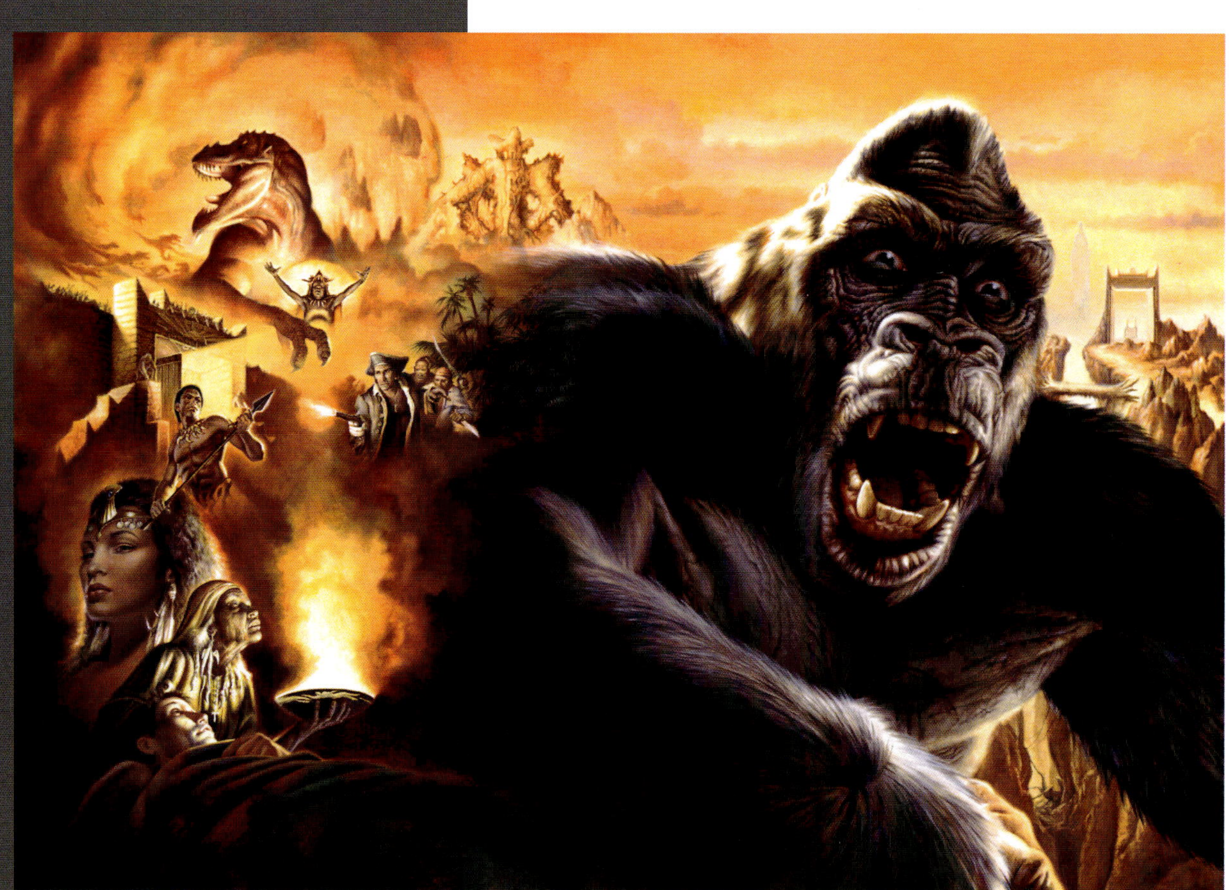

Kong: King of Skull Island, 2003
Oil on paper. Collection of the artist.

Vincent DI FATE

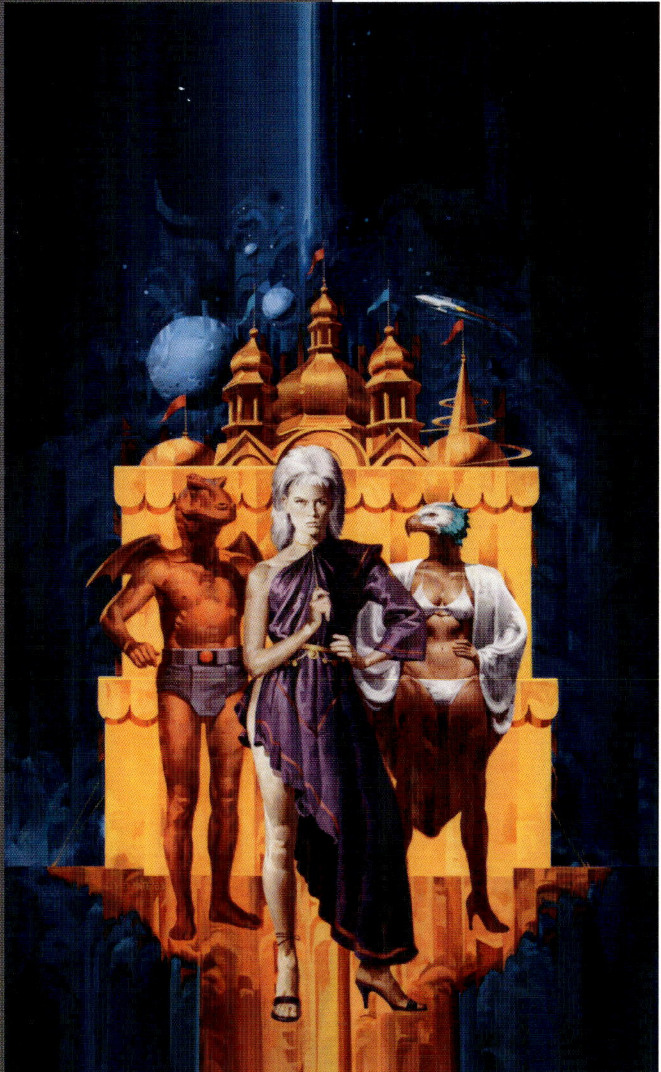

Melome, 1983
Oil on board. Collection of Vincent Di Fate.

American, born 1945

Di Fate's impact on the field is twofold: not only is he a highly prolific and highly decorated painter in the genre, he has also been one of the field's leading historians and scholarly critics for nearly forty years. Having created approximately four thousand images for publication during his career, Di Fate has worked for nearly every imaginable client from *Reader's Digest* to NASA. His seminal book *Infinite Worlds* (1997) remains the finest work ever written on the art of science fiction.

Melome shows Di Fate at his best, demonstrating a clear connection to the earlier tradition in the field while mixing a classic science-fiction feel and appreciation of the mid-century artists with the technical influence of the Brandywine and associated painters.

Tony DiTERLIZZI

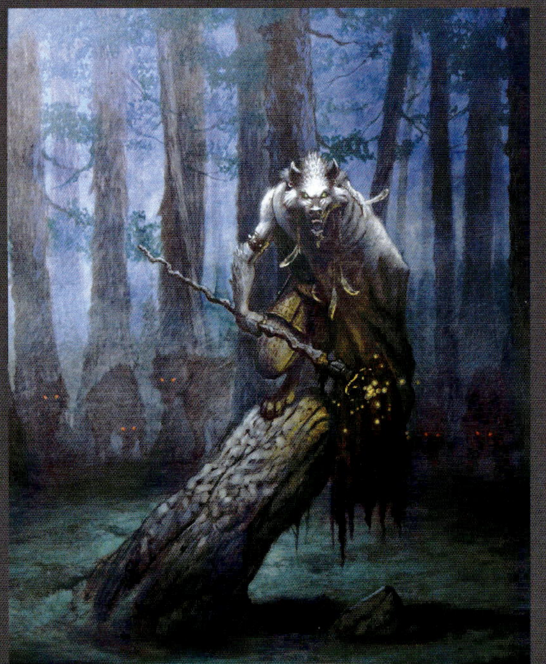

Gnoll Shaman, 2000
Acrylic, gouache and watercolor on paper.
Private collection.

American, born 1969

DiTerlizzi first reached prominence producing imaginative illustration for TSR's *Dungeons & Dragons*, utilizing a classical ink-and-watercolor style highly reminiscent of Arthur Rackham. In the early part of the twenty-first century, he began to create his own worlds in best-selling children's books, including the 2003 Caldecott Honor Medal–winning *The Spider and the Fly*. Together with writer Holly Black he created the *New York Times* bestselling *Spiderwick Chronicles* series and feature film. Most of his later work exhibits a more involved style, using a wide range of media including gouache, acrylics, and colored pencils in addition to inks and watercolors.

Gnoll Shaman shows, in one piece, two distinct segments of DiTerlizzi's career. One of his final pieces for TSR before moving exclusively to his own book creations, this piece demonstrates the mixed media approach that DiTerlizzi would utilize for his own work while still showcasing his treatment of "adult" imaginative themes.

Jeff EASLEY

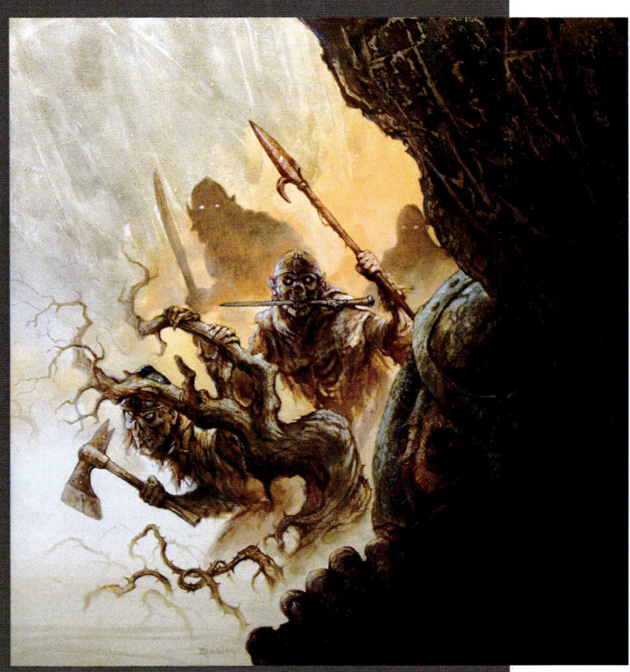

Dymrak Dread, 1993
Oil on board. Private collection.

American, born 1954

Easley is best known as one of the group of artists responsible for the creation of the look of the *Dungeons & Dragons* world, working with Clyde Caldwell, Larry Elmore, and Keith Parkinson. While Caldwell, Elmore, and Parkinson would all leave TSR by the early 1990s, Easley would continue to work for TSR (and subsequently Wizards of the Coast) until after the beginning of the twenty-first century. His work presents a unique sense of color and drama, and he excels at creating a sense of power and character within his nonhuman creations, particularly dragons and the undead.

Dymrak Dread is actually an atypical work in terms of its limited palette—Easley's work is normally ablaze with vibrant color—but it provides a superb example of the ability of his work to convey both character and mood. Even when the painting is stripped down to its bare essentials, his denizens radiate menace. Zombies, skeletons, vampires, and other undead have been popular themes for a long time—but no one has ever painted them more powerfully than Easley.

Bob EGGLETON

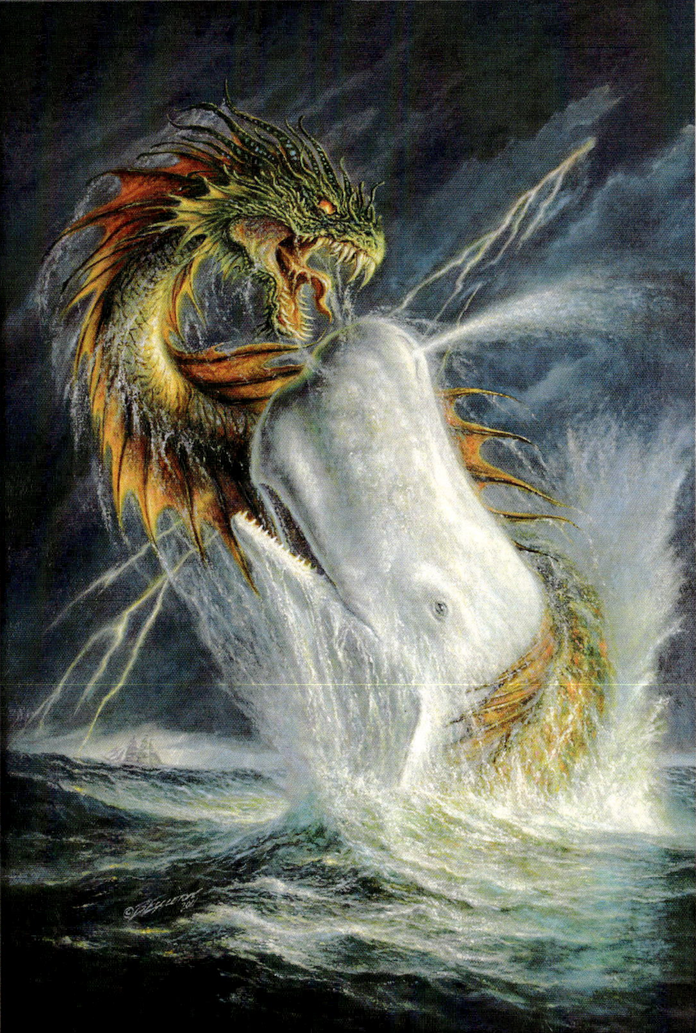

Moby Dick and the Sea Monster, 2011
Oil on canvas. Collection of the artist.

American, born 1960

Of all of the artists working in the field today, Eggleton may show the most direct connection to his nineteenth-century roots, particularly to romantic painters like J. M. W. Turner and John Martin. He began his career creating slickly airbrushed astronomical paintings, then shifted toward a more loosely painted style, working with both acrylics and oils, mastering a range of science fiction, fantasy, and horror themes. By the late 1990s, however, his work had shifted completely to oils and began to more strongly show his early influences. Eggleton is one of the most decorated figures in the field, winning immediate recognition in the early 1980s and maintaining—and expanding—that recognition as his career has progressed.

Moby Dick and the Sea Monster is a recent piece, showing the hallmarks of Eggleton's fully evolved style, bringing elements of the fantastic to dramatically created romantic landscapes and seascapes.

Larry ELMORE

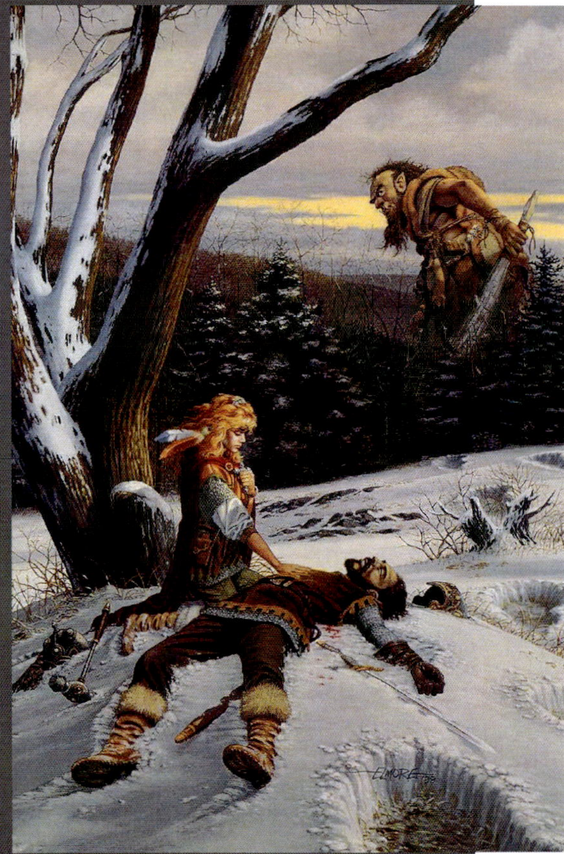

Avalyne the Life-Giver, 1988
Oil on Masonite. Collection of the artist.

American, born 1948

Of the four artists of TSR's *Dungeons & Dragons* team in the early 1980s, Elmore may be the one who is most closely associated with the shared world of *Dragonlance* created by the four artists. His best work tends to show a split personality, mixing distinctive characters—frequently beautiful women—with majestic, sprawling landscapes that often become characters in their own rights.

Avalyne the Life-Giver is one of Elmore's finest paintings, mixing a beautiful female character with strong narrative and wonderfully rendered landscape. This piece also demonstrates one of Elmore's strengths, which is his understanding of natural light and its interplay with colors.

Stephen FABIAN

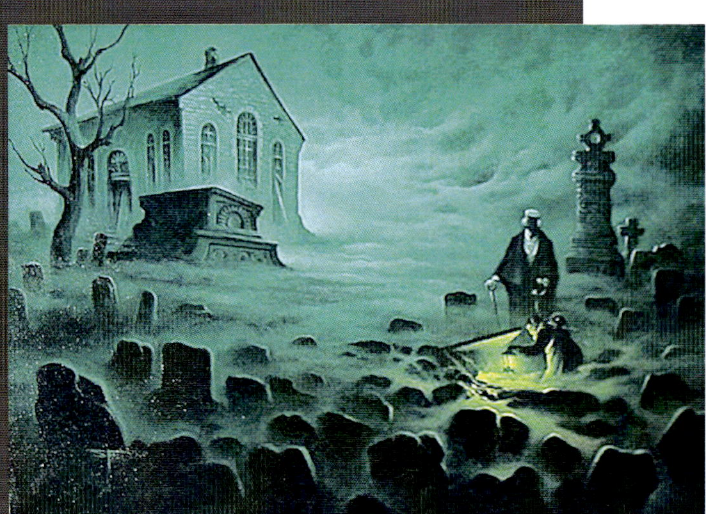

The Graverobbers, 1985
Oil on board. Collection of Stuart Schiff.

American, born 1930

Fabian came very late to the field—he did not start working as a professional artist until he was forty-three years old, after a layoff ended his previous career as an engineer. Completely self-taught, he became an almost immediate success when he began his freelance career in the early 1970s. He is best known for his sumptuous black-and-white work, producing hundreds of interior illustrations as well as several portfolios in a very unique style. His color work, although much more rare, demonstrates uncommon color solutions that create great drama and mood, often while working in a limited palette.

The Graverobbers is a perfect example of Fabian's unusual sense of color. Based strictly on its narrative elements, the painting is not fantastic in nature. However, the monochromatic green palette creates a tremendously eerie and otherworldly mood that clearly communicates the supernatural circumstances to the viewer.

Fred FIELDS

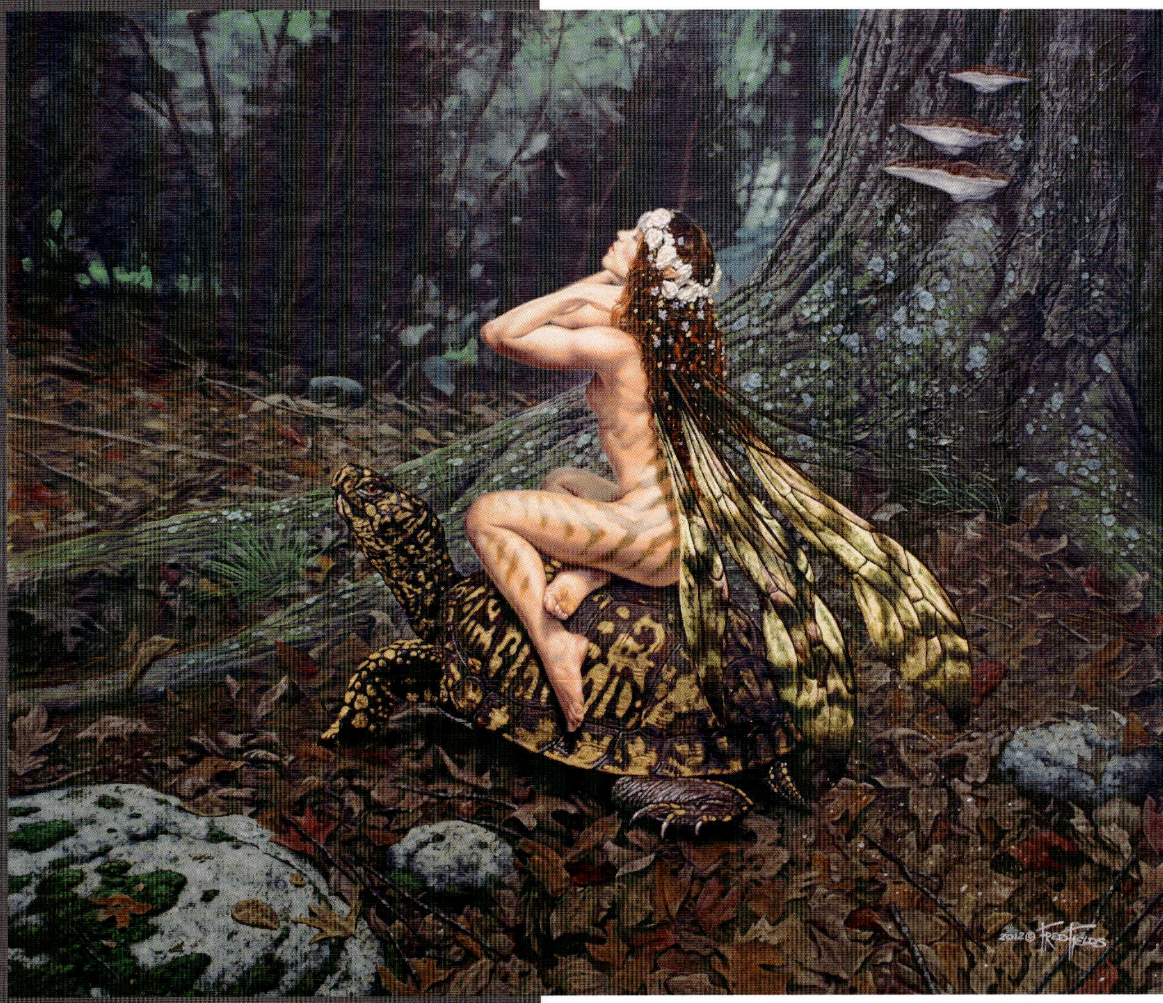

Patience, 2012
Oil on canvas. Collection of the artist.

American, born 1965

Fields began his career as a freelancer creating work for TSR, eventually becoming a staff artist and remaining with the company for ten years. After leaving TSR he took the unusual step of shifting to personal work in the western genre, building a significant following in the gallery market and honing his academic painting skills to high polish. After a long absence from imaginative imagery, Fields returned in 2010, creating both private commissions and personal works in the field but refraining from any commercial illustration.

Patience displays Fields at his finest, demonstrating his superb academic painting technique—examine the feet in the image—as well as his wry sense of humor, evidenced by the title.

Marc FISHMAN

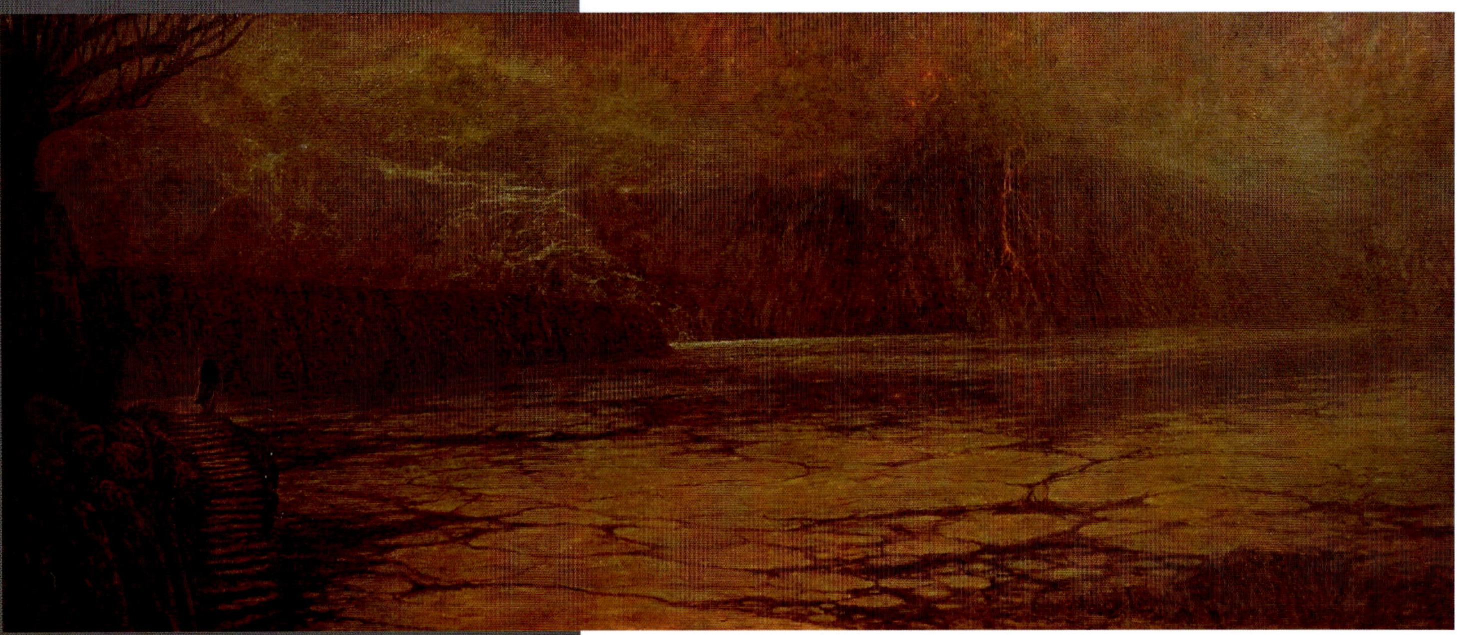

Dante on the Banks of the Styx, 2011
Oil on canvas. Collection of the Association of Fantastic Art.

American, born 1971

Fishman is somewhat of an anomaly in the contemporary imaginative realist field, which tends to focus on more tightly rendered works. Where many artists are striving to include more detail in their paintings, Fishman actively tries to display less, presenting just enough visual information to allow the viewer to complete the scene. Although heavily influenced thematically by the Pre-Raphaelites and post Pre-Raphaelites, Fishman's own painting style owes a greater debt to the more impressionistic trends of the late nineteenth century.

Dante on the Banks of the Styx is typical of Fishman's recent work, with details more suggested than clearly delineated, relying on mood and structure to transport the viewer into the scene.

Eric FORTUNE

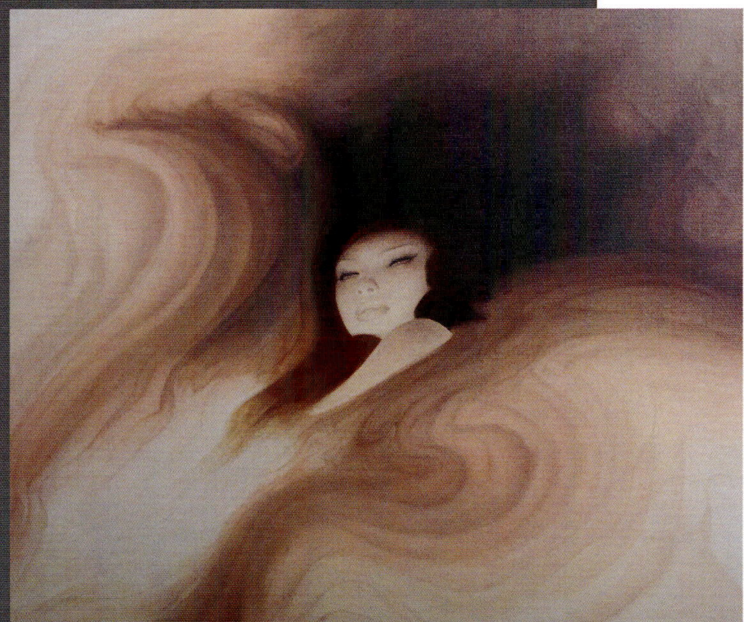

Oblivion, 2010
Acrylic on canvas. Collection of the Association of Fantastic Art.

American, born 1976

Fortune's work walks the line between imaginative realism and something closer to surrealism, presenting stylized figures in limbo-like settings. His work is at the same time nonnarrative and yet deeply character driven, created with a unique watercolor-like use of acrylic paint. Early in his career he worked at a very small scale, but as his gallery exhibitions have become more popular he has begun to paint on a fairly large scale.

Oblivion is representative of Fortune's current work, making his thematic approach even more explicit than usual as the female figure is, literally, nowhere, yet the painting crackles with action and dynamism.

Jon FOSTER

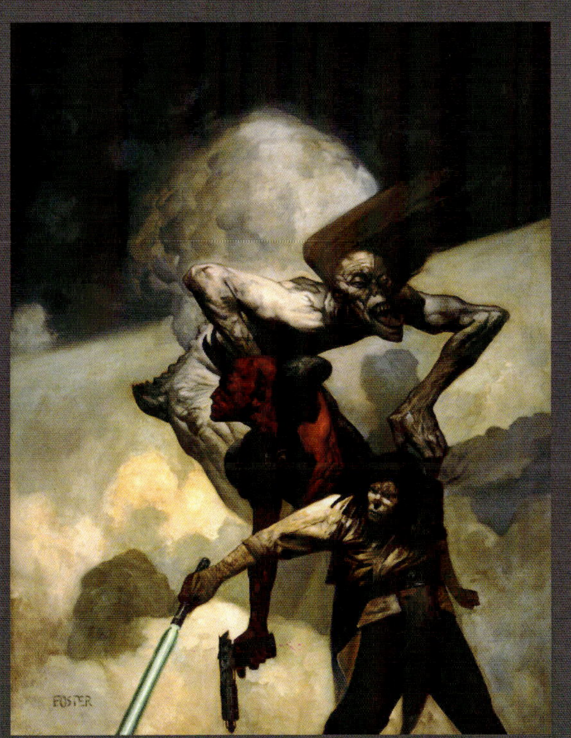

Star Wars: Anzati (Darkness #3), 2001
Oil on canvas. The Frank Collection.

American, born 1968

Foster was one of the principal artists to combine the kinetic painting styles of mentors Rick Berry and Phil Hale with the jagged, edgy feel typical of the beginning of the twenty-first century, creating a highly distinctive and influential look. Although he began his career working mainly in oils, Foster often completed his work digitally and now works completely in the computer, making major finished oils quite uncommon.

Star Wars:Anzati (Darkness #3), one of the last major Foster paintings to be completed in oils, clearly demonstrates the edgy kineticism typical of his work. Note how the exaggerated anatomy and limited palette produce a gritty, almost dystopian feel.

Brian FROUD

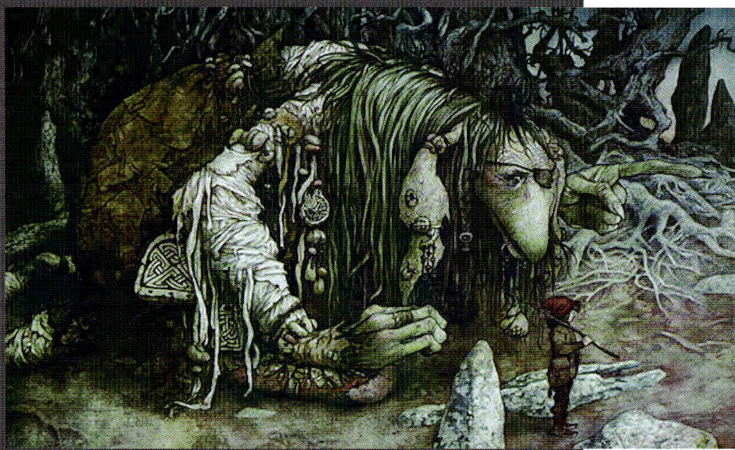

Land of Froud, 1977
Watercolor on paper. Collection of Robert Gould.

British, born 1947

Froud is renowned as one of the principal artists responsible for the rebirth of "fairy art" in the late 1970s with the publication of his book (with Alan Lee) *Faeries* (1979). *Faeries* has sold over three million copies to date, and Froud has completed several related books as well. In addition, he is a highly successful concept artist, having been predominantly responsible for the designs of such films as *The Dark Crystal* (1982) and *Labyrinth* (1986).

Land of Froud is the cover image for his first art book, *The Land of Froud*, published in 1977. This work is emblematic of Froud's approach to storytelling and legend, more akin to his concept work for *The Dark Crystal* than *Faeries*. This early major work clearly shows the influence of Swedish artists John Bauer and Gustave Tenggren.

Donato GIANCOLA

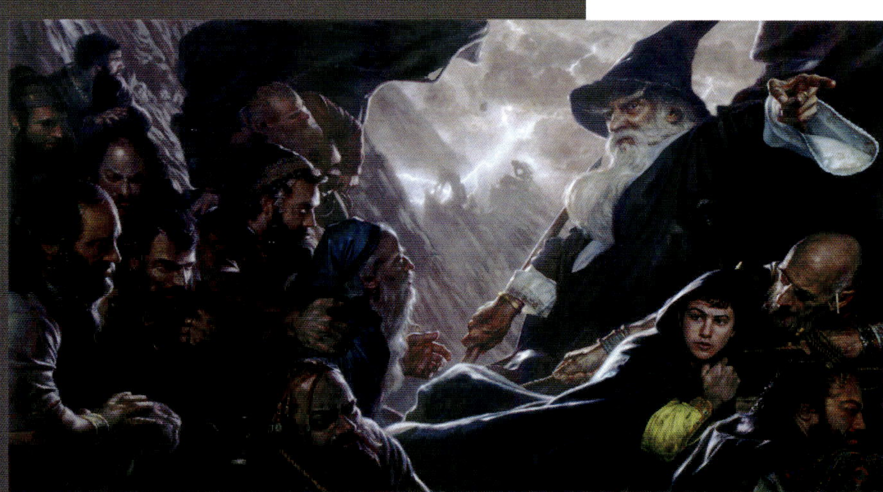

The Hobbit: The Expulsion, 2001
Oil on paper mounted to Masonite.
Collection of the artist.

American, born 1967

Donato (the artist's professional name) brings a unique presence to contemporary imaginative realism. While most contemporary artists' works are informed to some extent by their historical predecessors, Donato seeks to actively evoke the work of the old masters in his paintings, mixing their highly classical painting approach with contemporary subject matter. He is one of the field's finest and most recognizable painters, often working in very large scales. He is highly influential, but more from an inspirational standpoint than actual direct influence, as very few young artists are able to replicate his classical painting technique.

The Hobbit: The Expulsion is a prime example of Donato's work; grand in both scale and execution, it highlights his remarkable technical prowess as well as his exceptional narrative and compositional skills.

H.R. GIGER

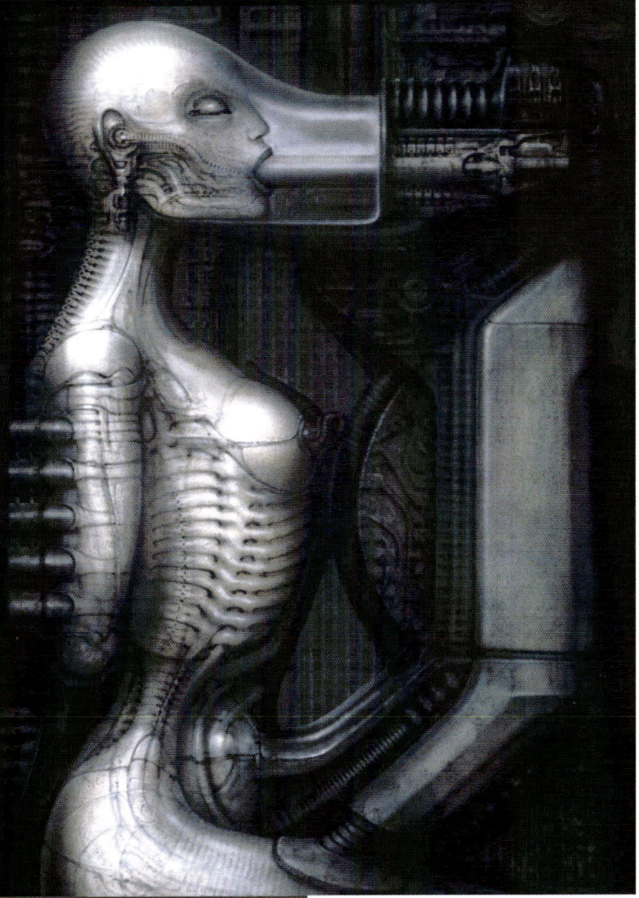

Biomechanoid II, Work 521,
c. 1975–1983
Acrylic on paper. The Frank Collection.

Swiss, born 1940

Giger is by far the most famous of the contemporary surrealist painters, eclipsing other notables such as Zdzislaw Beksinski, De Es Schwertberger, and Peter Gric. Although the surrealists come from a separate branch of the artistic tree than the imaginative realists (forking after the symbolists, in most cases), there is considerable crossover influence, especially in the case of Giger. While Giger is well known for his entire oeuvre, his greatest fame comes from his Oscar-winning visual design work on the iconic Ridley Scott film *Alien* (1979), which had a major impact on the look of science fiction throughout the visual arts. Since 1980 Giger has largely ceased painting to focus on sculpture, demonstrating the same biomechanical morphs that inhabit the majority of his painting.

Biomechanoid II, Work 521 comes from Giger's most famous collection of work, the *Necronomicon* (1977), and is a perfect example of his disturbing, often sexualized melding of flesh and machine. The *Necronomicon* works were what convinced Scott to hire Giger for the *Alien* designs.

Female Torso shows Giger's work brought into three dimensions, the female figure bound and machined. Although this sculpture was originally intended to be an edition of five, this piece was the only one ever cast.

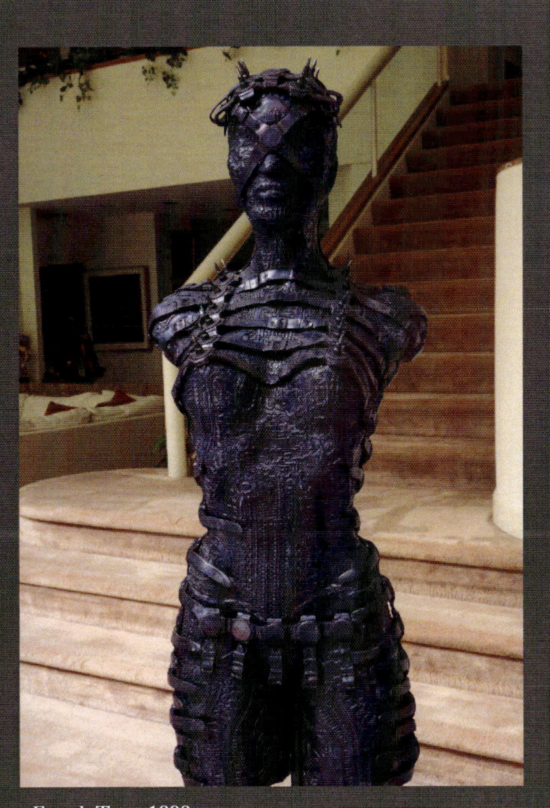

Female Torso, 1999
Bronze and aluminum. The Frank Collection.

GNEMO

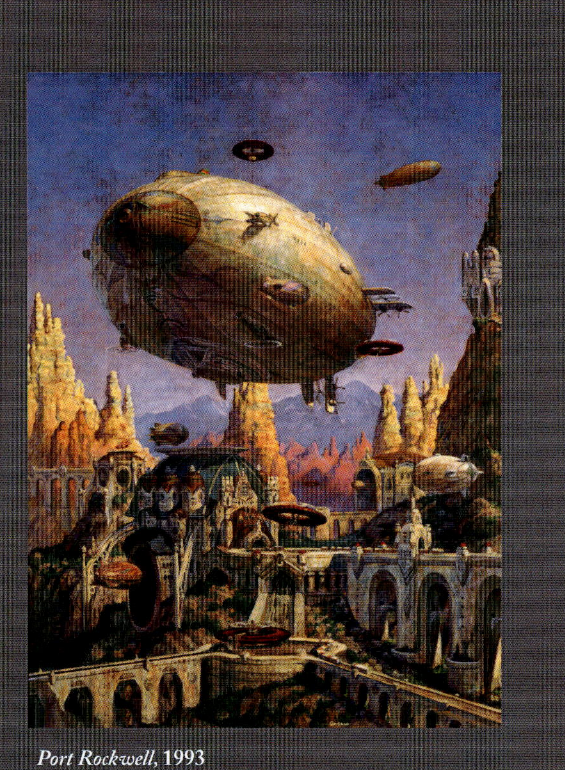

Port Rockwell, 1993
Oil on canvas. The Frank Collection.

American, born 1955

Gnemo (the artist works under this single name) has created a marvelous world that is a mix of Victorian England and fantasy, populated by extravagant cities, strange creatures, and airships. Gnemo works in a style that is highly reminiscent of the Brandywine painters, utilizing a soft palette and a loose, painterly style to create imagery that has a more romantic feel than that of many of his contemporaries.

Port Rockwell pays direct homage to one of Gnemo's artistic inspirations, Norman Rockwell. The structure, palette, and style of this piece harken directly back to the work of seminal golden age painter N. C. Wyeth.

Robert GOULD

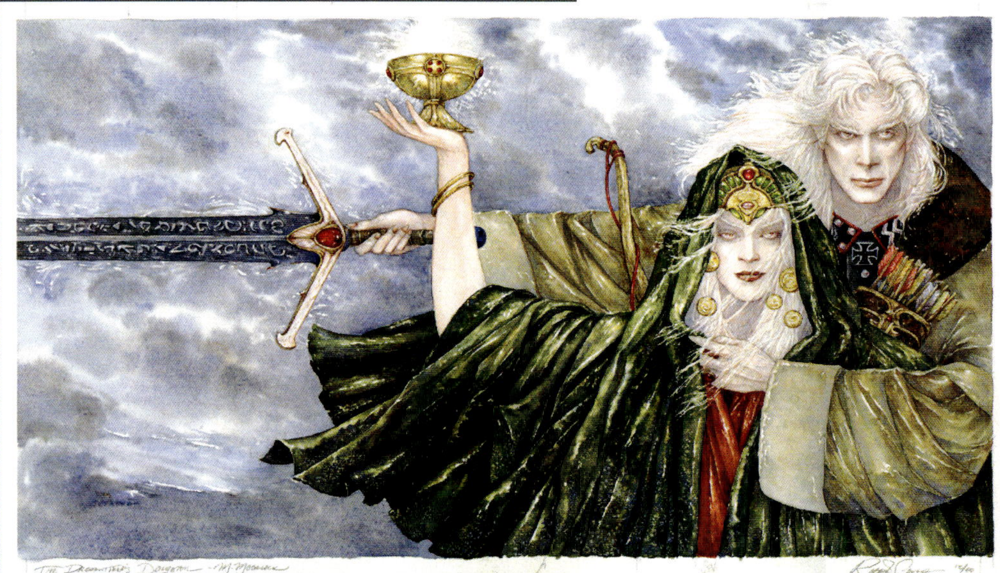

Dreamthief's Daughter, c. 1990
Watercolor on paper. Collection of Robert Gould.

American, born 1952

Gould is a proponent (along with Thomas Canty) of New Romanticism, drawing inspiration from the Pre-Raphaelite artists and combining it with a highly distinctive watercolor style. He is best known for his depictions of Michael Moorcock's antihero Elric of Melniboné, having established himself as one of the principal interpreters of that character.

The Dreamthief's Daughter is one of a series of Elric paintings created by Gould for Moorcock's novels. The influence of nineteenth-century artists like Sir Edward Coley Burne-Jones can clearly be seen in both the design and the execution of this piece.

Lars GRANT-WEST

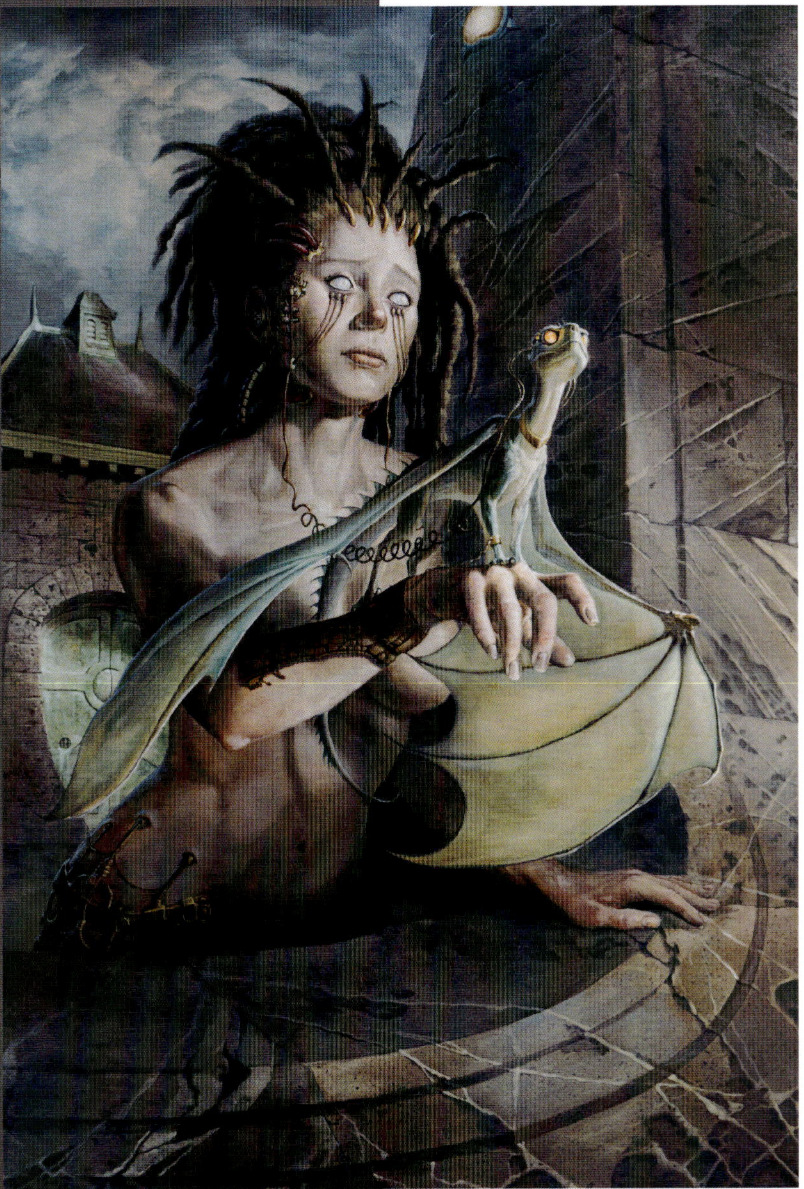

Pact of the Blind, 2010
Oil on canvas. Collection of the Association of Fantastic Art.

American, born 1968

Grant-West is best known for his stunning portrayal of dragons and other fantastic creatures that are drawn from the artist's extensive background in zoo science and biology. He has contributed extensively to both the *Dungeons & Dragons* and *Magic: The Gathering* worlds, mixing smaller-scale gaming art with his large-scale personal works.

Pact of the Blind is an example of Grant-West's narrative and technical abilities, as the painting tells the story of a blind young cyberprincess who must use the eyes of her dragon captive to see the sunrise.

Rebecca GUAY

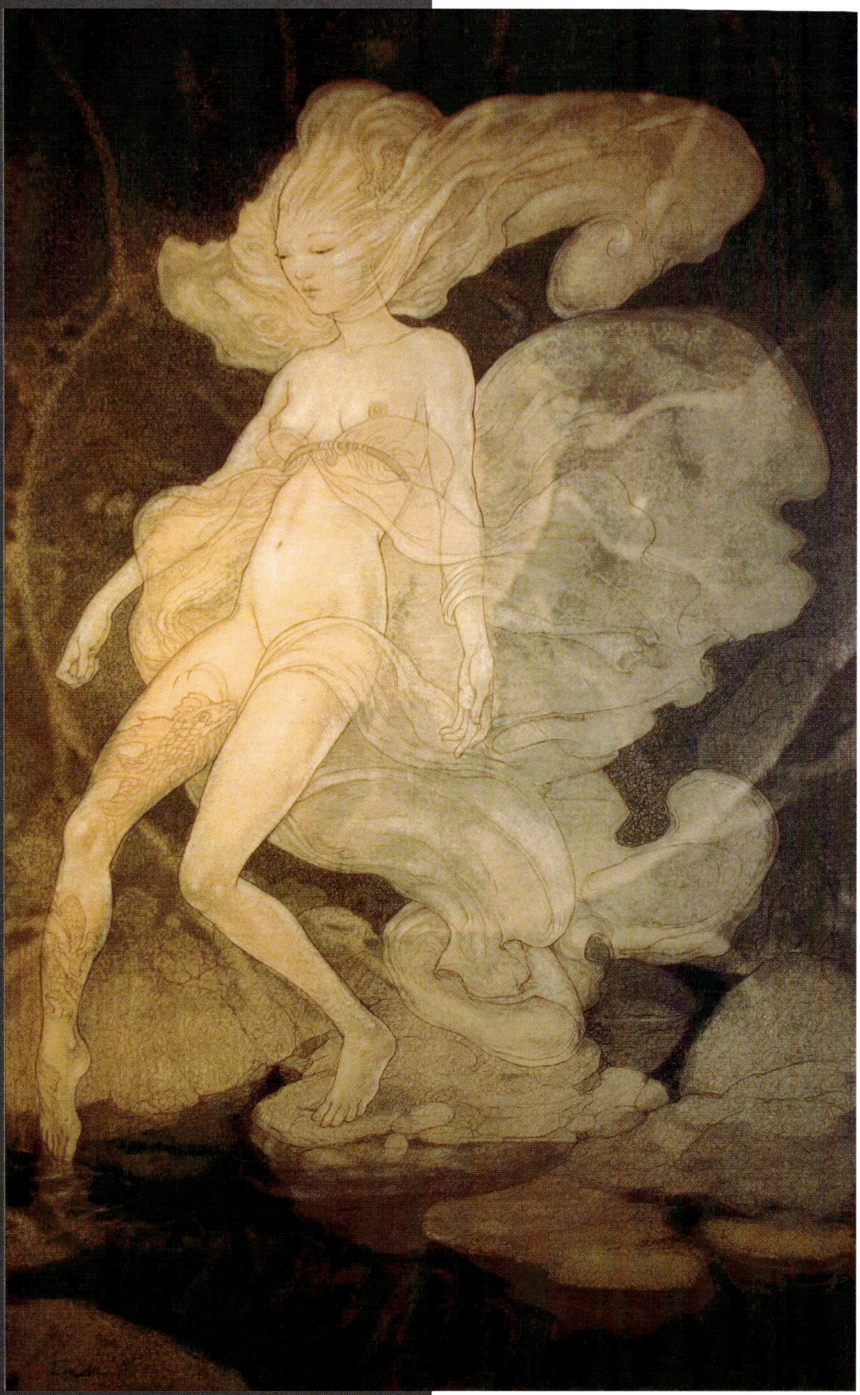

Pandora, 2011
Watercolor on board. Collection of the artist.

American, born 1970

Guay possesses one of the more distinctive styles in contemporary imaginative realism, working in watercolor in a style highly reminiscent of golden age painters such as Edmund Dulac and Kay Nielsen. Equally at home working with illustration, sequential storytelling, or gallery art, Guay's work blends mysticism with romance.

Pandora is an example of one of Guay's more recent gallery paintings, large in scale and highly romantic in tone.

James GURNEY

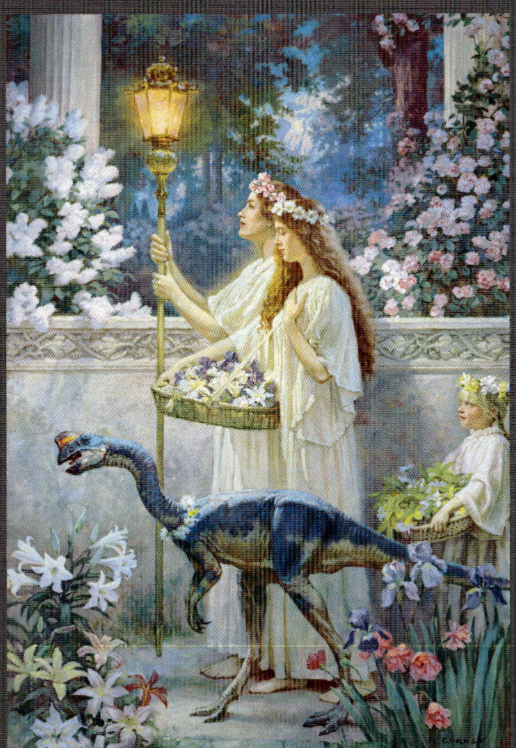

Garden of Hope, 1992
Oil on board. Collection of the artist.

American, born 1958

Gurney is one of the most famous contemporary imaginative realist painters. His tripartite fascination with ancient civilizations, dinosaurs, and nineteenth century academic painters led him, after a successful career as an illustrator, to create the bestselling *Dinotopia* book series, about a fabulous lost world of ancient cities and dinosaurs. He now spends much of his time split between researching and creating new books and teaching and lecturing to art students across the country.

Garden of Hope, an early *Dinotopia* painting, shows Gurney's more romantic influences, including the Pre-Raphaelites and other Victorian artists, as well as highlighting the artist's remarkable facility for creating carefully crafted, completely accurate depictions of known dinosaur species.

Dinosaur Parade is the cover painting for the original *Dinotopia* book that has been seen and enjoyed by millions of fans. This painting provides an excellent example of the influence of Sir Lawrence Alma-Tadema's history paintings on Gurney's work, as we can see clear echoes of Alma-Tadema's Rome in Gurney's Chandara.

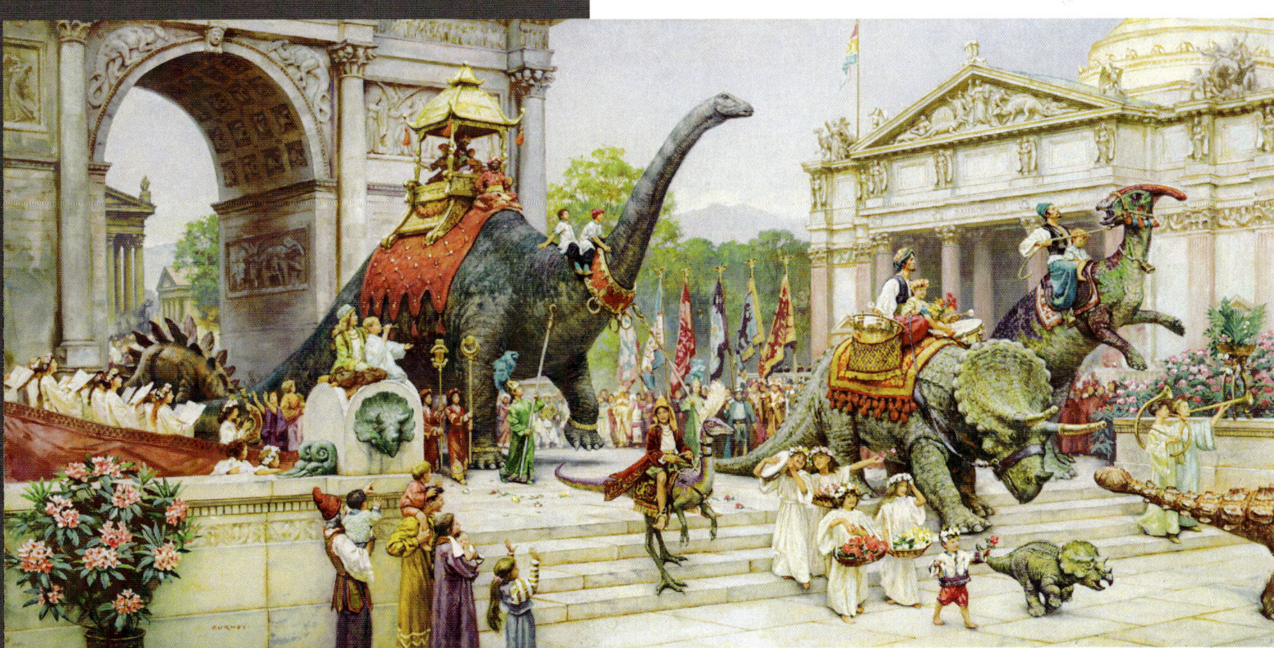

Dinosaur Parade, 1992
Oil on board. Collection of the artist.

Scott GUSTAFSON

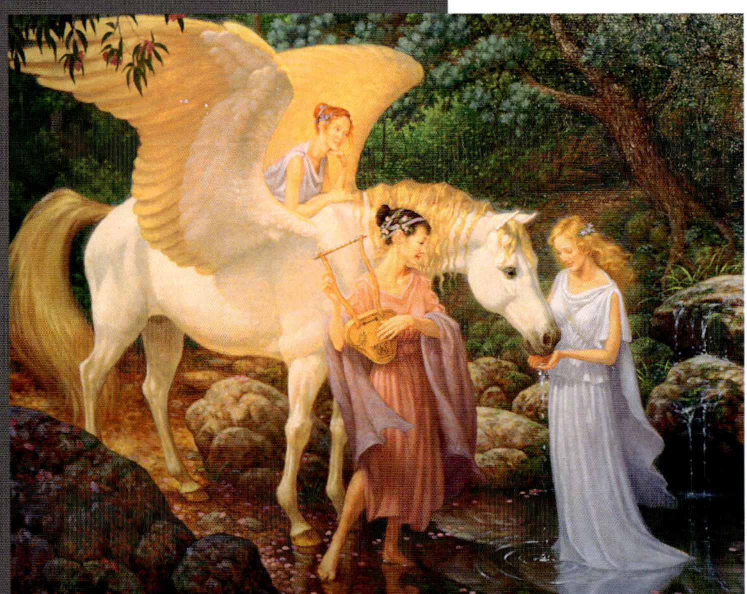

Pegasus and the Muses, 2007
Oil on Masonite. Private collection.

American, born 1962

Gustafson is world renowned for his warm, glowing depictions of classic fairy tales and children's stories. Having discovered the Brandywine painters at a fairly young age, Gustafson has followed in their footsteps in creating a wide range of beautifully illustrated books, including *Classic Fairy Tales* and *Peter Pan*.

Pegasus and the Muses is one of Gustafson's rare forays into adult fantasy. Created for a Greenwich Workshop limited edition, this painting is a beautiful example of the facility with light, color, and story that makes Gustafson's work so popular.

Phil HALE

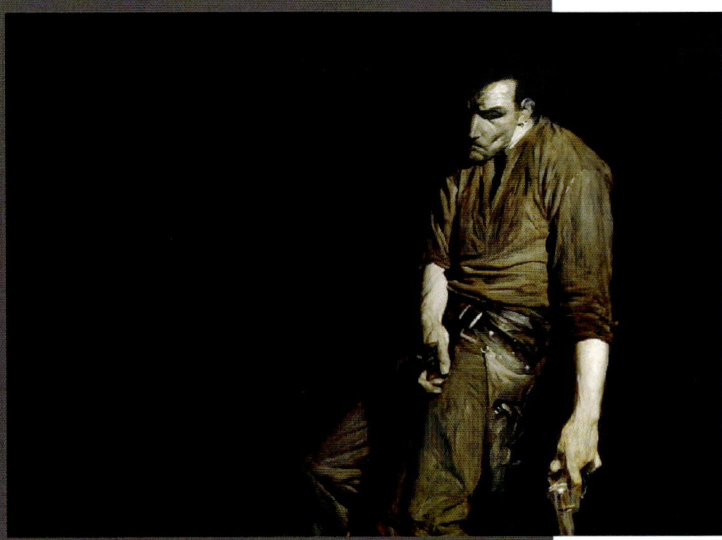

Roland Deschain, 1987
Oil on canvas. Collection of Robert K. Wiener.

American, born 1963

Hale burst on to the scene in the early 1990s, his stark, brushy painting style, limited palette, and kinetic, exaggerated figures having an immediate influence on the field. Hale's best imaginative work tends to be about movement, energy, and, frequently, the transfer of that energy from one character to another. Hale has won numerous awards and accolades for his portraiture, including being selected to paint the official portrait of former British prime minister Tony Blair.

Roland Deschain is an image done for one of Steven King's *Gunslinger* books, and it shows both sides of Hale's work: the awkward, moving position of the figure and its strong sense of personality.

Roger HANE

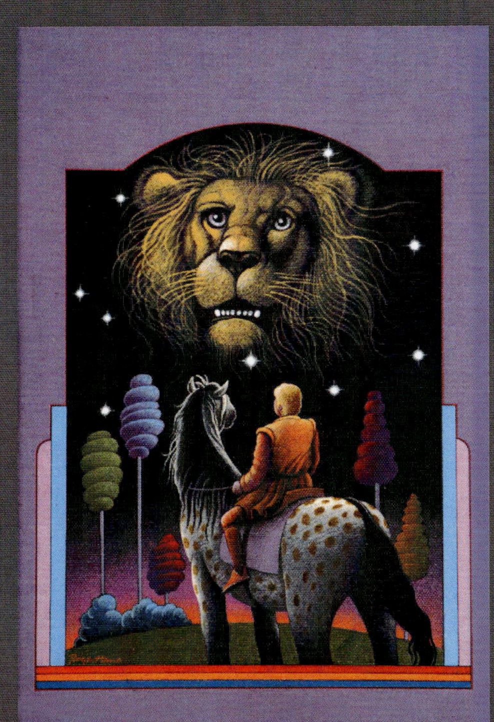

The Horse and His Boy, 1971
Acrylic on canvas. Collection of Robert Hunsicker.

American, 1939–1974

During Hane's brief eleven year career, he created over 300 illustrations, including the iconic covers for the Collier-Macmillan editions of C.S. Lewis' *The Chronicles of Narnia*, for which he is best known. His distinctively surrealistic flair and dynamic compositions make his work immediately recognizable. Sadly, his career was cut short by his death following a mugging in New York City's Central Park in 1974.

The Horse and His Boy is one of Hane's Narnia covers, demonstrating the distinctive style and palette that typified his work for the series, which are some of the most widely-recognized imaginative images of the twentieth century.

John HARRIS

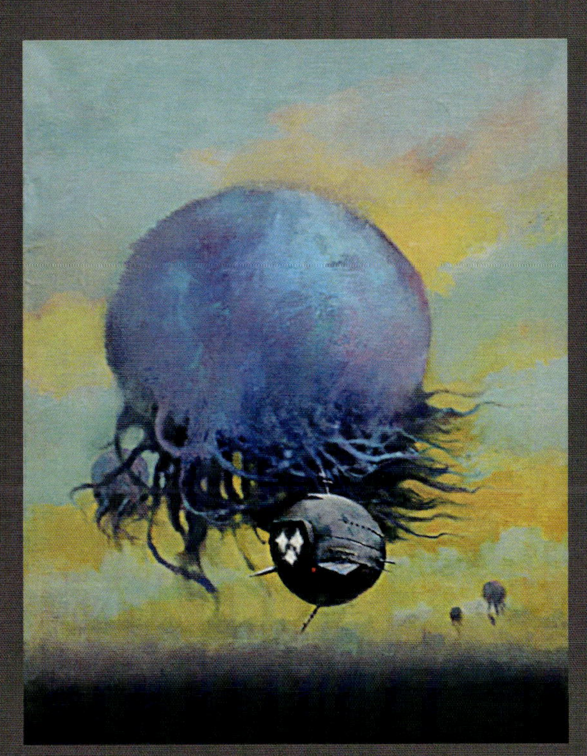

Leviathans of Jupiter, 2010
Oil on canvas. Collection of Paul and LizAnn Lizotte.

British, born 1948

Harris's work has changed over the course of his career. Beginning with tight works done in shellac inks over gouache, he has moved through acrylics and on to oils, his work gradually becoming more impressionistic over time. One thing that hasn't changed is his fascination with scale; Harris' works are filled with immense structures, ships, cities, and landscapes, all rendered in a stunning palette mixing deep, rich colors with pastel hues that are rarely seen in the field.

Leviathans of Jupiter is typical of Harris's recent work, featuring gigantic mechanical structures—in this case spaceships—on a uniquely colorful background.

Michael C. HAYES

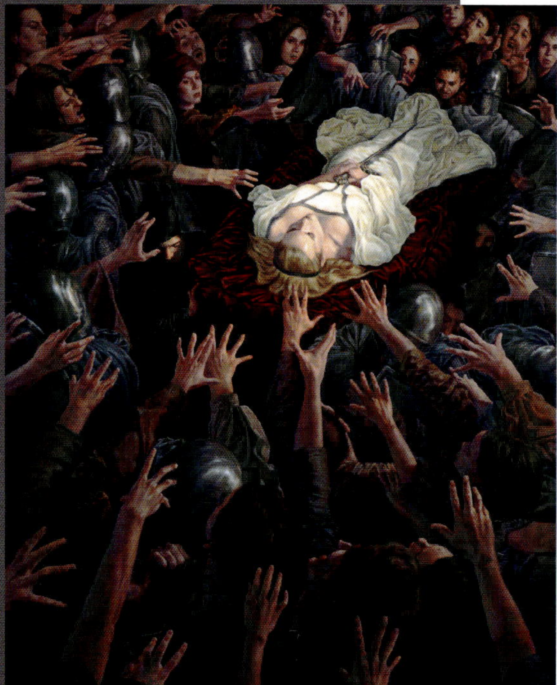

Procession, 2012
Oil on Masonite. Collection of the Association of Fantastic Art.

American, born 1982

Hayes is one of the finest young painters in the field, building an enthusiastic following around his classically painted figural works that often feature beautiful female figures. His personal work also tends to explore more introspective themes, particularly the themes of death and loss. Hayes is one of several major young artists in the field who teach at the Watts Atelier in California, along with E. M. Gist and Lucas Graciano.

Procession is the largest work Hayes has completed to date, and is an example of the artist's fascination with the idea of death and mourning. It was created for the 2012 IlluXCon symposium.

Richard HESCOX

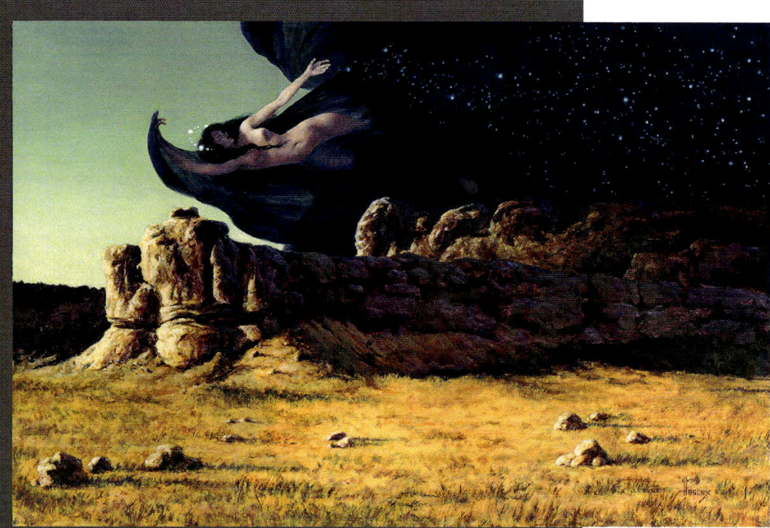

The Night, 2006
Oil on canvas. Collection of the artist.

American, born 1949

Hescox spent the majority of his career as a highly successful illustrator, beginning in the late 1970s. In the past ten years he has largely stopped accepting commercial assignments to focus on his personal visions. Although his commercial work showed the hallmarks of the Brandywine artists, they were created in the slicker, more tightly rendered style typical of book covers during the period. His personal work, by comparison, is much more strongly influenced by the imaginative painters of the Victorian era, whose imagery Hescox actively collects.

The Night is an example of Hescox's personal work, treating a classical theme in a nineteenth-century manner that would look perfectly at home next to works by Victorian artists Herbert Draper or Frank Dicksee.

Stephen HICKMAN

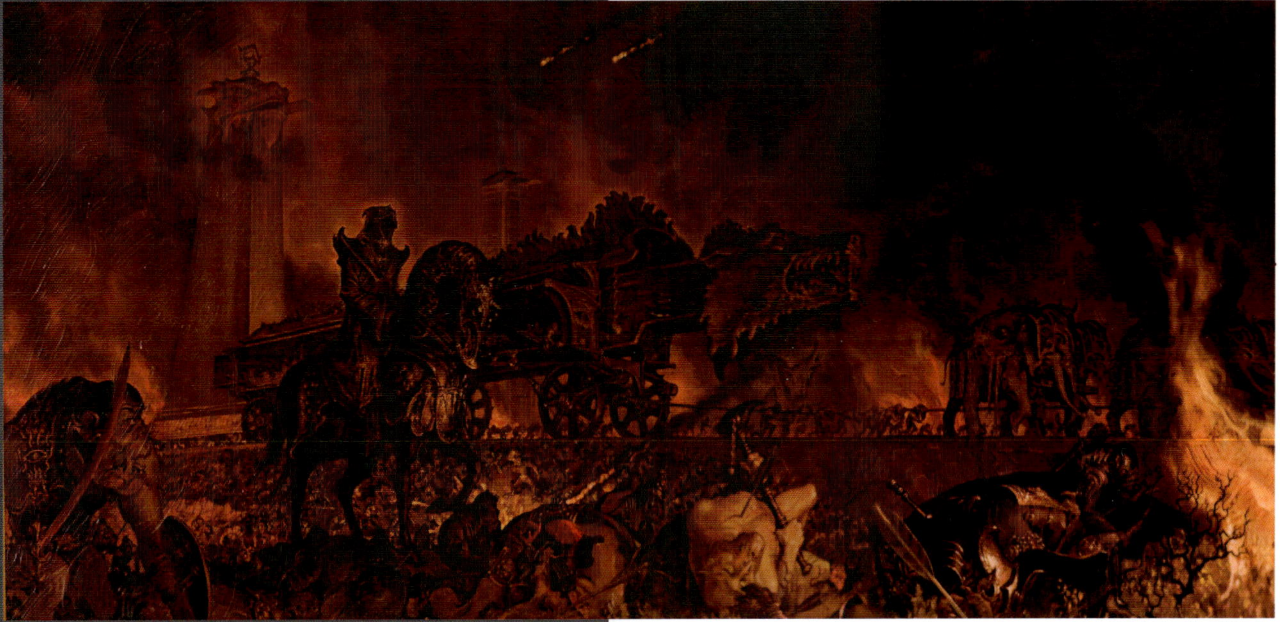

Siege of Minas Tirith, 1978
Oil on Masonite. Private collection.

American, born 1949

Hickman entered the field in the mid 1970s and serves as a prime example of an artist who followed Frazetta's lead back to earlier painters, but with his own twist. Hickman is an avid student of art history, and during various stages his work has shown strong influences ranging from the Dutch masters to art nouveau, whose highly decorative, organic style continues to inform much of Hickman's work.

Siege of Minas Tirith is a major early work of Hickman's, who has frequently explored the worlds of J. R. R. Tolkien in his personal works. This piece, never intended for publication, utilizes dark, rich colors and heavily stroked varnish to evoke the heat and despair of the successful siege, and is a prime example of the need to see imaginative realist works in person, as it—like the work of many other artists—is not served well by photographic reproduction.

Brothers HILDEBRANDT

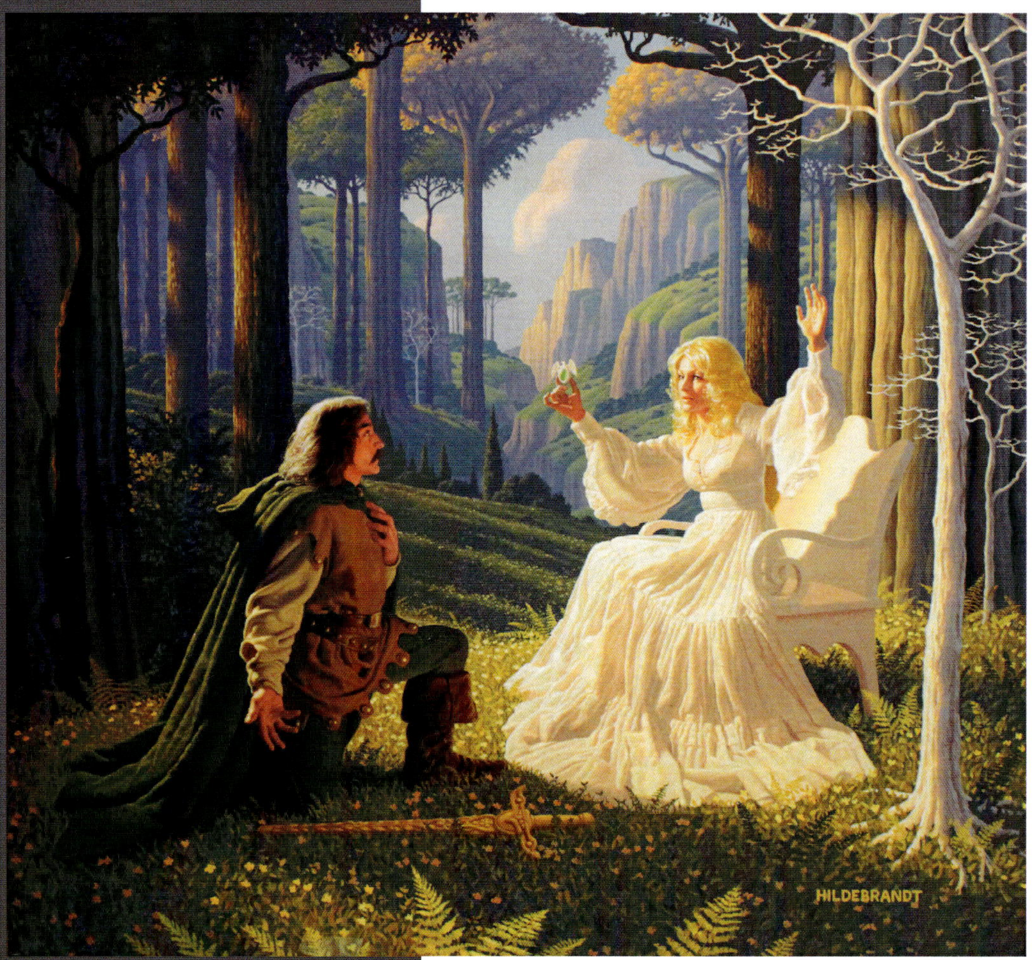

The Gift of Galadriel, 1977
Acrylic on board. Collection of Greg Hildebrandt.

American, Greg, born 1939; Tim,1939–2006

The Brothers Hildebrandt are synonymous with contemporary imaginative realism, recognized as key figures in the contemporary movement and hugely influential on most of the artists starting their careers in the 1980s or later. Twins Greg and Tim are best known for their depictions of the worlds of J. R. R. Tolkien in a series of 1970s calendars, as well as creating the original iconic movie poster for *Star Wars*. Their work showcases a beautiful handling of light and color, highly influenced by golden age artist Maxfield Parrish.

The Gift of Galadriel is an example of the Brothers' painting at its finest, depicting the elf princess Galadriel for their 1977 *Lord of the Rings* calendar. The beautiful luminescence of whites like Galadriel's gown is a hallmark of the Brothers' work, shown to full effect in this piece.

Greg HILDEBRANDT

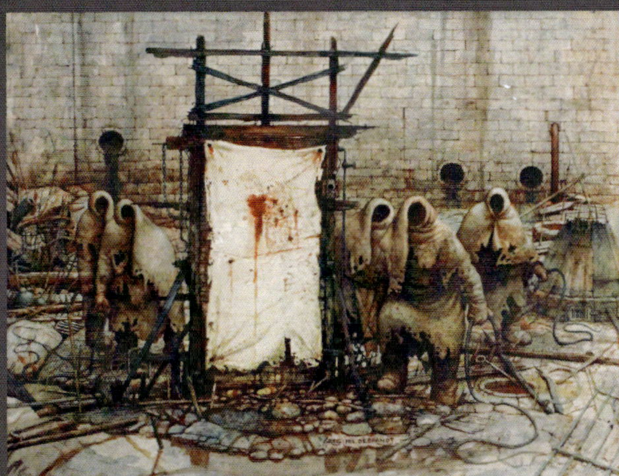

Dream 1: Crucifiers (Mob Rules), 1974
Acrylic on board. Collection of the artist.

American, born 1939

Hildebrandt's solo work is similar to and yet distinct from the work created in tandem with his twin brother, Tim. He continues to work in acrylics, but in a style that places greater emphasis on form and finish than the heavily glazed studies in light and color produced by the Brothers. Over the past ten years Hildebrandt has become increasingly interested in classic pin-up painting, building a huge following in that field and doing far less imaginative work, although the fantastic pieces he does produce are among the best of his career.

Dream 1: Crucifiers (Mob Rules) is, literally, a nightmare pulled from a dream that haunted Hildebrandt for years. It was painted in 1974 and stored in a closet until the band Black Sabbath asked to license the image for their 1981 *Mob Rules* album. This piece represents a side of Hildebrandt's art that rarely surfaces explicitly, but is often an undercurrent in many of his darker-themed works.

Smaug Destroys Laketown is Hildebrandt's revisitation of one of the Brothers' most famous paintings, a 1976 image of Smaug created for that year's Tolkien calendar. Created specifically for the 2010 IlluXCon symposium, a significant portion of the piece was painted live during the event.

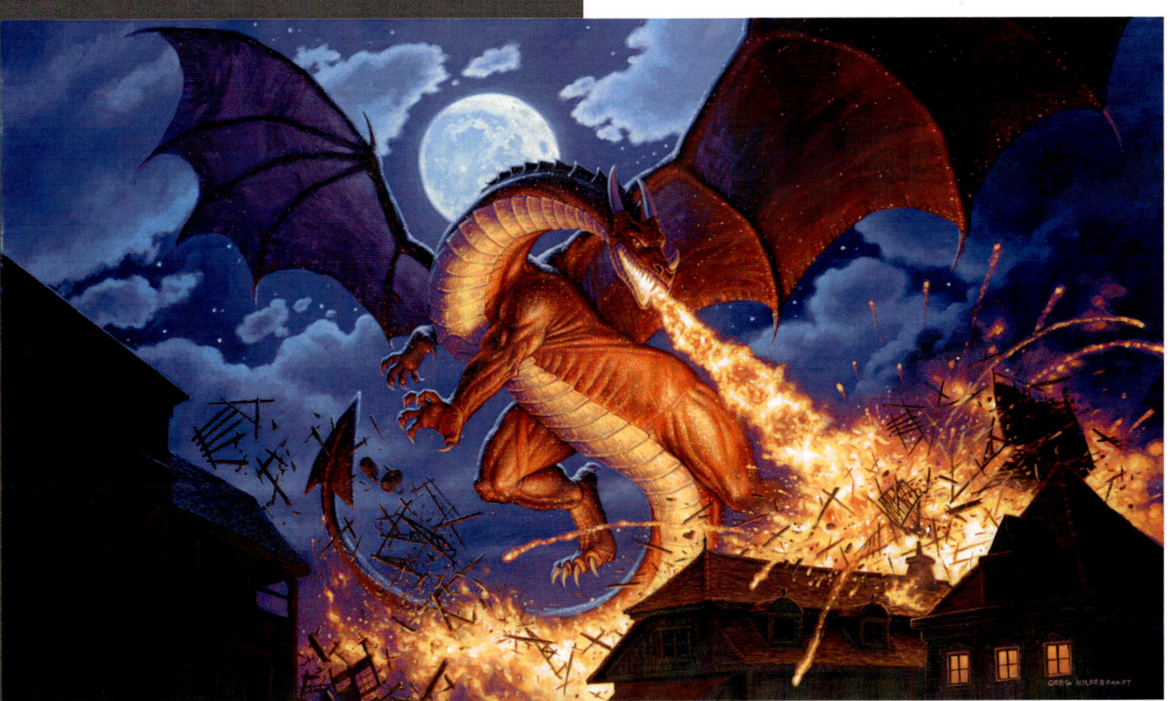

Smaug Destroys Laketown, 2010
Acrylic on canvas. Collection of the artist.

Jason HITE

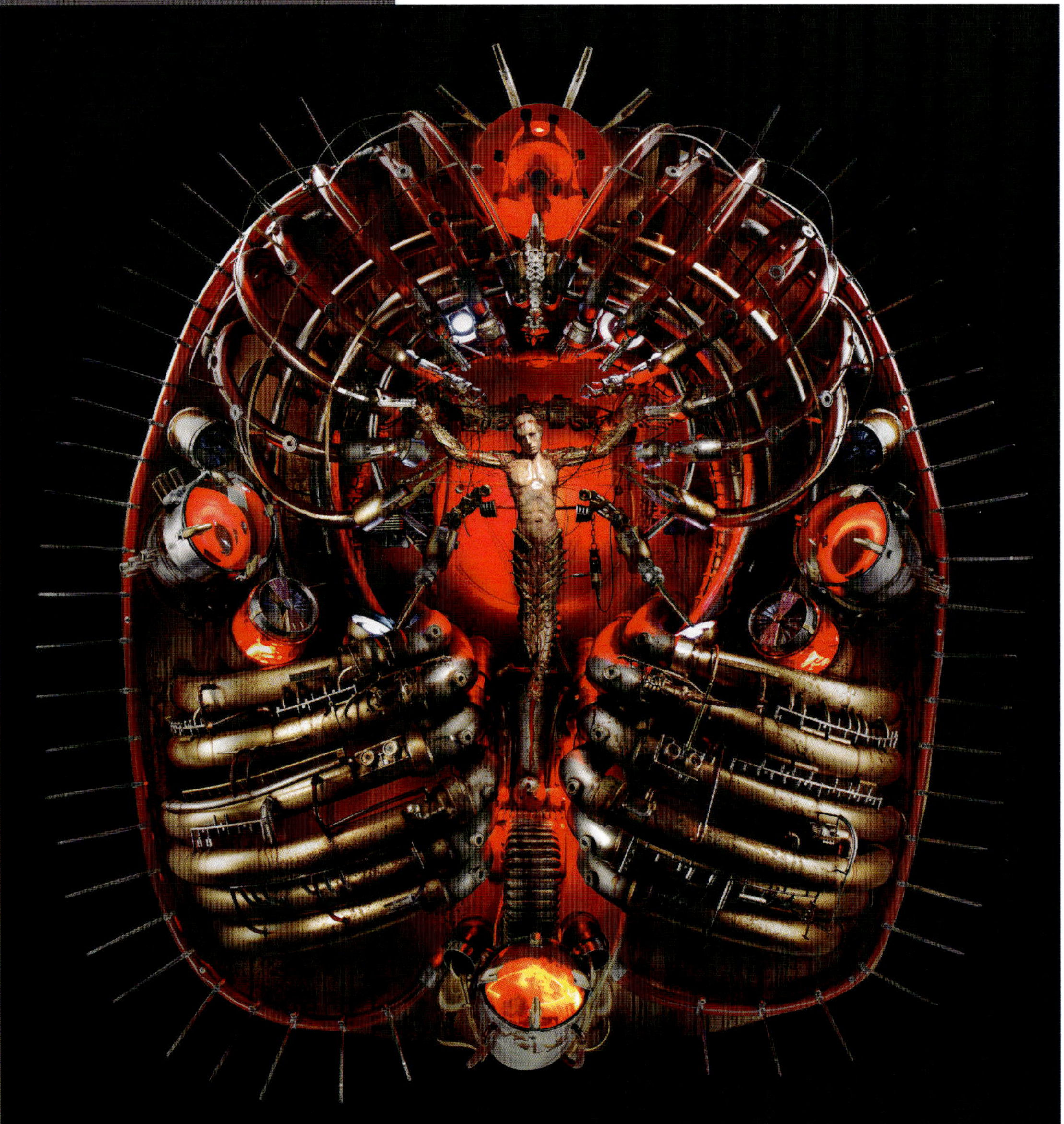

Technological Crucifixion, 2010
Mixed. Collection of the artist.

American, born 1976

Hite has created sculptural works for a diverse range of companies, from Hasbro to Disney. His own personal visions frequently explore our delicate and sometimes hazardous modern relationship with machines and technology.

Technological Crucifixion examines the question of our reliance on modern media. If we could subsist solely by this mechanism, how many machines would it take to sustain a human being, and what might that look like?

John HOWE

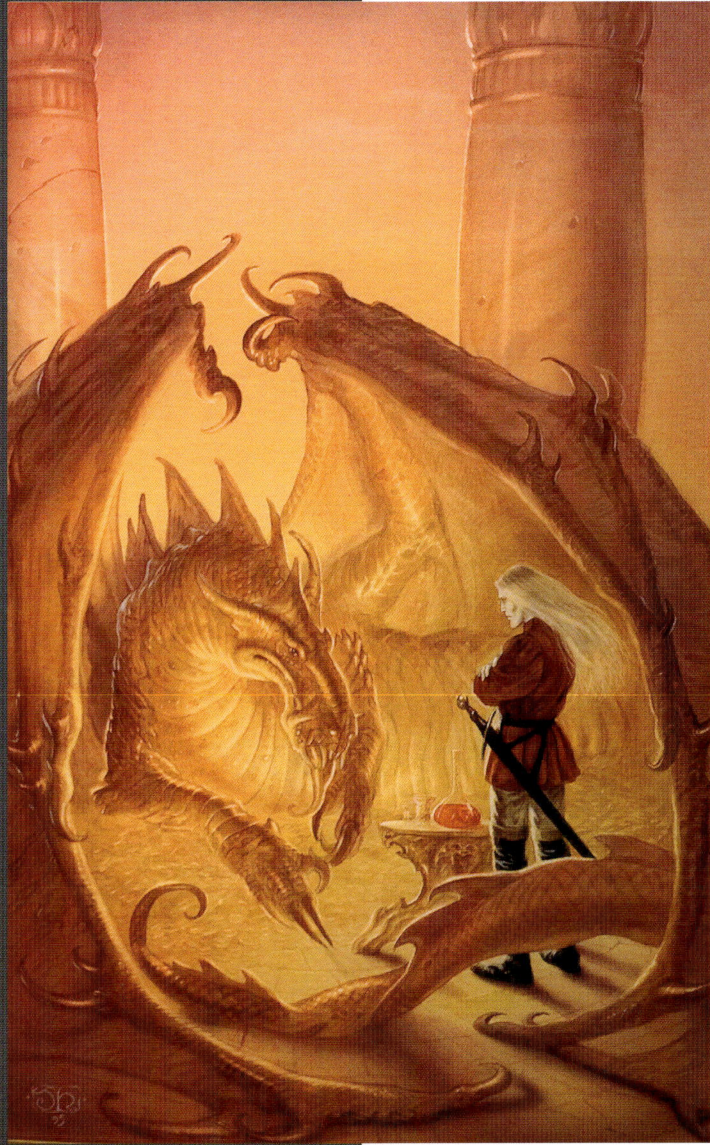

Cup of Morning Shadows, 1995
Watercolor on paper. Private collection, New York.

Canadian, born 1957

Howe is best known for his work with Tolkien's *Lord of the Rings* series, having served as one of the two principal concept designers (along with Alan Lee) for Peter Jackson's film trilogy, as well as one of the most significant illustrators of Tolkien's work in recent years. Howe demonstrates a unique style, handling watercolors like acrylics, working more in opaques than is typical for contemporary watercolorists.

Cup of Morning Shadows demonstrates Howe's deft handling of a monochromatic palette as well as his flair for painting dragons, something for which he is justly renowned.

Bruce JENSEN

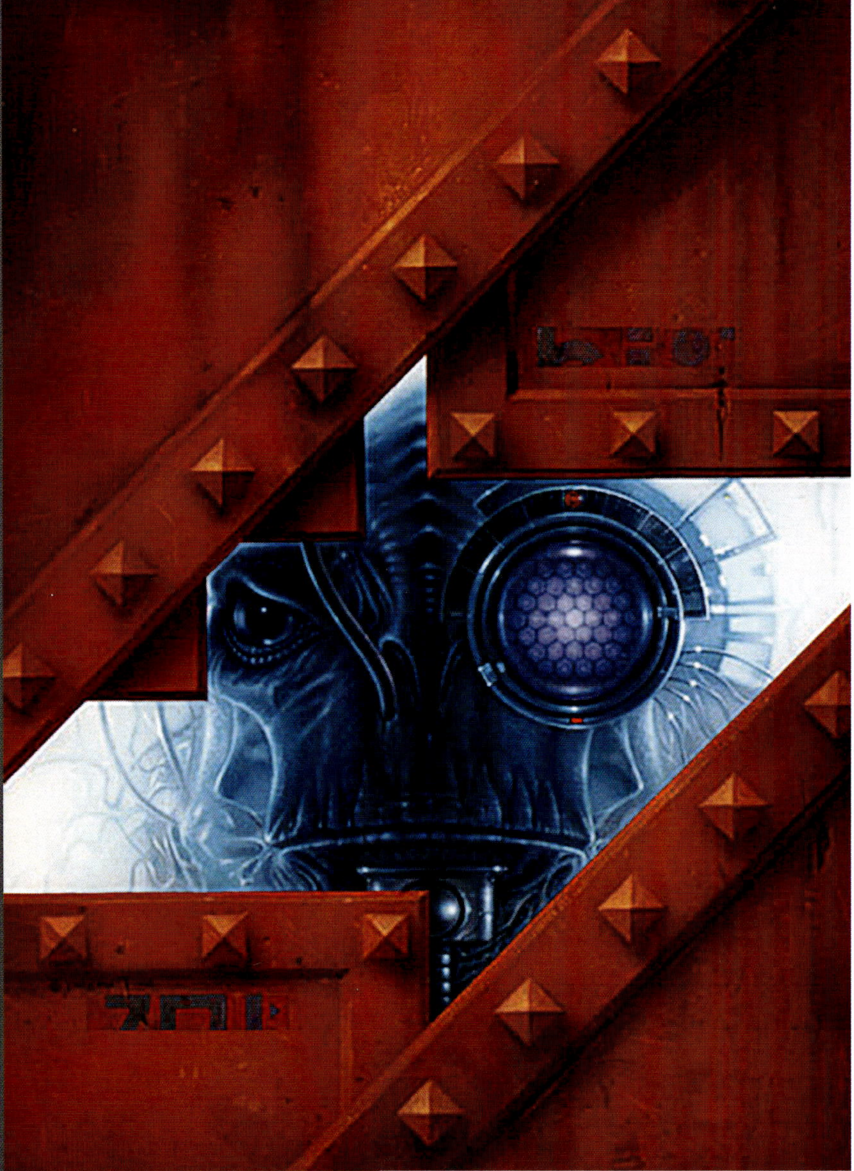

Final Battle, 1994
Acrylic on board. Collection of the artist.

American, born 1962

Jensen's work is characterized by a more modernist approach to imaginative realism, making extensive use of collage and trompe l'oeil realism to create strikingly composed images combined with vibrant color. His work was extremely popular in the late 1980s and 1990s. He has since moved predominantly to computer-generated graphics, working as an animator and designer for CBS News since 1999, the sole exception being his *Alien Menagerie* series of personal works.

Final Battle is an excellent exemplar of what Jensen's imaginative painting is all about: a striking composition, eye-fooling texture and form, and a brilliant use of color to create an image that demands the viewer's attention.

Jeffrey JONES
Catherine

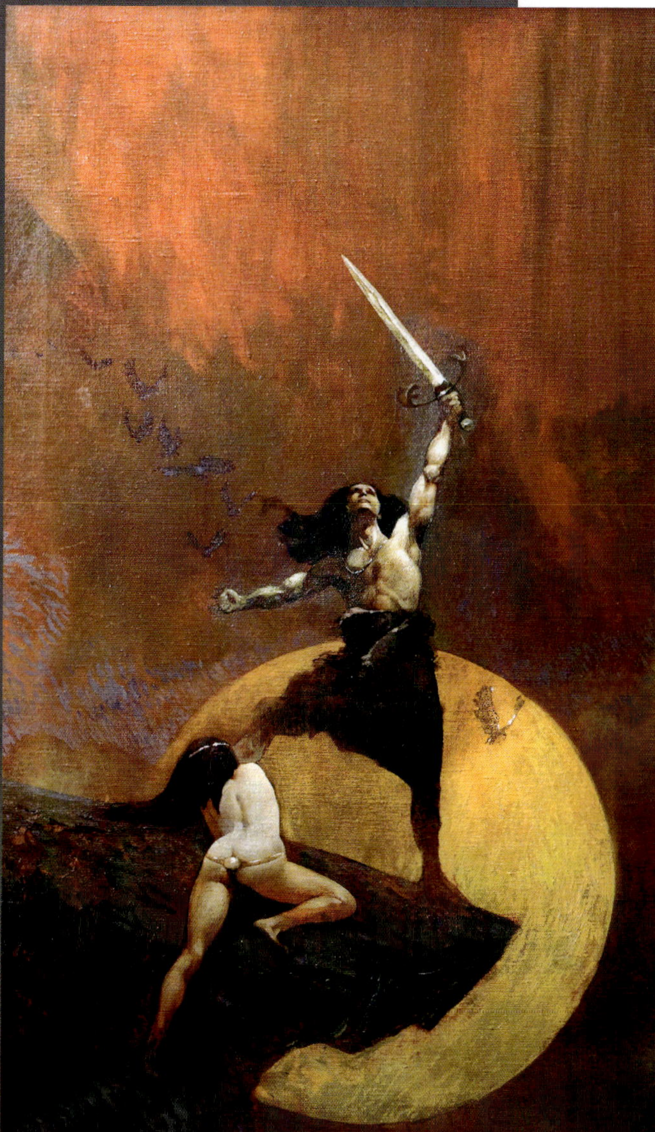

Messenger of Zhouvastou, 1973
Oil on linen. Private collection.

American, 1944–2011

Jones may have been the best pure painter of the 1970s. Although he lacked Frazetta's raw power, Jones was a more thoughtful artist and demonstrated a much wider range, from his classic heroic covers of the early decade through his time in the Studio—an artistic collective with Michael William Kaluta, Barry Windsor-Smith, and Bernie Wrightson—in the mid-1970s where his work took a sharp turn toward romanticism and the Pre-Raphaelites. Later in his career his work became increasingly loose and impressionistic, utilizing rich color and shadow more than rendered forms.

Messenger of Zhouvastou is a classic early work, clearly showing the influence of both the Brandywine artists and Frazetta on the young Jones, and yet it is distinctive in both its composition and its paint quality, mixing the suggested and the delineated in a way that typified Jones' finest work during this period.

Patrick JONES

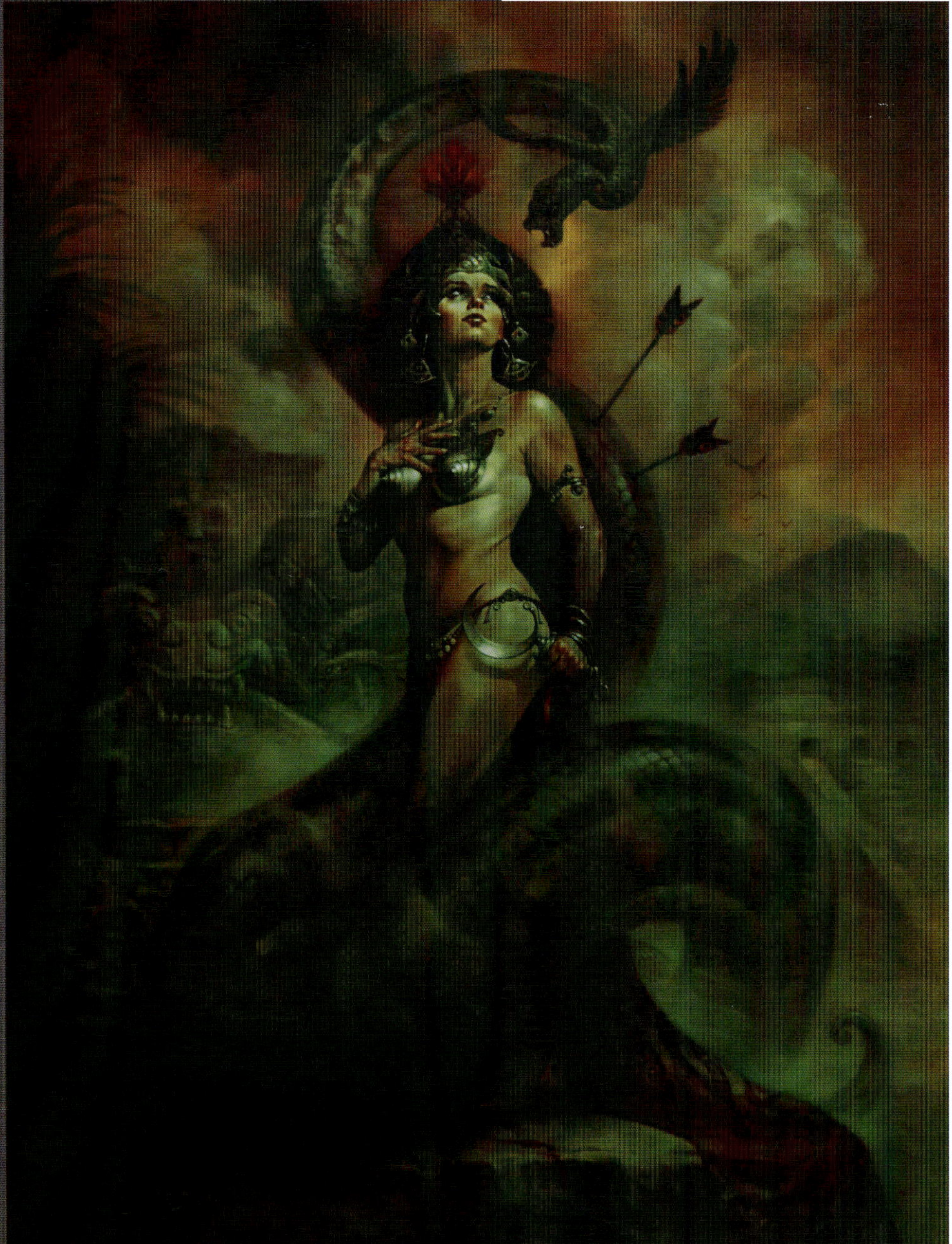

The Sacrifice, 2012
Oil on canvas. Collection of Gareth Knowles.

Irish, born 1970

Patrick Jones is one of the rare artists in the field equally at home in either traditional or digital media. Heavily influenced by both the nineteenth century academic painters as well as contemporary artists like Vallejo and Frazetta, Jones tends to create near-classical compositions with a highly distinctive limited palette, giving his works a feeling of mood and, in many cases, darkness that would be missing in a more traditional color scheme.

The Sacrifice clearly demonstrates Jones' classical figure-painting skills as well as his ability to create mood and atmosphere from color and light.

Michael William KALUTA

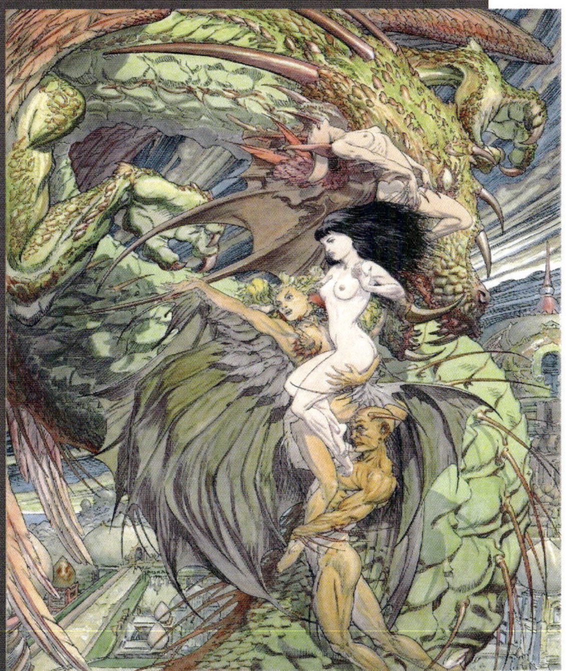

Vampirella #4, 1991
Watercolor and ink on paper.
Collection of Jim Reid.

American, born 1947

Kaluta was one of the founders of the Studio artist collective (with Barry Windsor-Smith, Jeffrey Catherine Jones, and Bernie Wrightson) in the mid-1970s, an endeavor that saw all four artists turn sharply toward earlier artistic influences. In Kaluta's case his strongest influences came from art nouveau and the golden age ink and watercolor artists, an association that can clearly be seen in his work. Kaluta works in ink and watercolor, only very rarely turning his hand to other mediums, and has achieved great success and recognition in both comic and illustrative mediums.

Vampirella #4 is a typical Kaluta image, mixing swirling, stylized shapes with sharply defined, often elongated figures. While his Studio work tended toward darker, more opaque colors, his later work tends to be lighter and more transparent, more colored line than painted forms.

Ken KELLY

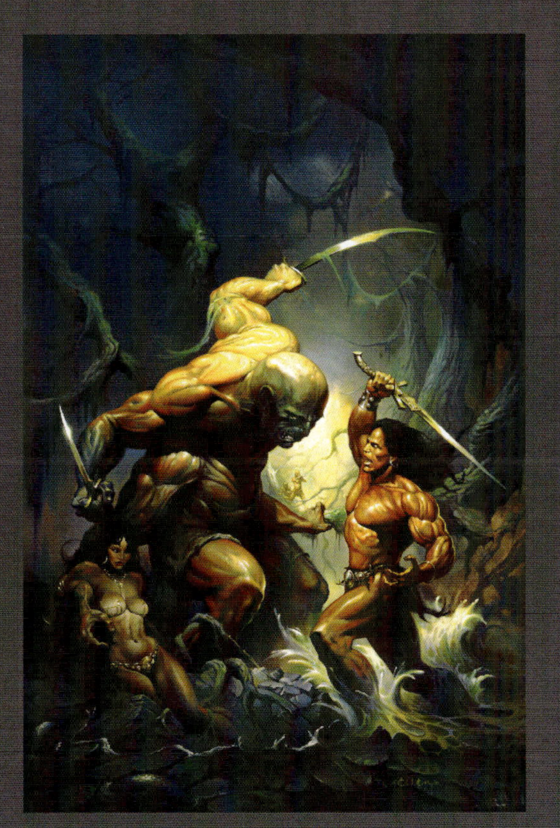

American, born 1946

Kelly rose to prominence in the early 1970s, following in Frazetta's footsteps to create powerful, dynamic compositions with blazing color and high action. As his career progressed, Kelly's figural style became more rendered, creating even more "pop" in his illustrations. He is best known for his depictions of barbaric warriors, particularly Conan, and for his early work for the various Warren magazines such as *Creepy*, *Eerie*, *Vampirella*, and *Famous Monsters*.

Conan the Formidable is a particularly good example of Kelly's style, with his highly rendered figures standing out from the richly colored and more loosely handled background. Like Frazetta, Kelly paints to the high point of action, his figures usually in dynamic poses at the height of conflict.

Conan the Formidable, 1990
Oil on Masonite. The Frank Collection.

Thomas KUEBLER

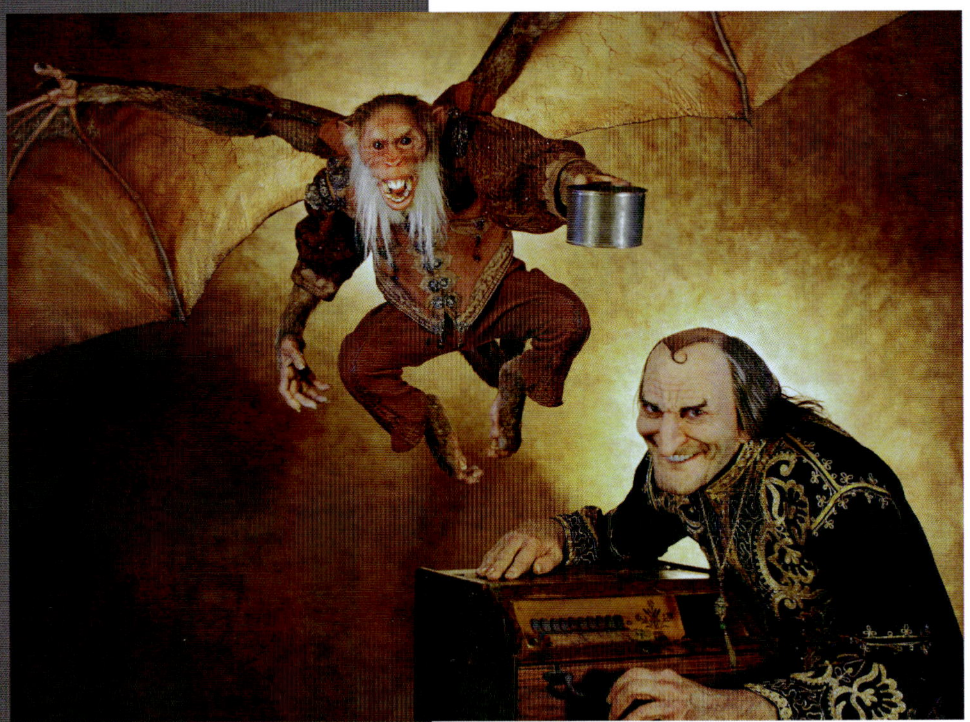

The Mythical Menagerie of Doctor Baltus Bagoon, 2010
Silicone and mixed media.
Collection of the artist.

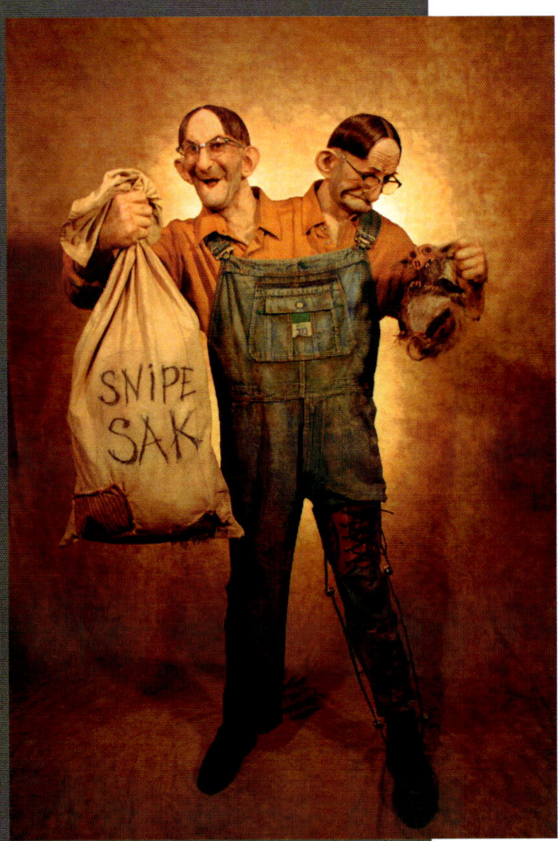

Cletus & Shorty Hunt Snipe, 2011
Silicone and mixed media. Collection of the artist.

American, born 1960

Kuebler is renowned for his large-scale sculptural works, often depicting freakish characters drawn from history, film, or his own imagination. His work is extremely lifelike and is created using a wide array of techniques, many invented by the artist himself. He is easily one of the most recognizable sculptors working in the imaginative realm today, and his work is highly sought by collectors.

The Mythical Menagerie of Doctor Baltus Bagoon is the largest work Kuebler has created to date, developed for display at the 2010 IlluXCon symposium. In typical Kuebler fashion, the organ in the piece is a fully functional, extremely rare antique rescued and restored by the artist as part of the work.

Cletus & Shorty Hunt Snipe is a revisitation of an earlier work featuring Cletus and Shorty, this time adding in the elusive snipe, which was created with a mixture of sculpting, furrier techniques, and taxidermy, as the creature's feet and tail come from an expired opossum that was "collected" by the artist for future use.

Todd LOCKWOOD

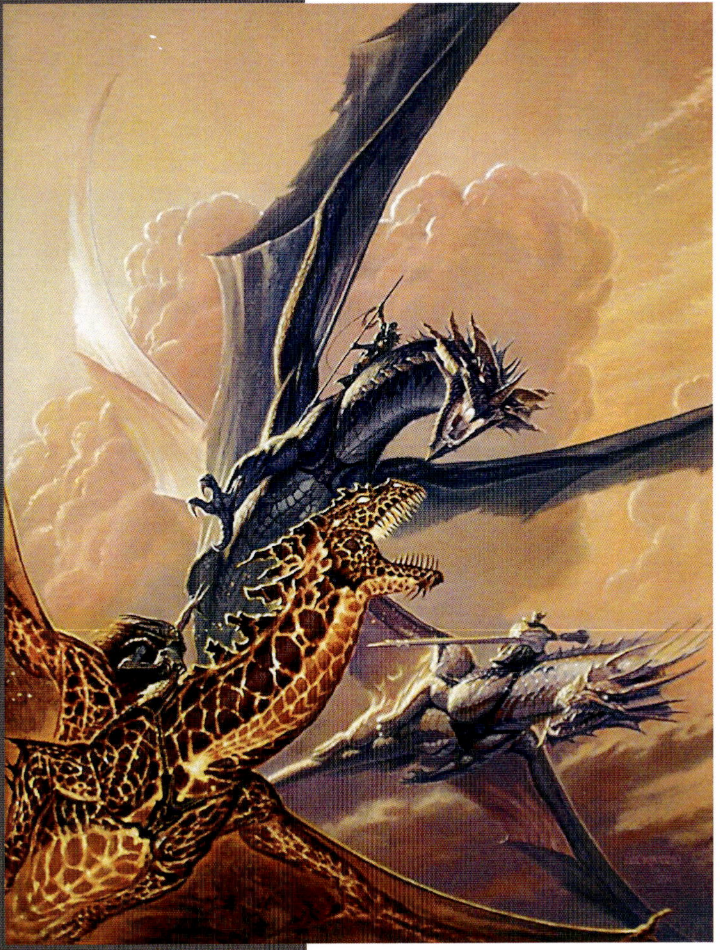

Chaos Spawn, 1999
Oil on Masonite. Collection of Greg Obaugh.

American, born 1957

Lockwood is most recognized for his contributions to the *Dungeons & Dragons* universe, having been responsible for a significant amount of the current artistic direction and visual style in the game. Having worked exclusively digitally since 2000, Lockwood has recently returned to painting in oils, translating the slight shift in style brought about by working digitally smoothly back into traditional media.

Chaos Spawn is an earlier work, dating from before Lockwood's shift to working digitally. However, it is late enough that many of the stylistic hallmarks—such as the edgy, "pointy" designs and pearlescent colors—that would typify his later work are already present.

Don MAITZ

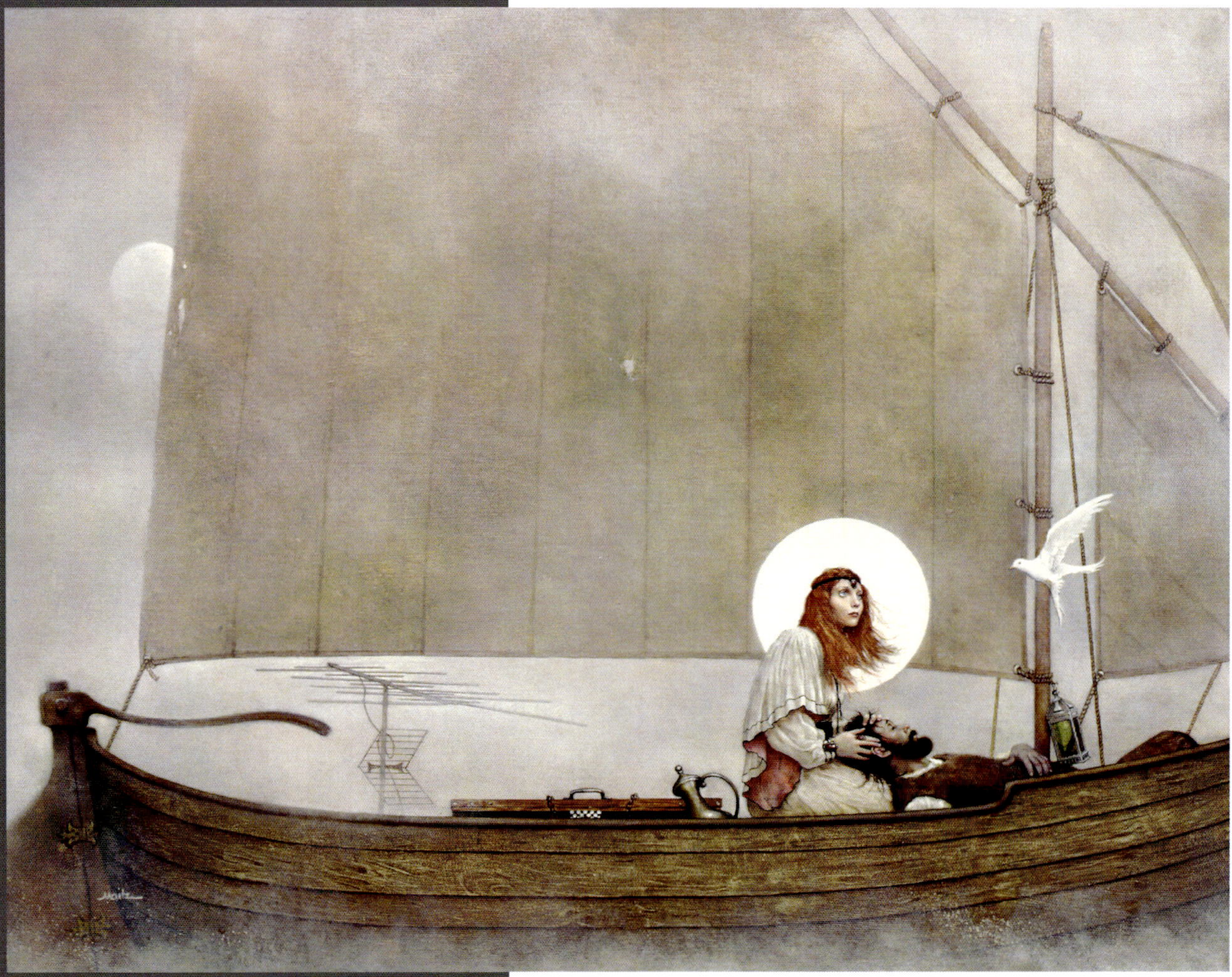

Second Drowning, 1979
Oil on Masonite. Collection of the artist.

American, born 1953

Although Maitz is one of the best-known figures in contemporary imaginative realism, beginning his career in the mid-1970s, his single most famous work demonstrates his second love—pirates—as he is the artist responsible for creating Captain Morgan for the rum of the same name. His work is a delightful blend of classic Brandywine style and a slicker, more highly rendered modern approach.

Second Drowning shows Maitz earlier in his career, working in a slightly looser style more closely related to the nineteenth and early twentieth century artists than the tighter approach he would favor later on. *Second Drowning* portrays the aftermath of a second great flood brought about by the worship of technology, setting the woman adrift both physically and spiritually.

Greg MANCHESS

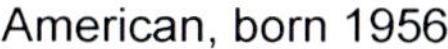

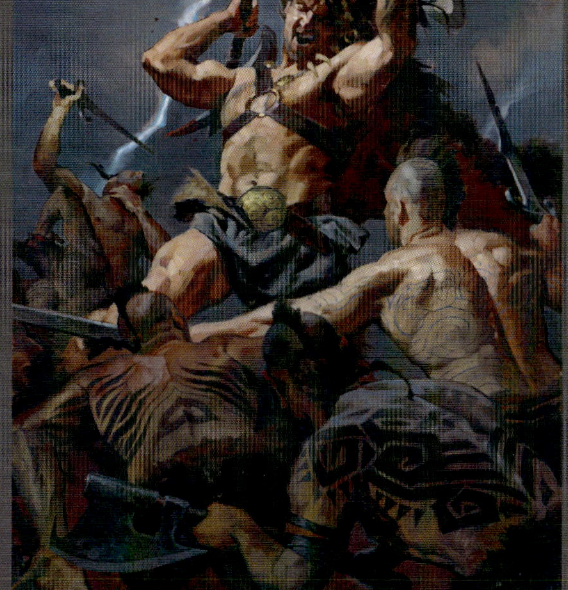

American, born 1956

Manchess is a classical illustrator in the true Brandywine sense, working with a wide range of themes including historical, portraiture, and the fantastic. His work is marked by a brushy, painterly style that frequently suggests as much as renders, and vivid, dramatic colors.

Conan Lightning Battle is Conan not as Frazetta or Beekman would render him, but as he might have been conceived by Schoonover—much more realistic but still in a frenzy of action that demonstrates why Manchess is considered to be one of the finest "painterly" artists working in the field today.

Conan Lighting Battle, 2004
Oil on canvas. Collection of the artist.

Rodney MATTHEWS

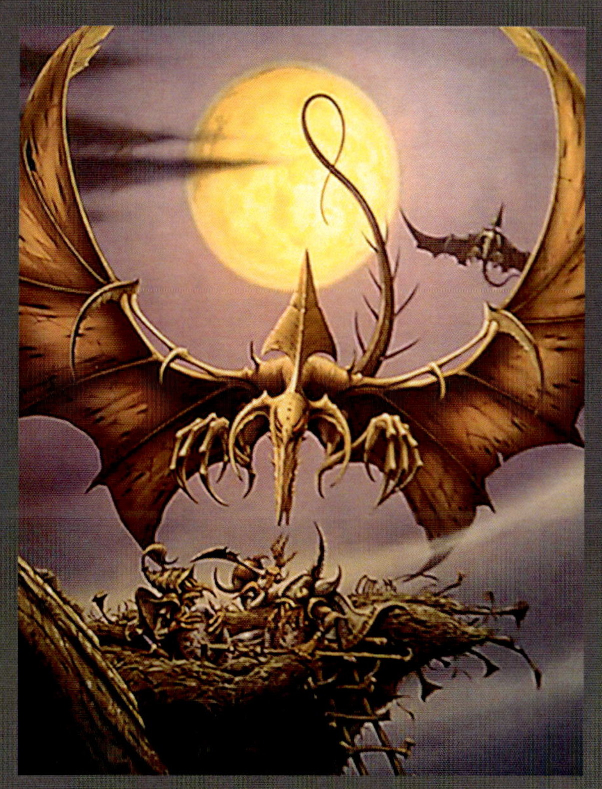

British, born 1945

Matthews, one of the defining voices of the rebirth of British imaginative realism in the 1970s, is best known for his album cover work for Nazareth, Asia, Magnum, The Scorpions, and many others. At the same time he has created a highly influential career as a freelance illustrator, utilizing a dreamlike approach that runs as a common thread through many of his British contemporaries and is clearly distinct from American fantastic art.

Caught in the Act is a private commission created by Matthews. It is somewhat more highly rendered than some of his earliest paintings but still maintains the same use of gouache, inks, and airbrush and the highly distinctive characters that have marked his work throughout his career.

Caught in the Act, 2006
Gouache and ink on paper. Collection of Greg Obaugh.

Iain McCAIG

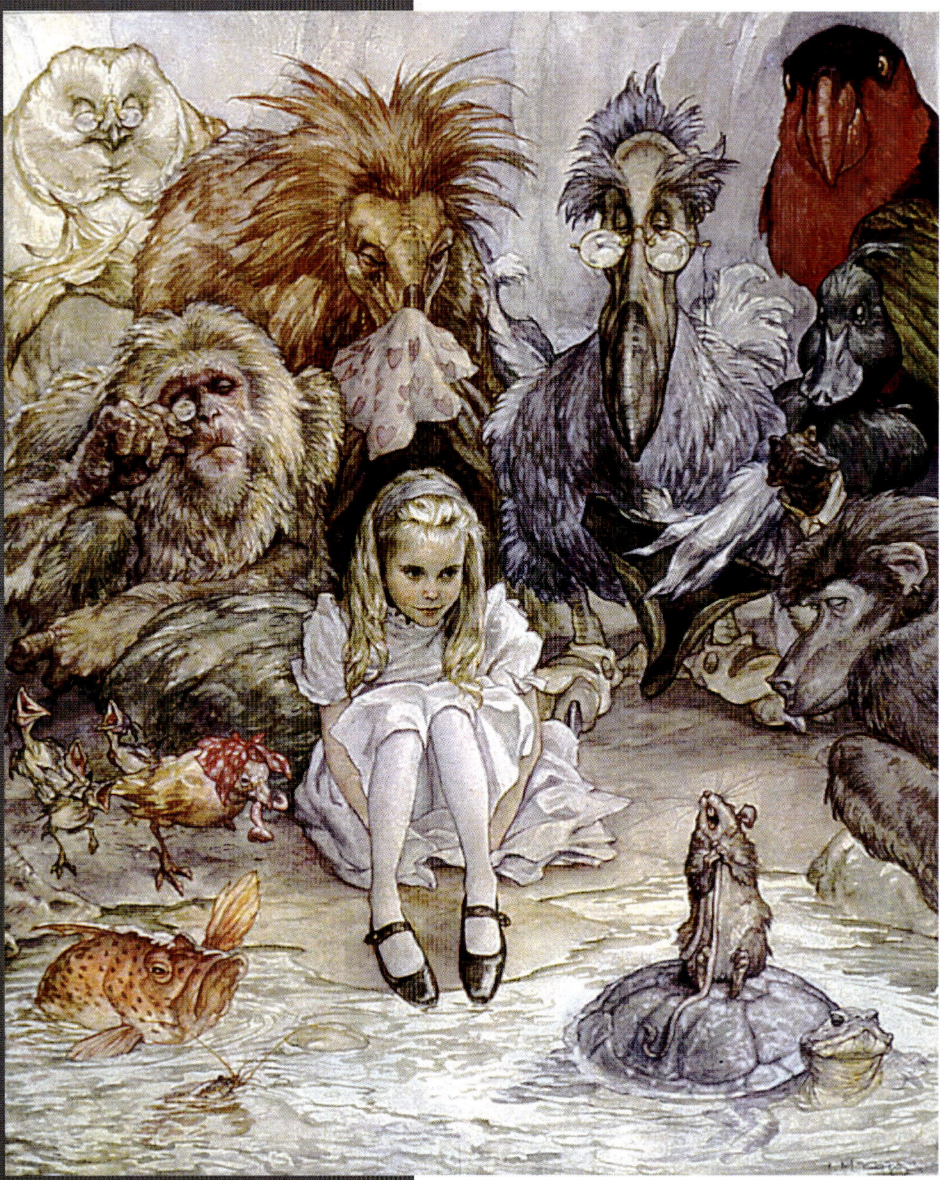

Alice, 2001
Watercolor on paper. Private collection.

Canadian, born 1957

McCaig, one of the finest contemporary imaginative watercolorists, left the field of illustration in the early 1990s to pursue concept work in Hollywood. Since then he has become one of the best known conceptual artists in the film industry, having created iconic characters like Darth Maul and Padmé Amidala for the *Star Wars* prequels as well as having worked on *Terminator 2*, the *Spiderwick Chronicles*, and numerous other films.

Alice represents one of very few traditional media works McCaig has created since transitioning to digital concept work. The delicacy of his watercolor painting is unparalleled, as is his ability to create characters—which has stood him in good stead as a concept artist.

Daniel MERRIAM

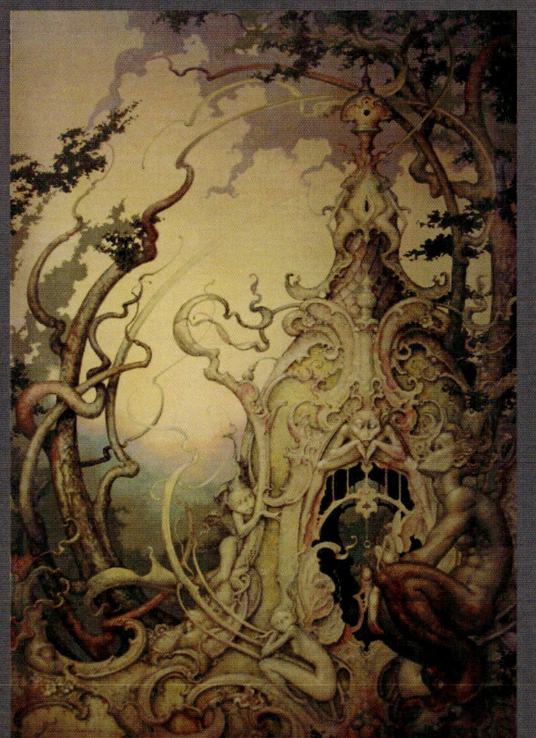

Hideaway, 2008
Oil on canvas. Collection of the artist.

American, born 1963

Merriam is a highly regarded contemporary artist who straddles the line between surrealism, magic realism, and narrative imaginative painting. His elaborate, organic forms and figures give Merriam a unique artistic voice and make his work readily identifiable, even as compared to his closest peers like Gil Bruvel or Michael Parkes.

Hideaway provides a perfect example of perhaps Merriam's most distinctive stylistic feature, his use of elaborate, dreamlike architectures that bring to mind an organic version of art nouveau, with the beautiful form and slight untidiness that comes with biological shapes.

Petar MESELDZIJA

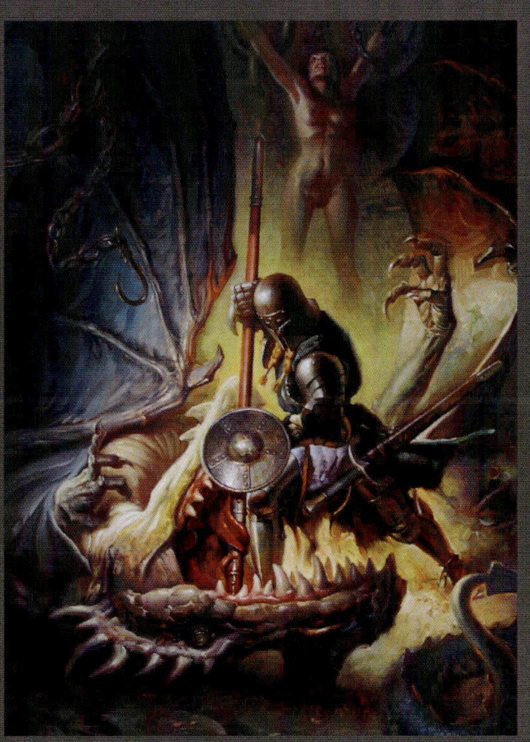

Serbian, born 1965

Meseldzija's painting style is highly classical, drawn from centuries of European painting, and his work is often informed by classical Serbian myth and legend. His powerful brushwork and palette are reminiscent of Frazetta, but Meseldzija is also capable of painting with great restraint and subtlety.

The Rescuer may read, at first, as a simple variation on the St. George legend, but Meseldzija is able to utilize this classic narrative structure to create a work that supersedes the narrative, bringing a sense of universal good versus evil to the painting. This work, created in 2011 for the IlluXCon symposium, is impactful in both execution of color and composition.

The Rescuer, 2011
Oil on Masonite. Collection of the Association of Fantastic Art.

Ian MILLER

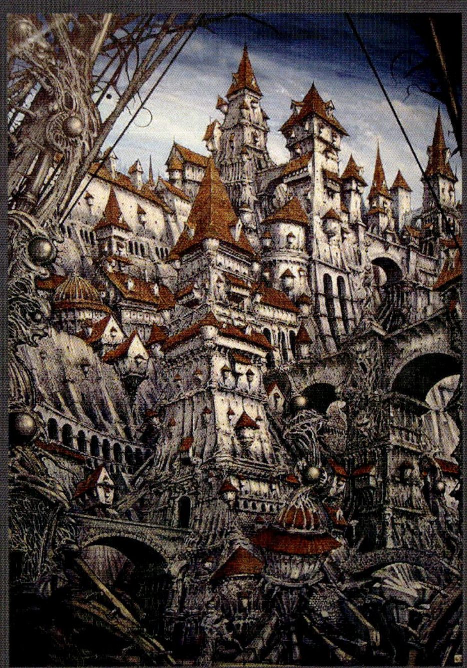

Turris 10:25 a.m., 2007
Watercolor and ink on paper. Collection of Paul and LizAnn Lizotte.

British, born 1946

Miller is inarguably the finest pen-and-ink artist since Virgil Finlay, and arguably the finest technically to ever to work in the imaginative field. His style might be best described as gothic grotesque, incredible detail mixed with a unique sense of design and geometry. Miller is best known for his work for the British company Games Workshop in the 1980s creating artwork for the *Warhammer* and *Warhammer 40k* games.

Turris 10:25 a.m. is a perfect example of Miller's architectural works: impossibly complex, extremely ornate structures towering over the mandatory tiny figure, providing scale.

(Jean Giraud) MOEBIUS

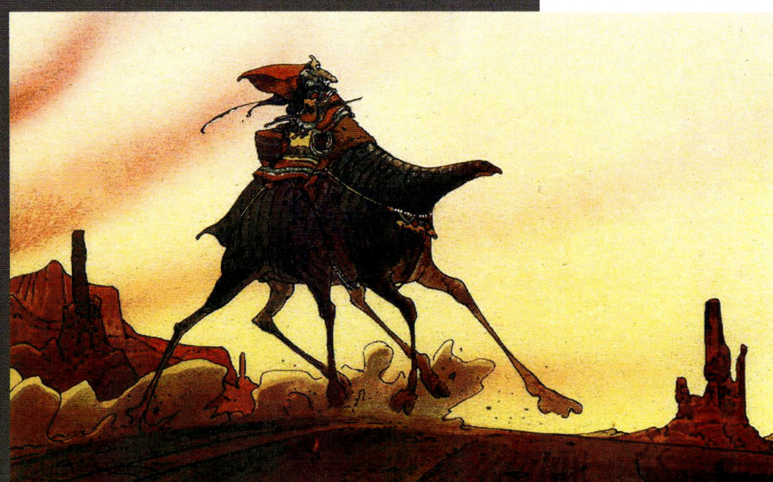

The Desert, 2001
Ink and dye on paper. Collection of Henry Mayo.

French, 1938–2012

Giraud, a French comic artist, did most of his fantastic work under the pseudonym Moebius, producing a body of work that has proven extremely influential. His groundbreaking work in the 1970s French magazine *Metal Hurlant* helped to revitalize sequential fantasy and science-fiction narrative, and his stark, almost surreal style has influenced creators from Hayao Miyazaki to Ridley Scott.

The Desert is a small, personal work created by Giraud as a gift for a friend. Its simple, stark composition and strange creatures are typical of Giraud's work in the imaginative field, demonstrating his uncanny ability to create mood and character from the barest of visual clues.

Clayburn MOORE

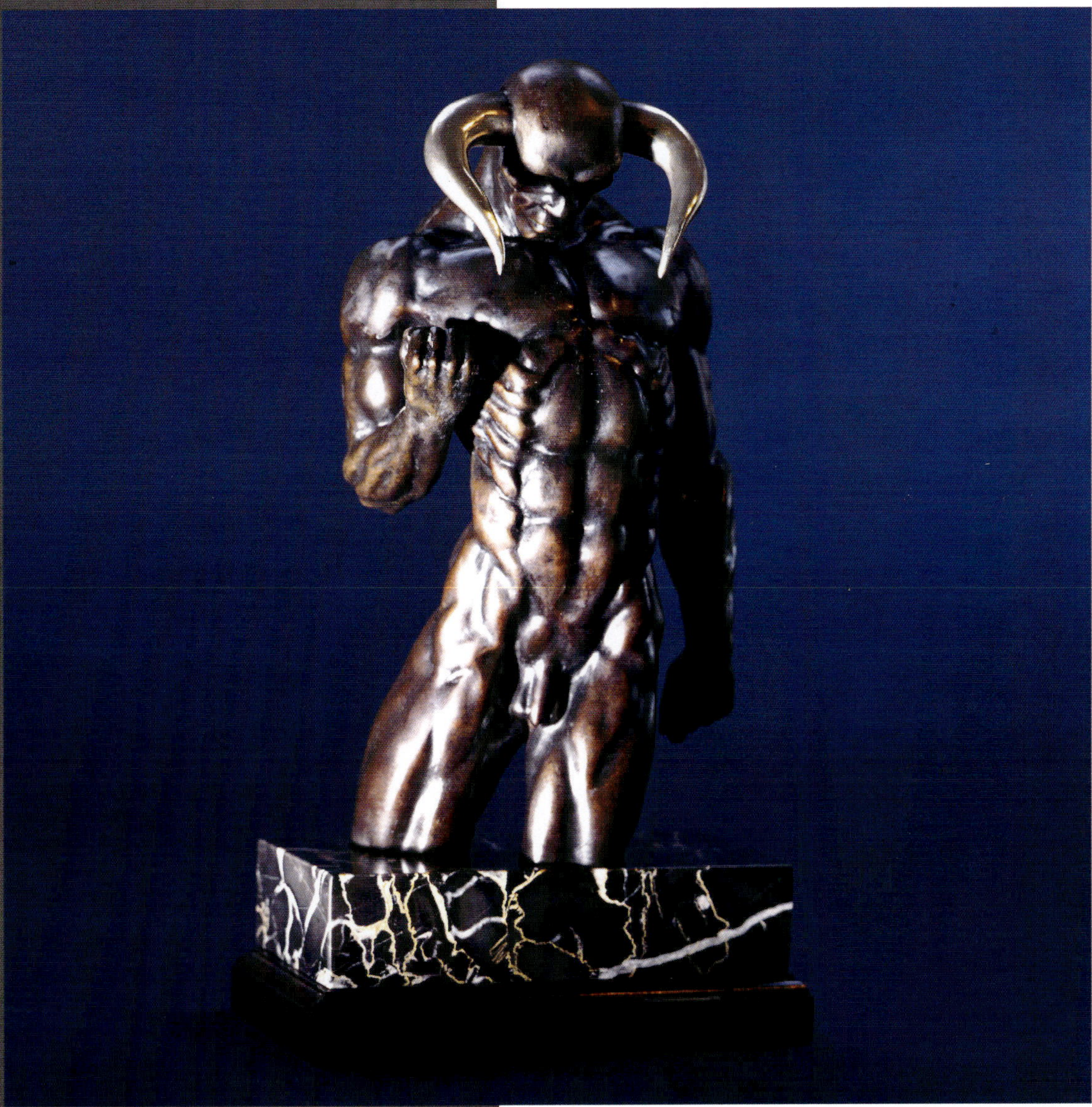

Taurus, 1985
Bronze. The Frank Collection.

American, born 1965

Moore is one of the most recognized sculptors in the field of imaginative realism, specializing in a blend of classically accurate anatomy and fantastic imagery. His bronzes are renowned for their figurative impact and powerful economy of composition.

Taurus clearly demonstrates Moore's facility with classical anatomy, in this case providing a contemporary spin on the mythological minotaur.

Rowena MORRILL

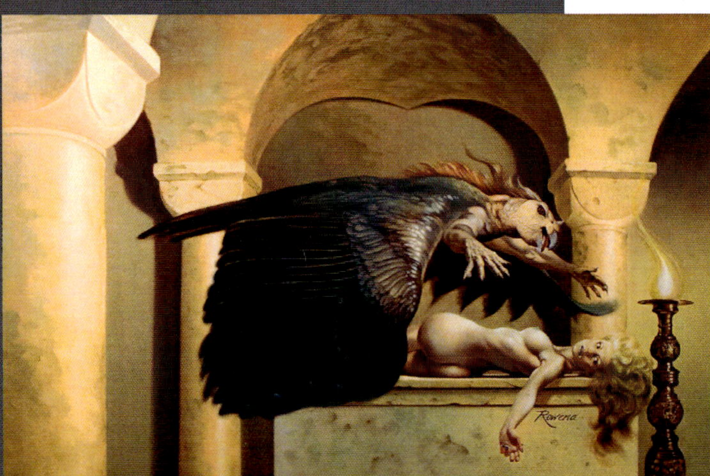

Madwand, 1982
Oil on board. Private collection.

American, born 1944

Morrill (who paints under the name Rowena) is one of the most significant female artists in the field, a key figure of the 1980s and early 1990s and the first major contemporary female imaginative realist. Although there were many female artists working in the field early in the twentieth century, there were none between 1940 and the 1970s, when Rowena's career began. Her painting style is typified by highly rendered, tightly detailed pieces with an almost impossibly smooth surface, produced by working with very few layers of extremely thin oil paints.

Madwand is Rowena's second most famous painting, next to *King Dragon,* which became infamous for turning up in the palace of Sadaam Hussein's son. It showcases the polish and luminosity for which her paintings are famous, as well as her remarkable ability to reproduce human skin tones.

John Jude PALENCAR

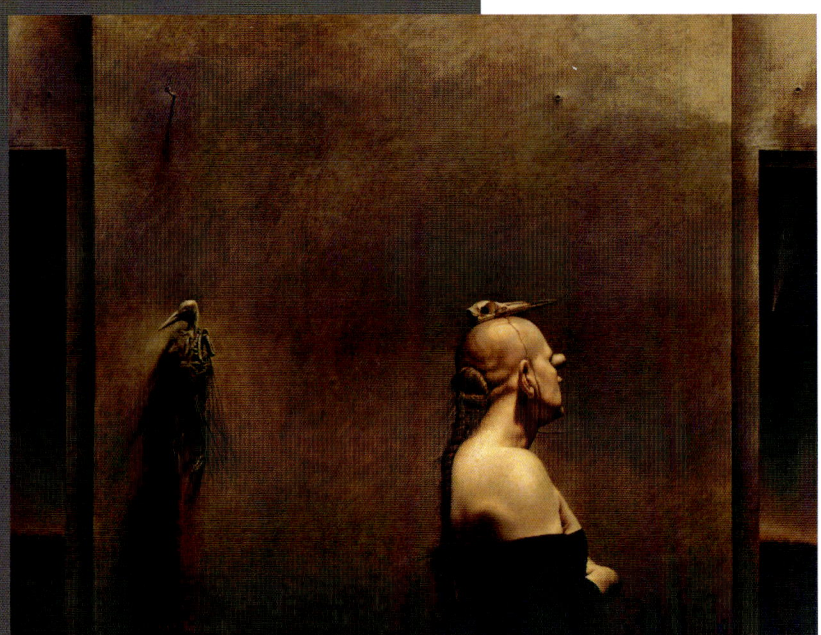

Comet Rider, 2001
Acrylic on paper. Collection of the artist.

American, born 1957

Palencar has one of the most distinctive styles of any contemporary artist in the field, working with acrylics and a very dark-toned palette to produce works that are as much symbolist as realist, showing the influence of Bosch as much as Pyle with a technical approach that owes little to either.

Comet Rider is an example of one of Palencar's personal works, exploring the themes of death and transmigration with a disturbing twist.

David PALUMBO

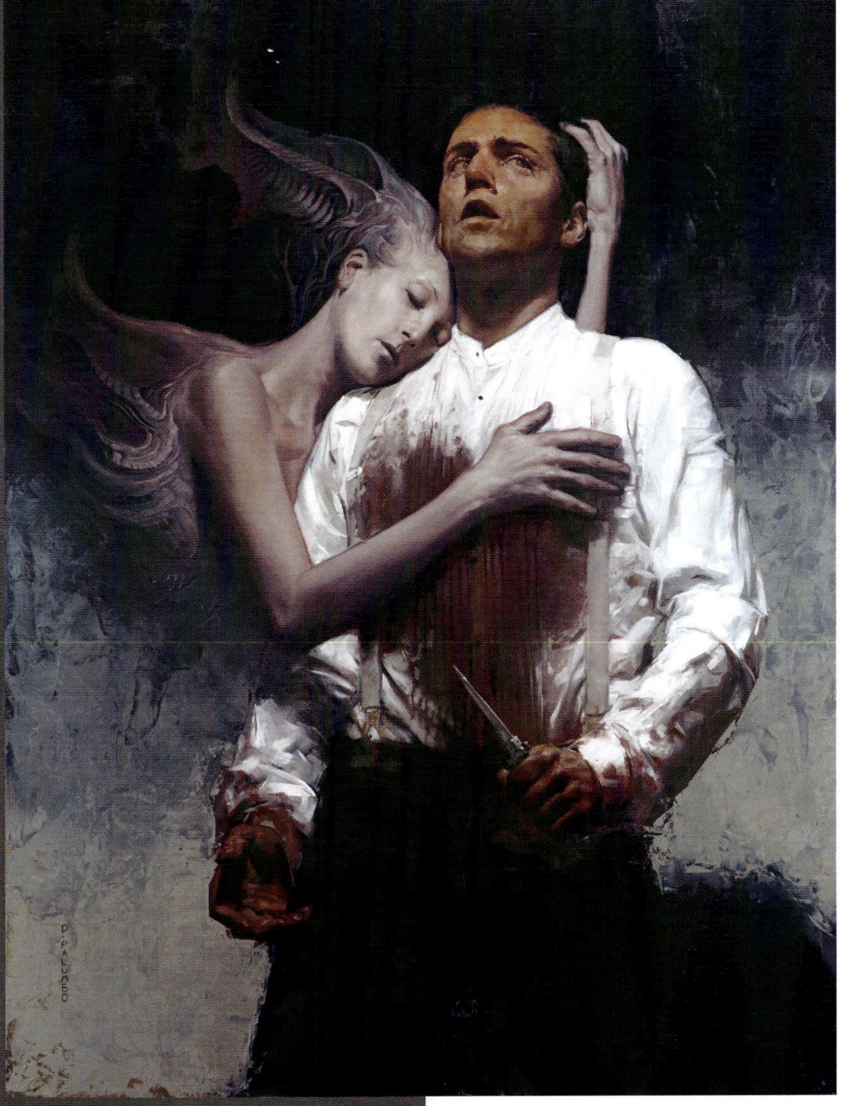

Terrible Weakness, 2012
Oil on wood panel. Collection of the artist.

American, born 1982

Palumbo is one of the brightest young talents in imaginative realism. Although he is the son of artist Julie Bell and stepson of Boris Vallejo, his work references a distinctively different approach than either of them, working in a much more painterly style. He does, however, share their fascination with the female form; Palumbo's oeuvre is a mix of imaginative realism, classical nudes, and uniquely unidealized pin-up.

Terrible Weakness marks a shift in direction for Palumbo, reaching toward works that are less traditional and more studies in mood and emotion, yet still captured in his brushy, highly textural style.

Michael PARKES

Angel of August, 2011
Bronze. Courtesy of Swan King International.

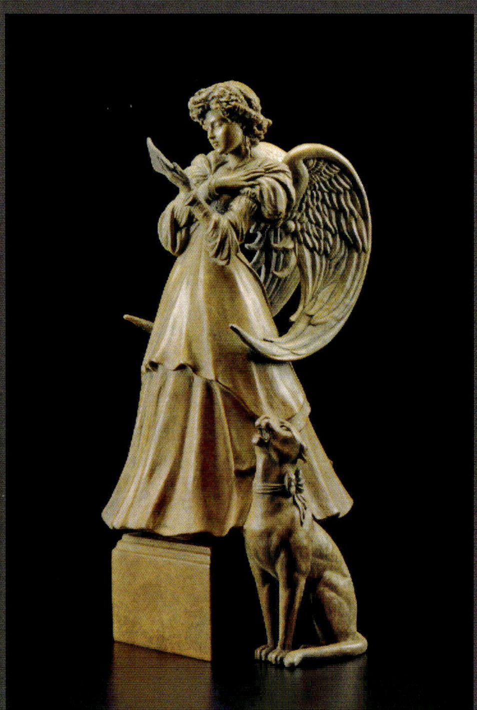

The Letter, 2011
Bronze. Courtesy of Swan King International.

American, born 1944

Parkes is the world's best-known artist working in the magic realist tradition, drawing inspiration from widely ranging mystical sources such as the cabalistic and the tantric. His work is highly realist in its figural depictions but more surrealistic in structure, presenting dreamlike imagery rather than logical narrative.

Angel of August and *The Letter* represent the newest direction in the artist's work, sculpture in bronze. Featuring the same iconography as his two-dimensional work, his sculptures have quickly attracted a worldwide following, allowing the artist to concentrate almost exclusively in this medium at the present time.

Quetzal is typical of more recent works by the artist, showcasing his delicate drawing and color skills rather than oil painting, which he does fairly rarely.

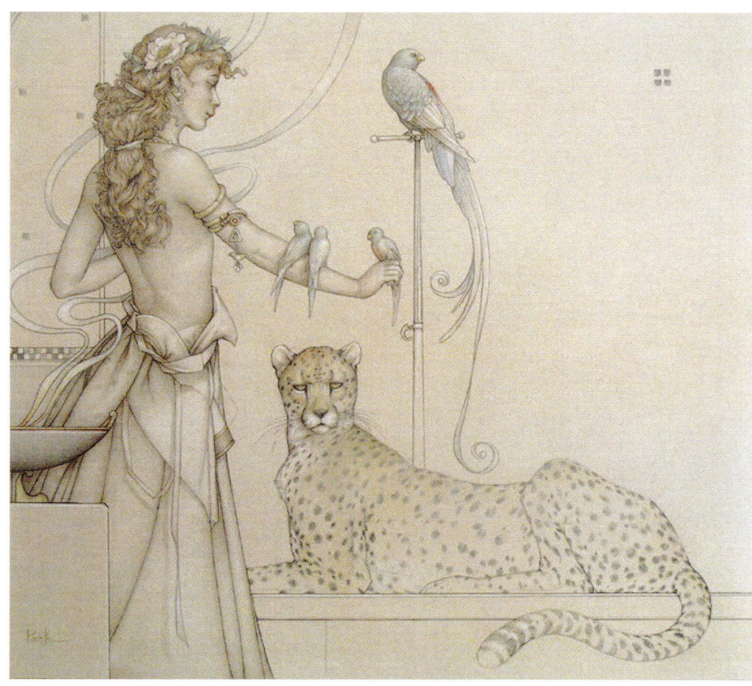

Quetzal, 2008
Mixed media on paper. Private collection, New York.

Keith PARKINSON

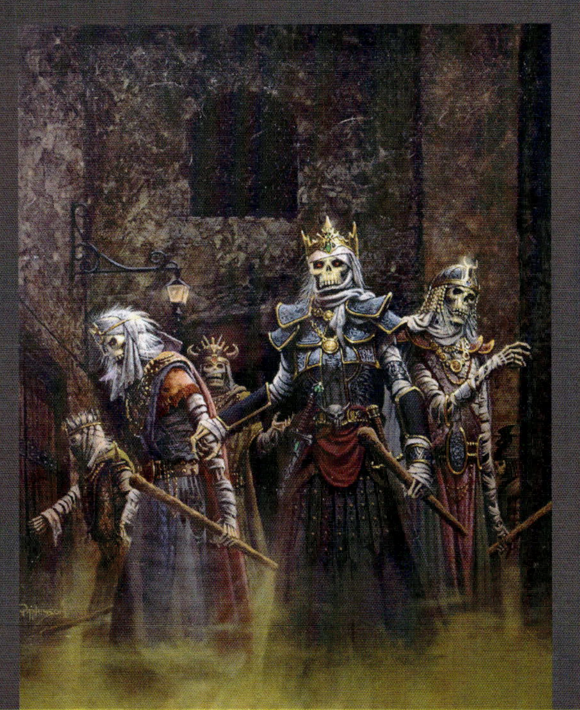

Gods of Lankhmar, 1986
Oil on board. Private collection.

American, 1958–2005

Parkinson rose to prominence in the field as part of the group of staff artists at TSR in the early 1980s (along with Larry Elmore, Clyde Caldwell, and Jeff Easley), although he was the first of the four to leave TSR. Renowned for his instinctual sense for color solutions and lighting as well as his sometimes wry sense of humor, Parkinson's work became even more polished after beginning his freelance career. He was also highly in demand as a concept artist, being one of the formative artistic voices behind the *Everquest* computer role-playing game.

Gods of Lankhmar is an example of Parkinson's earlier work, done for TSR in the mid-1980s. While his command of color and lighting is apparent, the style is slightly rougher than it would appear in his later work.

Omar RAYYAN

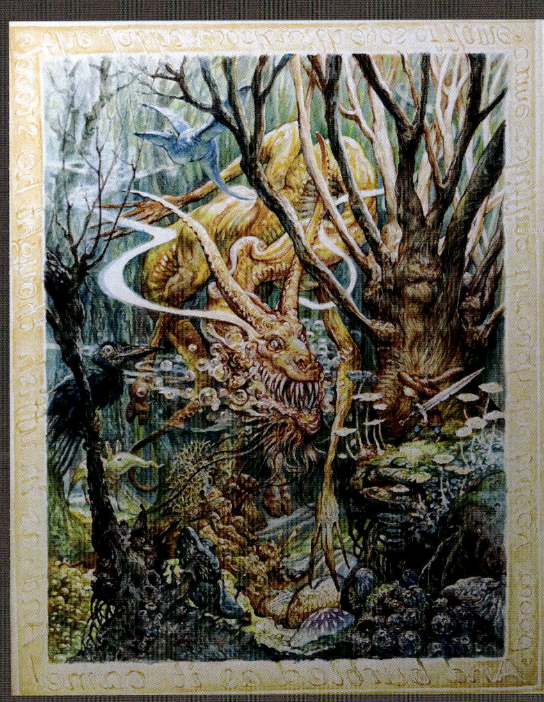

Jabberwocky, 2011
Watercolor on paper. Private collection.

American, born 1968

Rayyan is one of the foremost watercolorists in the field, with work harkening back to the late nineteenth and early twentieth centuries and reintroducing much of the whimsy that rarely appears in contemporary imaginative realism. His paintings are filled with anthropomorphized animals presented in a style that is more detailed than most watercolors, a nod to the fact that Rayyan's main inspirations are nineteenth century oil painters.

Jabberwocky demonstrates Rayyan's approach to both technique and style, presenting a highly detailed image, beautifully painted, that retains a lighthearted approach without being childish.

Kirk REINERT

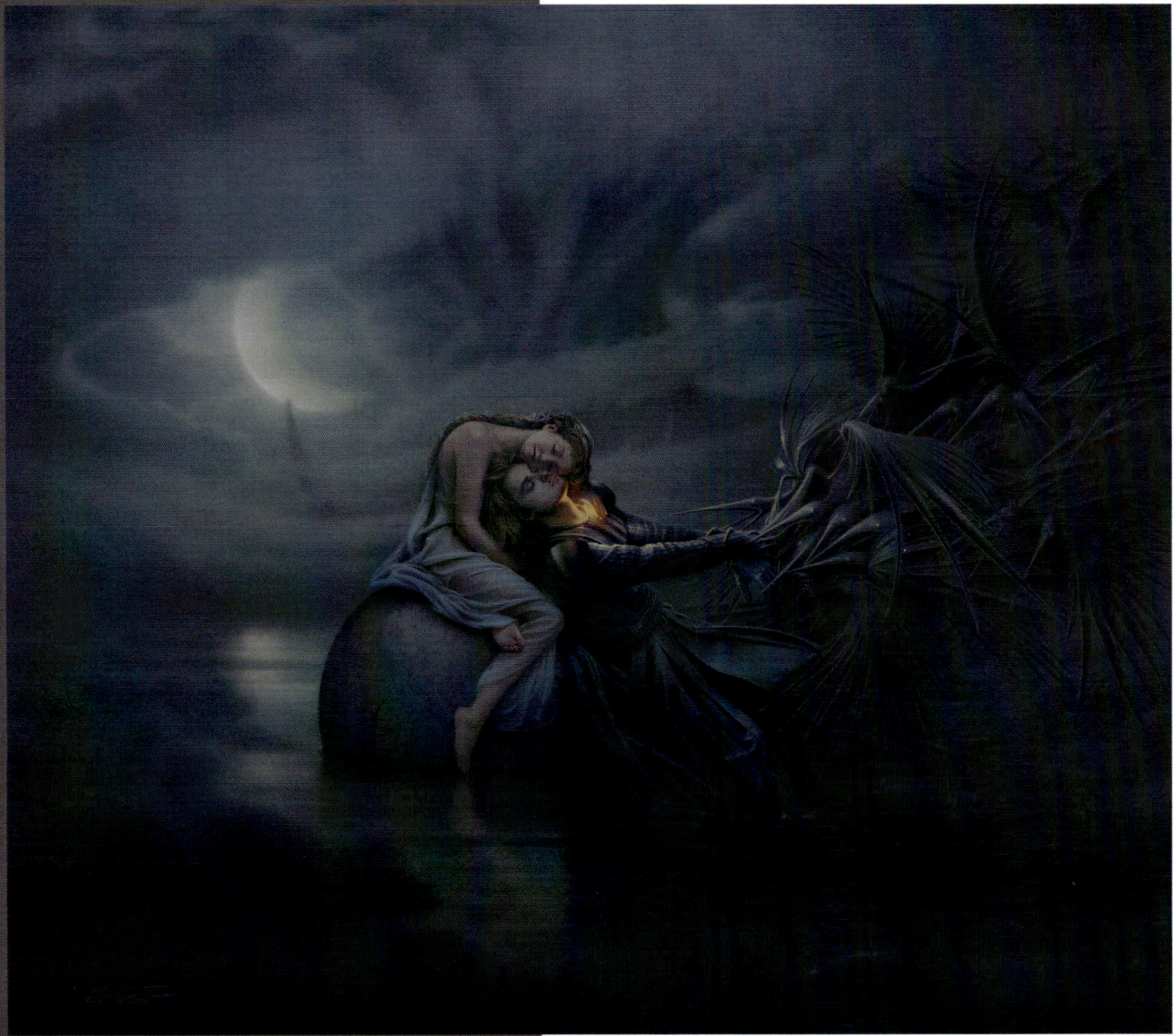

Vader's Dream: A Visitation from Padme, 2010
Acrylic on canvas. Private collection.

American, born 1955

Reinert began his career working for the classic Warren magazines such as *Eerie* and *Creepy*, then moved into working for a wide range of publishing clients. In the early 1990s, Reinert began producing high-end lithographs of personal works, quickly building a large following, particularly in Japan. He works in a highly detailed style, always painting in acrylics, and covering a wide thematic range.

Vader's Dream: A Visitation from Padme is Reinert's contribution to a collection of paintings inspired by *Star Wars*, shows the artist at his most visionary.

Luis ROYO

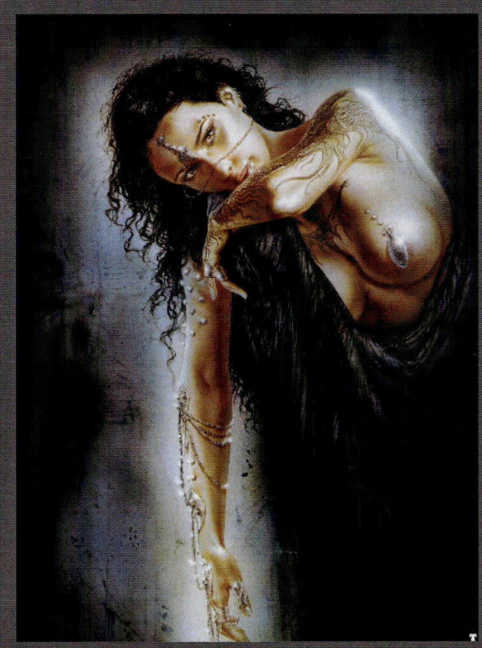

Sodom's Princess, 2000
Acrylic and watercolor on paper. Collection of Jim Reid.

Spanish, born 1954

Royo is world renowned for his blend of sensuality and fantasy, having authored a series of books and portfolios featuring his work. Although he started his career producing book covers, he has worked largely on his personal visions since the early 1990s. Over the years his style and palette have changed significantly, from highly rendered, brightly colored early work to a sketchier style and much darker palette, as his themes have also shifted from the sensual into the outright erotic.

Sodom's Princess shows Royo in mid-transition from his earlier style to his more recent work. It demonstrates the greatly subdued palette of his recent creations and features a highly rendered figural style, but with a looser, less defined background.

Robh RUPPEL

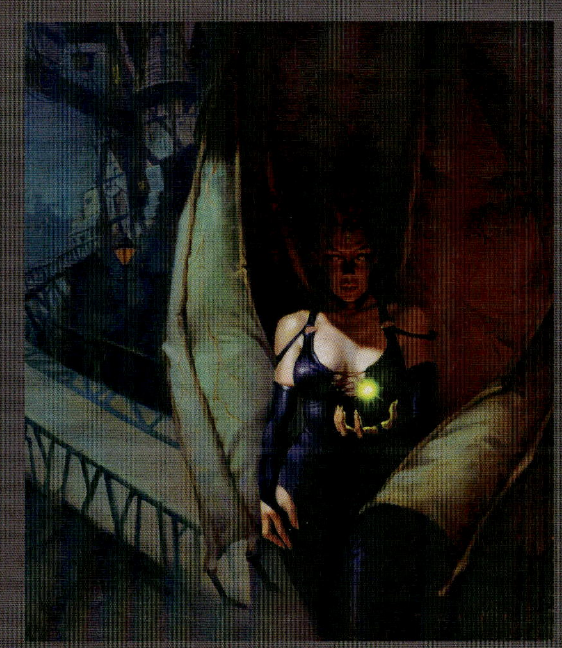

Harbinger House, 1996
Oil on canvas. Private collection.

American, born 1963

Ruppel is something of a modern-day Renaissance man, having made his mark as painter, film concept artist and art director, and, most recently, art director for the award-winning *Uncharted* video-game franchise. After freelancing in a variety of genres, he entered the fantastic art field as an artist for TSR in the mid-1990s, then left TSR—and illustration—after four years to join Disney Studios, first as a concept artist and then as an art director, before moving full-time to gaming in 2007. Since his time at TSR, Ruppel has worked almost exclusively digitally. For someone who has spent relatively little time as a traditional painter, the impact of his work is exceptional.

Harbinger House is one of Ruppel's most famous oil paintings, dating from his time at TSR working on the *Planescape* system.

Ruth SANDERSON

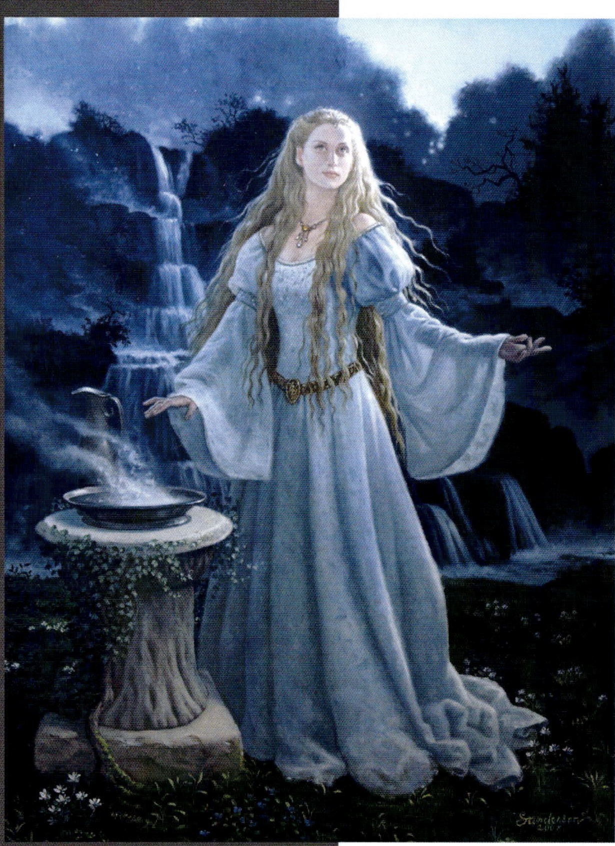

American, born 1951

Sanderson is best known as an award winning children's book illustrator. Although she did many book covers earlier in her career, she specializes in fairy tales, both classic and self-penned. Her work is heavily influenced by both the Victorian romantic painters and the Brandywine artists, as she paints in a classical style while often favoring the somewhat stylized figures of the nineteenth century.

Galadriel is one of Sanderson's rare recent forays into non-fairy-tale imaginative subject matter, featuring Tolkien's iconic elven princess.

Galadriel, 2008
Oil on Masonite. Private collection.

Manuel SANJULIAN

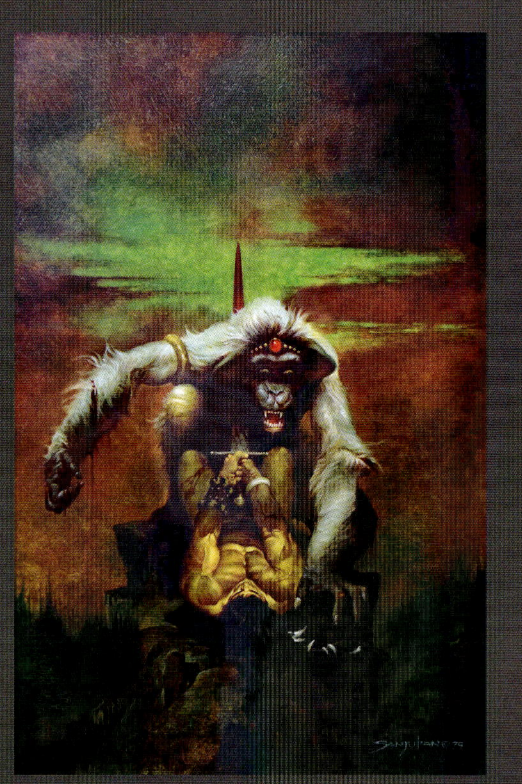

Spanish, born 1941

Sanjulian first achieved prominence in the field in the 1970s working for Warren Publishing's trio of magazines *Eerie*, *Creepy*, and *Vampirella*. Although his early work drew justifiable comparisons to Frazetta, as he matured his work began to show more and more influence from the Spanish old masters. Sanjulian has always worked comfortably in a variety of genres, and much of his current output is classical realist painting targeted at his considerable following among European art collectors.

Conan and the Flame Knife is one of Sanjulian's most famous imaginative works and clearly shows the strong influence of the Spanish old masters as well as his remarkable compositional skills.

Conan and the Flame Knife, 1978
Oil on board. Private collection.

Jordu SCHELL

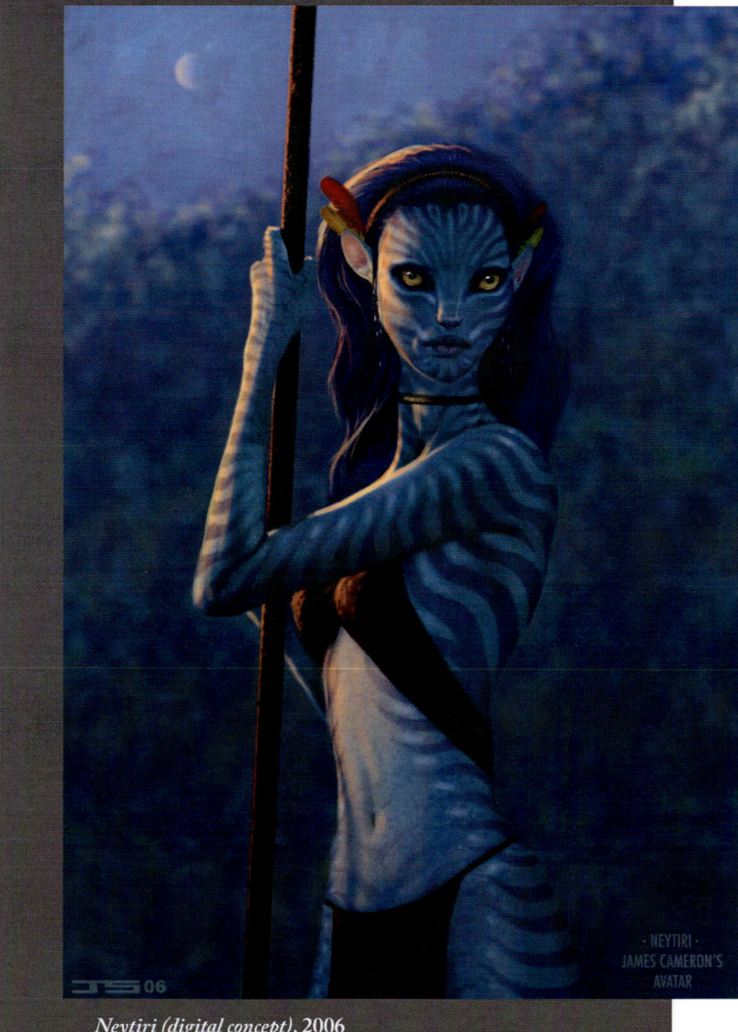

Neytiri (digital concept), 2006
Digital. Image courtesy of the artist.

Neytiri (sculpture), 2006
Mixed media. Collection of the artist.

American, born 1967

Schell is one of the premier creature designers and sculptors in the film industry, having lent his talents to a wide range of major film projects. He is best known for having designed the Na'vi for James Cameron's film *Avatar*. Unlike many creature designers in today's field, Schell sculpts exclusively in traditional media, even turning down major projects that require digital sculpture, although he does do his initial conceptual work digitally.

Neytiri is the original concept design created by Schell to demonstrate to James Cameron how *Avatar*'s alien race would appear. Pictured here is the initial digital painting Schell created. The *At the Edge* exhibition includes the cast and hand-painted half-head sculpture Schell created based on this digital painting, which is not pictured in the catalog. The sculpture is cast in latex from the original molds and hand-painted by the artist.

Hyde is a superb example of Schell's mask designs, completely hand finished by the artist.

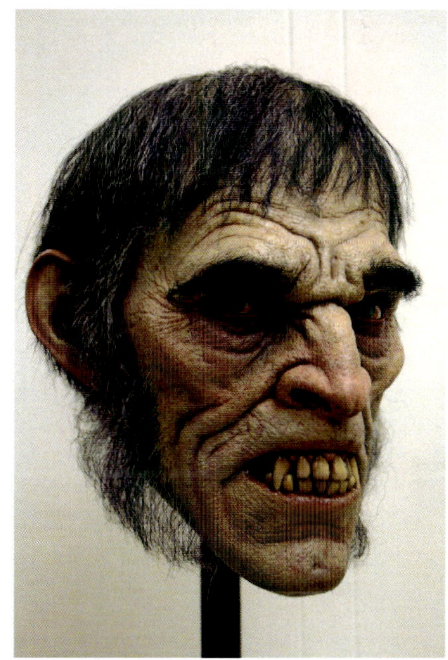

Hyde, 2012
Mixed media. Collection of the artist.

Dave SEELEY

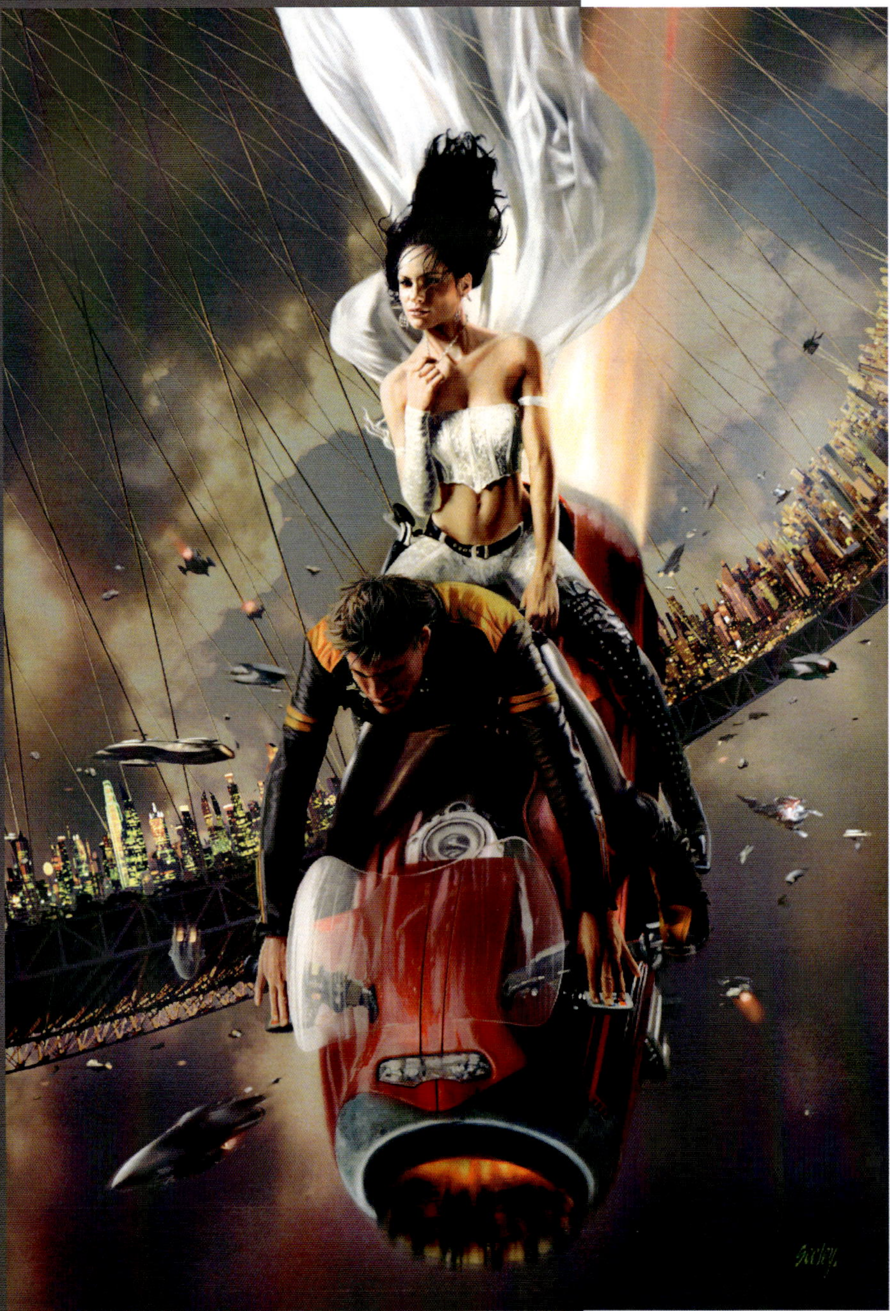

Virga, 2008
Mixed media on paper. Collection of the artist.

American, born 1960

Seeley's work is instantly recognizable for its mix of digital and traditional imagery, vibrant color, and near photorealistic figurative work. A significant percentage of Seeley's work is in the field of advertising, which allows him to create his imaginative work as he sees fit, at large scale and with a high degree of complexity. Most of his paintings consist of digitally created backgrounds with traditionally painted figures, although his painting technique is so refined as to make it difficult to tell where the computer ends and the painter begins.

Virga is typical of Seeley's work: highly energetic, visually complex, and spectacularly rendered to a high degree of realism.

Lisa SNELLINGS

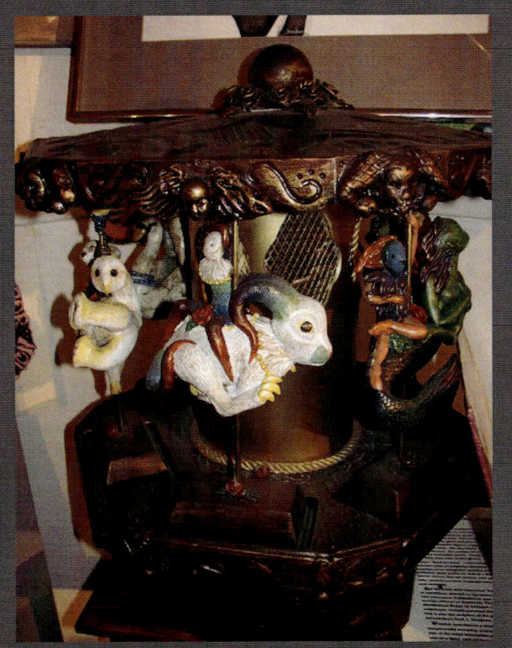

Carousel, 2005
Mixed media. Collection of Stuart Schiff.

American, born 1958

Snellings is best known as a sculptor specializing in dark, edgy characters that are at the same time childish and maturely disturbing. Many of her larger-scale sculptures have kinetic elements, including her most famous series, *Dark Caravan*, which features several large, dark amusement park rides populated by all manner of strange visions. In recent years she has focused on limited-edition pieces featuring strange harlequin like creatures called Poppets.

Carousel is not part of the *Dark Caravan* series but features the same thematic elements as those larger works. The characters are childish and yet quite dark in tone.

James STERANKO

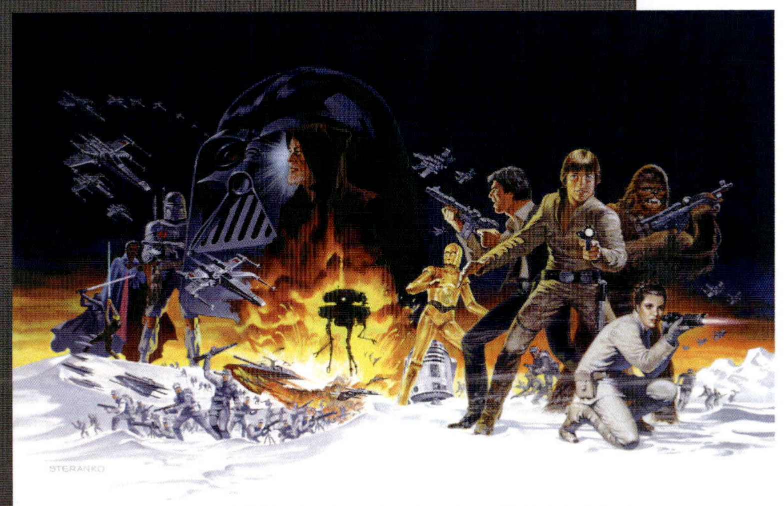

Star Wars: The Empire Strikes Back, 1980
Oil on board. Collection of the artist.

American, born 1938

Steranko, one of the most important comic artists in the history of the field, also spent a considerable amount of time bringing his distinctive style and vision to books, magazines, and films over the course of his career. His film concepting credits include *Raiders of the Lost Ark* and Coppola's *Dracula*. He has also been a remarkable historian of his fields, both writing on comic history and amassing a significant private collection of original pulp illustrations.

Star Wars: The Empire Strikes Back is an iconic image that represents the film, created for Steranko's own *Prevue* magazine's exclusive preview of the film in 1980, shortly before it was released to theaters.

Matthew STEWART

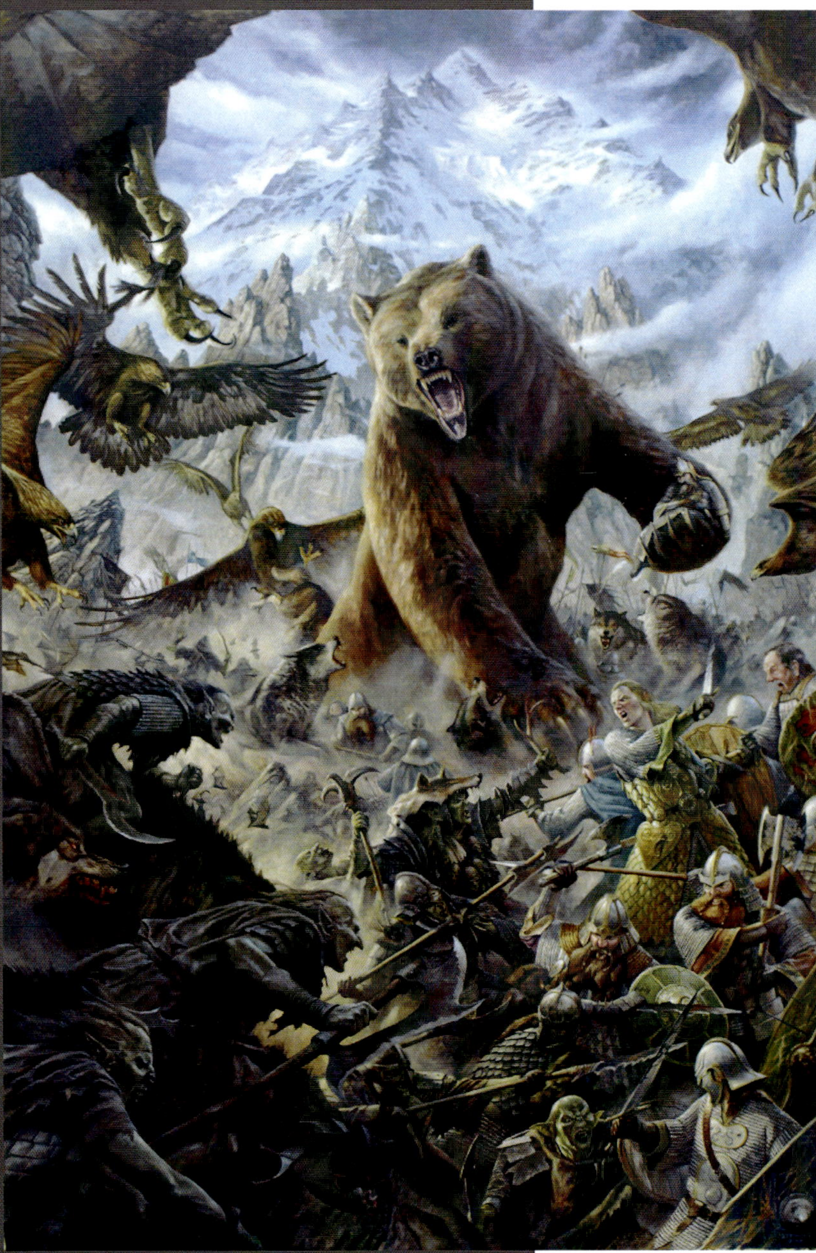

Battle Under the Mountain, 2010
Oil on Masonite. Collection of the Association of Fantastic Art.

American, born 1977

Stewart broke into the fantastic art field working for *Magic: The Gathering* but has since successfully branched out to create award-winning works for a variety of clients. His style is a mix of classical fantastic imagery with just a touch of the contemporary edgy/pointy design features so prominent in the field today.

Battle Under the Mountain is Stewart's largest and most ambitious work to date, in which he fully indulges his personal passion for the worlds of J. R. R. Tolkien. Created in 2010 for the IlluXCon symposium, the painting references but does not exclusively follow the cinematic designs of Howe and Lee. It won the 2010 Chesley Award for Best Product Illustration.

Darrell SWEET

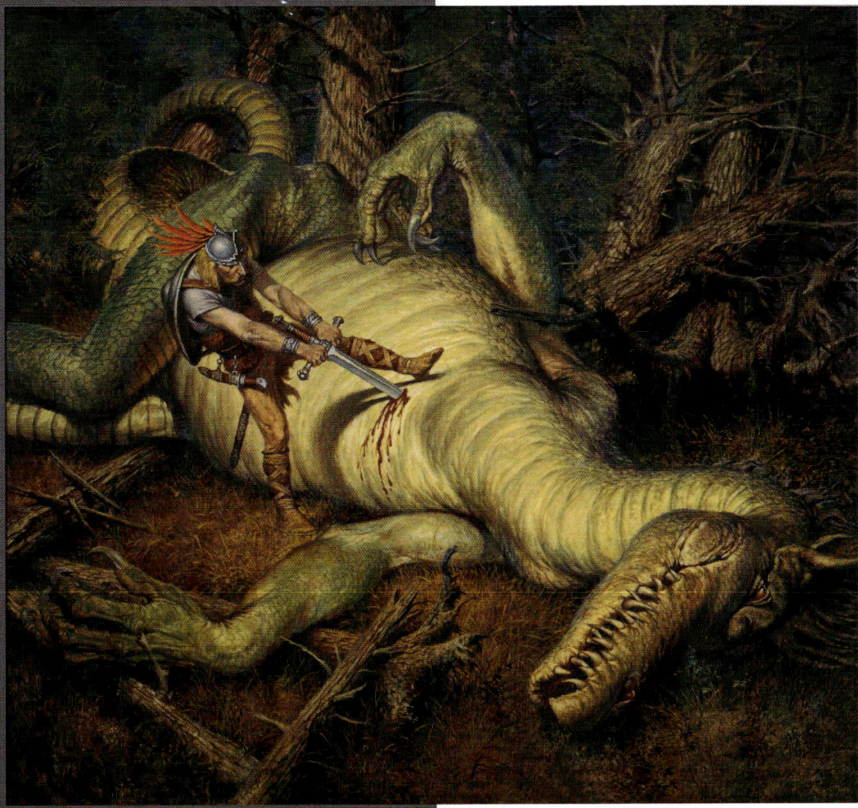

The Slaying of Glaurung, 1982
Oil on canvas. The Frank Collection.

American, 1934–2011

Sweet is best known for his colorful works for fantasy and science-fiction book covers in the 1970s and 1980s, although he worked in a variety of genres over the course of his long career. His work has defined the visuals for a number of best-selling series, including Piers Anthony's *Xanth* books and Robert Jordan's *Wheel of Time* series. His work shows a wide range of influences from the nineteenth century all the way to the present, but they are so well blended into Sweet's own style that no specific influences are readily apparent beyond the near-ubiquitous debt to the Brandywine artists, particularly N. C. Wyeth.

The Slaying of Glaurung depicts a scene from J. R. R. Tolkien's *Silmarillion*, showing Sweet's wonderful narrative skills to full effect, from the downed trees to the dragon's broken form and the effort of the valiant warrior to retrieve his sword.

Justin SWEET

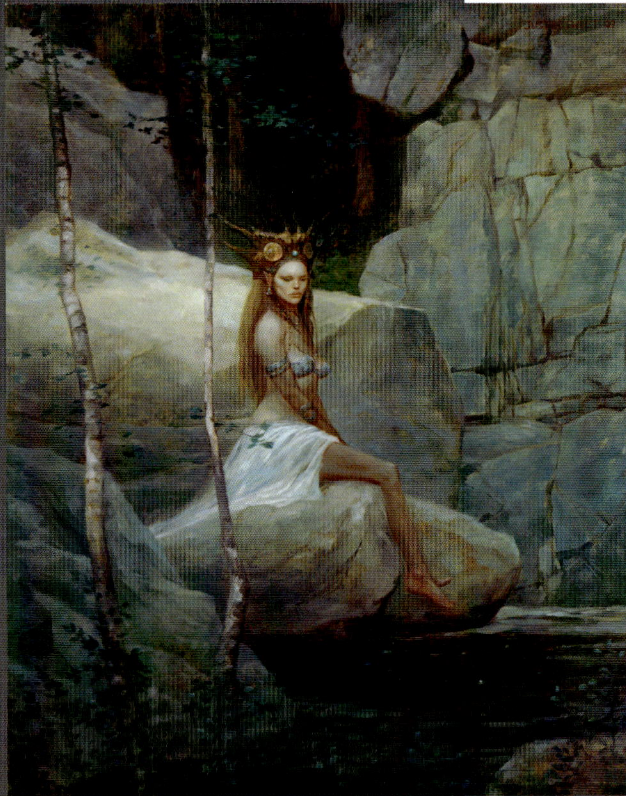

Elf Princess, 2009
Oil on canvas. The Collection of the Association of Fantastic Art.

American, born 1968

Sweet—no relation to Darrell—is one of the major voices of twenty-first century imaginative realism. He is highly sought after for film-concept design, including the *Narnia* films and the recent *John Carter of Mars*, for which he works predominantly digitally. For the occasional cover project or his own personal work he switches to oils, demonstrating the same powerful, loose, sweeping brushstrokes and visual energy that typifies his digital work. His dark, edgy characters and visceral impact have spawned legions of imitators in the digital-art world, but none have so far been able to approach his mastery of traditional media.

Elf Princess is a personal work of Sweet's, created for exhibition at the 2010 IlluXCon symposium. The lack of tension in this piece is unusual in Sweet's work, but the mood of beauty and serenity created is no less impactful than his more energetic works.

Tom TAGGART

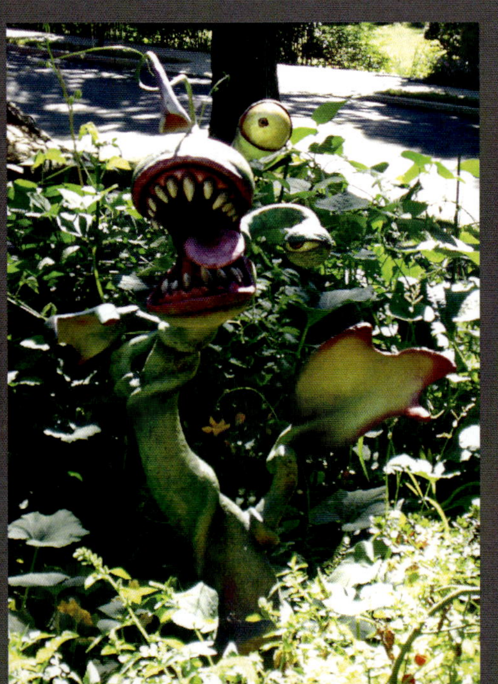

Carnigourd, 2009
Mixed. Private collection.

American, born 1965

Taggart is well known for his work in a variety of media, both two dimensional and three dimensional. His work tends to display a unique sense of ironic humor, unusual in the field, and is often stylized to the point of being closer to lowbrow art than mainstream imaginative realism in its use of brilliant colors to reflect emotional states and attitudes.

Carnigourd is a perfect example of Taggart's exaggerated humor, blending goofiness with just enough edge to create a compelling work.

Boris VALLEJO

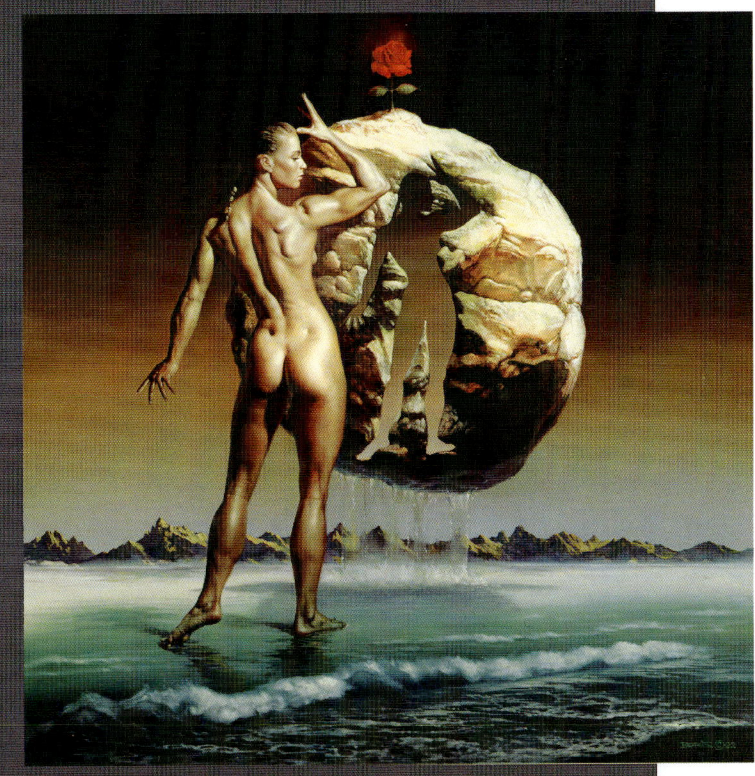

Peruvian, born 1941

Vallejo is one of the masters of contemporary imaginative realism, and one of the most recognized figures in the field worldwide. His extremely tightly rendered, figure-centric compositions of beautiful, powerful women and mighty beasts dominated the field in the late 1970s and 1980s, and his work continues to define fantastic art for millions of fans around the globe. He is married to artist Julie Bell, and they often collaborate on paintings as their styles are different but complementary.

A Rock By Any Other Name demonstrates the lush figural work that defines Vallejo's work, in this case demonstrating that the artist is just as comfortable with more conceptual designs as with strongly narrative pieces.

A Rock By Any Other Name, 1992
Oil on board. Collection of the artist.

Charles VESS

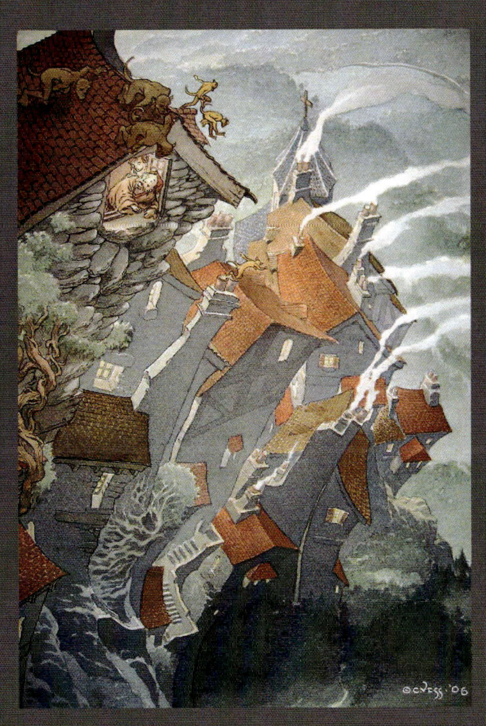

The Village of Wall, 2006
Watercolor and ink on paper. Collection of Paul and LizAnn Lizotte.

American, born 1951

Vess is one of the numerous artists who straddle the line between comics and illustration, working in both arenas in a style uniquely suited to both. He works in thin layers of watercolor over ink linework and is heavily influenced by artists such as Arthur Rackham and Willy Pogany. This style makes his work suitable for both audiences and fits perfectly with his rather Victorian approach to fairies, goblins, and similar themes.

The Village of Wall is a work created for a new limited edition of Vess's most famous work, *Stardust*, created in collaboration with writer Neil Gaiman. It demonstrates both his technique and his vision, with its otherworldly architecture and goblinlike creatures.

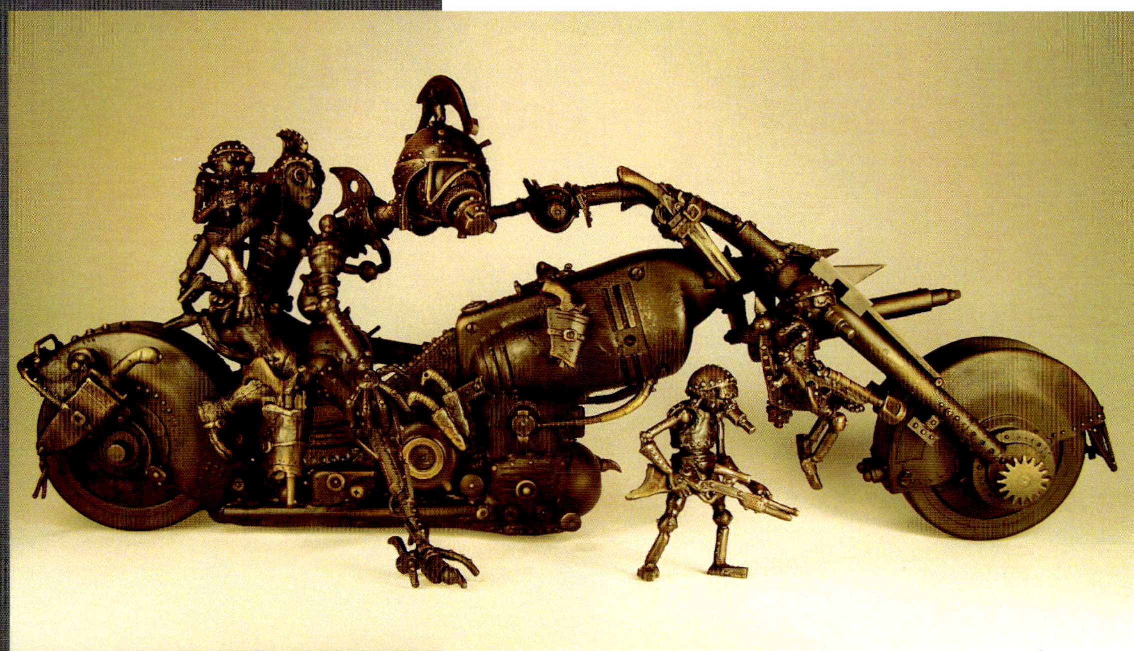

Robo-Bike, 2011
Bronze. Collection of Paul and LizAnn Lizotte.

Vincent VILLAFRANCA

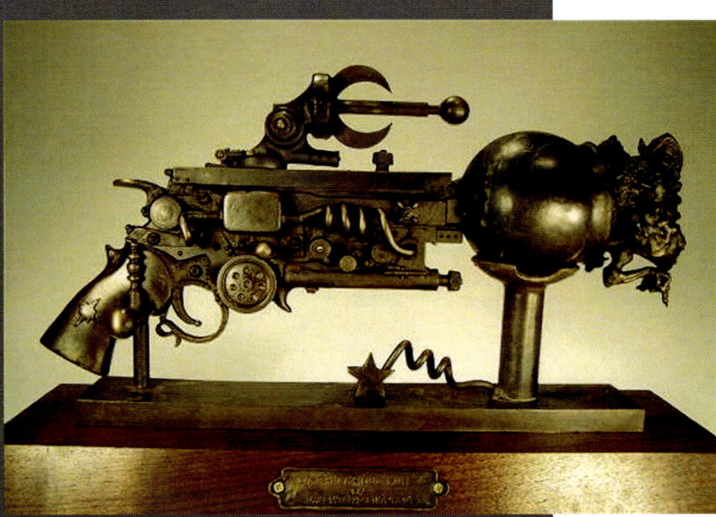

Astro Ghoul Gun, 2009
Bronze. Collection of Paul and LizAnn Lizotte.

American, born 1969

Villafranca is one of the most talented and popular bronze sculptors in the imaginative realist field today. His work is characterized by an odd blend of humor and solemnity that makes viewers simultaneously smile and gasp. On occasion Villafranca has forgone his trademark lightheartedness and created powerful, moving works commemorating human tragedies such as the First World War.

Robo-Bike is more "cool" and less humorous than many of Villafranca's creations, demonstrating what the artist can do with a straight science-fictional theme.

Astro Ghoul Gun provides a fine example of Villafranca's approach to his work, the finely wrought futuristic gun loaded with Rackham-esque goblins demonstrating both facets of his style.

Raoul VITALE

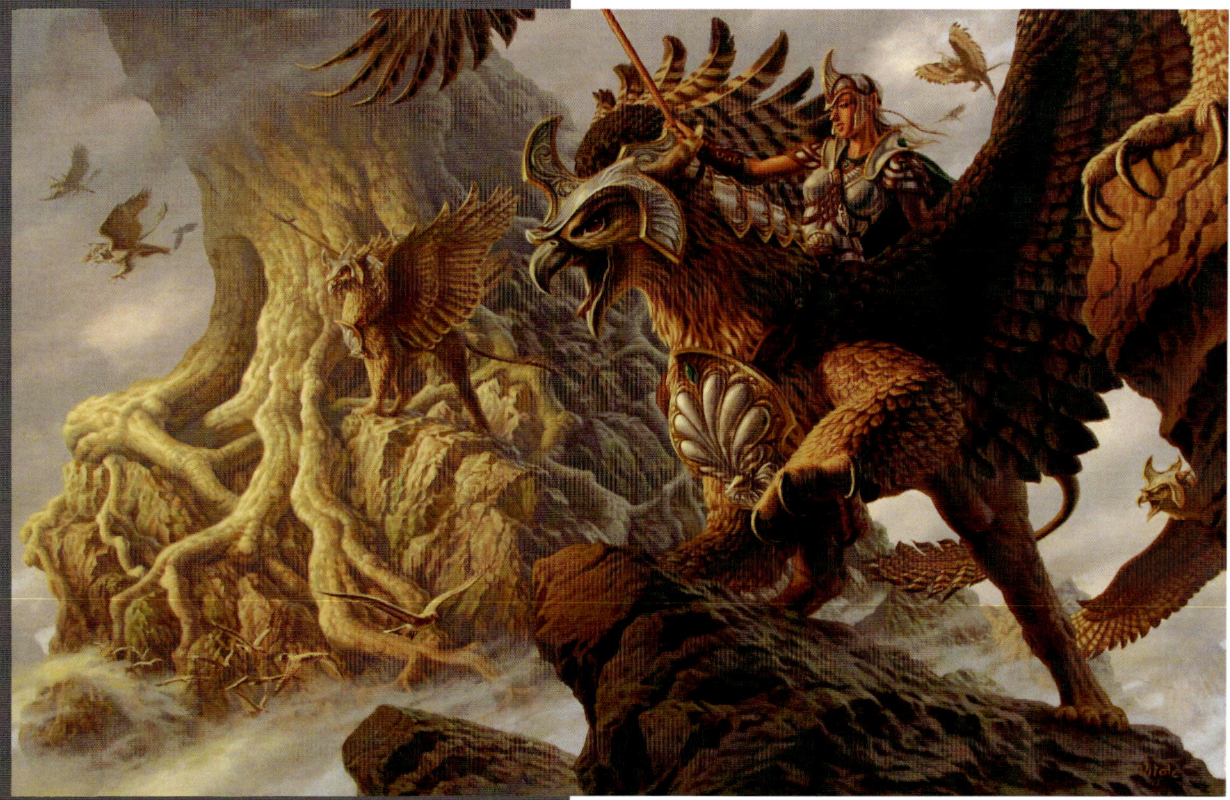

Torin's Quest, 2011
Oil on Masonite. Collection of Greg Obaugh.

American, born 1955

Vitale spent twenty-five years working as a stained-glass artist before seriously entering the imaginative realist field as a painter in 1998. Since then he has created a devoted following of fans and collectors drawn to his work by his blend of brilliant draughtsmanship and an amazing understanding of light and color, the latter of which is clearly informed by the earlier works of the Brothers Hildebrandt as well as the great Victorian painters.

Torin's Quest clearly demonstrates Vitale's lighting techniques as well as his depiction of trees, which has become something of a hallmark of his painting.

Michael WHELAN

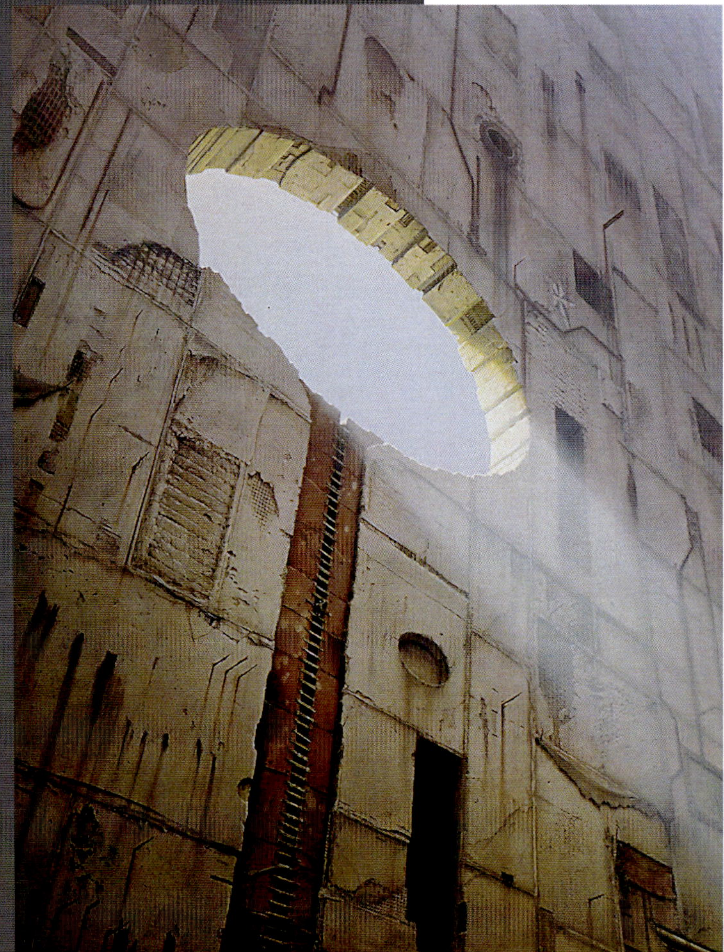

Lumen IV, 1997
Acrylic on canvas. Collection of the artist.

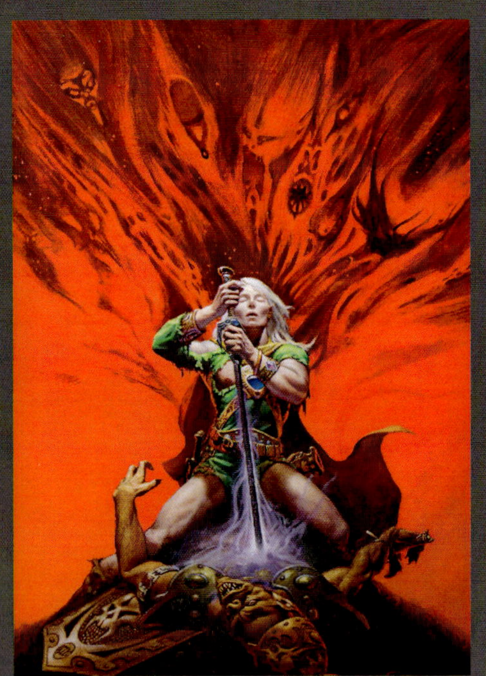

Weird of the White Wolf, 1976
Acrylic and oil on board. Private collection.

American, born 1950

Whelan has created iconic works in every decade since the 1970s, and as he has transitioned from illustration to purely personal paintings his technique and vision have only expanded. Working predominantly in acrylics for his entire career, his tightly rendered and highly realistic approach helped drive a sea change in the field in the late 1970s, along with artists like Boris Vallejo and Rowena Morrill.

Lumen IV is an example of Whelan's more recent work, as he has turned to more personal, visionary explorations of space, scale, and light. His stylistic hallmarks remain, even as the scope and symbolism of his work increases.

Weird of the White Wolf is one of Whelan's more well-known paintings, a depiction of Michael Moorcock's albino warrior, Elric. This painting is a superb example of Whelan's illustration, combining color, composition, and character in a single iconic image.

Allen WILLIAMS

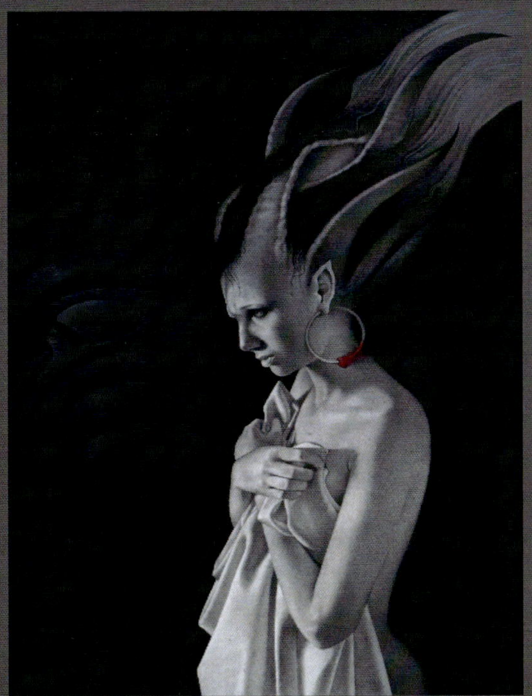

Love Lost, 2010
Graphite and oil on paper. Private collection.

American, born 1965

Williams began his career doing predominantly card art for various gaming companies, moving increasingly toward digital work as time passed. His personal work, however, was always handled in traditional media, and in a unique blend of black-and-white graphite and paint. In recent years this unusual technique combined with Williams's remarkable ability to create bizarre but believable creatures, has led to a high demand for his work as a concept artist for the film industry. At the same time, the refinement of his graphite/oil technique has led to an increasing demand for his original works.

Love Lost represents a new stage in the evolution of Williams' s oil/graphite technique. It also demonstrates his stunning draughtsmanship and his uniquely narrative conceptual style.

Barry WINDSOR-SMITH

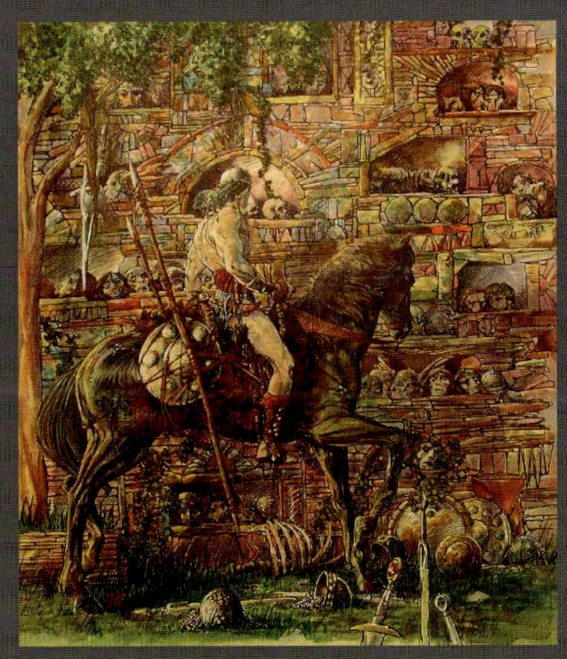

Conan Saga #3, 1987
Watercolor and ink on paper. Collection of Scott Williams.

British, born 1949

Windsor-Smith gained international attention in the comic-art field in the early 1970s as the artist for Marvel Comics' *Conan the Barbarian*, bringing his diverse artistic influences to that medium for the first time. It was his time as part of the Studio collective (with Jeffrey Catherine Jones, Bernie Wrightson, and Michael William Kaluta) in the 1970s that created the largest impact on imaginative realism. Of the four, Windsor-Smith was the most influenced by the Pre-Raphaelites, and his influence helped to repopularize artists like Dante Gabriel Rossetti and Sir Edward Coley Burne-Jones with a younger group of artists.

Conan Saga #3 demonstrates Windsor-Smith's stylized, elegant approach to the fantastic art field—vastly different from the painted rage that typified the treatment of artists like Frazetta.

Bernie WRIGHTSON

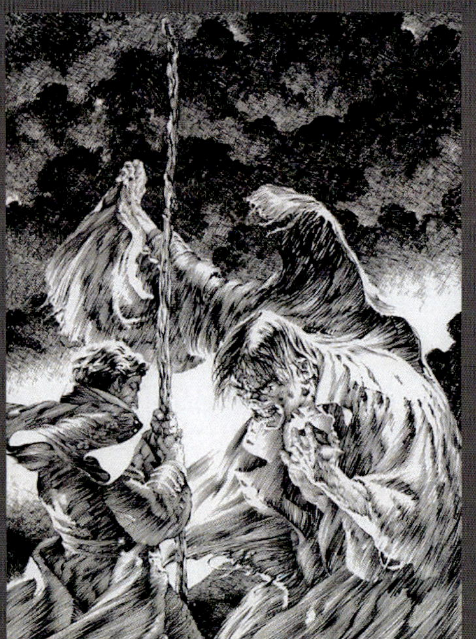

Frankenstein, 1983
Ink on paper. Collection of Scott Williams.

American, born 1948

Wrightson is best known for his work in the comic industry, where he is an icon of the field. Beginning in the mid-1970s, however, he joined with artists Barry Windsor-Smith, Jeffrey Catherine Jones, and Michael William Kaluta to create the Studio, an artist collective, and began developing more illustrative work, both in black and white and, more rarely, in color. By far the most famous project of his career so far has been his fully illustrated version of Mary Shelley's *Frankenstein*, first published in 1983. These plates, created in a style designed to evoke nineteenth century woodcuts and engravings—much like the work of Franklin Booth inadvertently replicated engraving styles during the golden age—are considered among the finest black-and-white pieces ever produced in the field.

Frankenstein is a magnificent example of Wrightson's work for his most famous project. The horror of the monster, the resoluteness of Dr. Frankenstein, and the power of the overall image are immediately apparent to the viewer. With repeated viewings it becomes possible to truly appreciate the staggeringly detailed linework in the piece, much of which is always lost to reproduction, no matter how faithful.

Mark ZUG

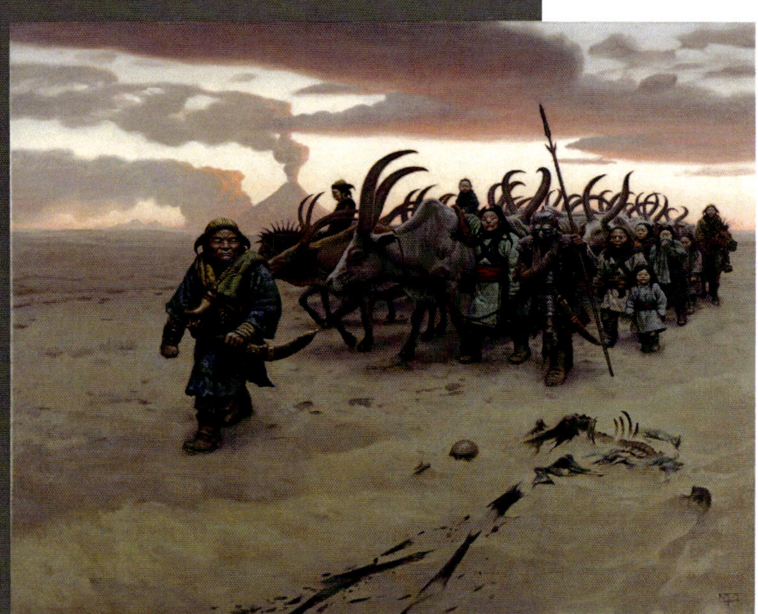

Sands of Gorgoroth, 2011
Oil on canvas. Collection of the Association of Fantastic Art.

American, born 1959

Zug has a reputation among his peers of being a painter's painter, a gifted artist whose paintings are carefully crafted layer by layer, utilizing a distinctive and sophisticated palette. Zug is heavily influenced by the Brandywine artists but is also a student of nineteenth century painters.

Sands of Gorgoroth, created for the 2011 IlluXCon symposium, is the first in a series of paintings examining Tolkien's *Lord of the Rings* trilogy from an alternate, almost deconstructionist approach. Here, the ravaging orcs are seen fleeing the scene of a titanic battle, but they are depicted as nearly human—a real race of creatures as opposed to mere foils to be massacred by the forces of good.